Practical Guide
to Computer Applications
for Architecture and Design

Practical Guide
to Computer Applications
for Architecture and Design

David Kent Ballast

Prentice-Hall, Inc.   Englewood Cliffs, New Jersey

720.28
B18p

Prentice-Hall International, Inc., *London*
Prentice-Hall of Australia, Pty. Ltd., *Sydney*
Prentice-Hall Canada, Inc., *Toronto*
Prentice-Hall of India Private Ltd., *New Delhi*
Prentice-Hall of Japan, Inc., *Tokyo*
Prentice-Hall of Southeast Asia Pte. Ltd., *Singapore*
Whitehall Books, Ltd., Wellington, *New Zealand*
Editora Prentice-Hall do Brasil Ltda., *Rio de Janeiro*
Prentice-Hall Hispanoamericana, S.A., *Mexico*

© 1986 *by*
PRENTICE-HALL, INC.
Englewood Cliffs, N.J.

All rights reserved. No part of this
book may be reproduced in any form
or by any means, without permission
in writing from the publisher.

Library of Congress Cataloging-in-Publication Data

Ballast, David Kent.
  Practical guide to computer applications for
architecture and design.

  Includes index.
  1. Architectural practice—Management—Data
processing. 2. Interior decoration—Management—
Data processing. I. Title.
NA1996.5.B35 1986   720′.28′5   86-9524

ISBN 0-13-690686-9

Printed in the United States of America

About the Author

David Ballast is a consultant and owner of Architectural Research Consulting, Denver, a firm offering applied research and information services to architects, interior designers and others in the building industry. In addition to consulting, he teaches part time in the graduate interior design program of the College of Design and Planning at the University of Colorado at Denver.

As a licensed architect, Mr. Ballast has worked in all phases of practice, including interior architecture. Before starting his own firm, he worked for Gensler and Associates, Architects, as a project manager.

The author received a Bachelor of Architecture degree with special honors from the University of Colorado. He is a member of the American Institute of Architects and the Construction Specifications Institute. Mr. Ballast has written for *The Construction Specifier* magazine and is the author of *The Architect's Handbook*, published by Prentice-Hall.

v

UNIVERSITY LIBRARIES
CARNEGIE-MELLON UNIVERSITY
PITTSBURGH, PENNSYLVANIA 15213

What This Book Will Do for You

The Architect's and Designer's Guide to Computer Applications provides practical, proven ways to successfully use computers for a wide variety of applications in the architectural and interior design office. The emphasis is on those uses that can yield the greatest increases in productivity, improved service and expanded business. Each chapter is packed with direct explanations of how you can apply the computer as a *tool* to help do your work better. Although computer-aided design and drafting has received most of the attention of design professionals, it is the day-to-day administration and production areas where the architect and interior designer can quickly realize the benefits of low-cost computers and software.

This *Guide* shows how you can use computers with readily available software to manage this ever-increasing flow of information. Most of the applications in this *Guide* can be implemented with one of three types of software—spreadsheet programs, data base management systems and word processing. A few others require specialized application packages. With an inexpensive nucleus of software, you can develop a powerful arsenal of functions customized to your needs to improve your practice.

This *Guide* has been carefully constructed and written as a self-contained guideline for implementing a particular application. You can select the applications that will be the most beneficial to you and go directly to those sections. All the information you need is there—application requirements, hardware and software requirements, cost variables, step-by-step implementation procedures, examples, additional tips and pitfalls to avoid. Later, when you have put the first few applications to use, you can go to other sections, each time making your computer more valuable and useful.

Among other benefits, you will find this *Guide* . . .

- *shows* how to control the hundreds of marketing contacts that are crucial to your firm's success. See Chapter 1.
- *illustrates* ways to both speed up and improve the appearance of proposals. See Chapter 1.

- *explains* methods of putting your fee estimates on target to help you land a job. See Chapters 1 and 2.
- *helps* get you started on your way to an organized system of records management. See Chapter 2.
- *dispels* the mystery of computerized financial management and takes you step by step through the implementation of an integrated system. See Chapter 2.
- *identifies* means of using microcomputers to expand your business with additional programming services. See Chapter 3.
- *describes* the procedure for setting up a data base management system to produce superlative programming reports. See Chapter 3.
- *presents* a shortcut method of completing a space-needs study for small to medium-size clients. See Chapter 3.
- *shows* ways to improve your design process without expensive computer-aided design software. See Chapter 4.
- *tells* how you can make the best use of checklists during the schematic and design development phases of your projects. See Chapter 4.
- *cuts* through the mystique of low-cost CADD and presents the essentials of what you need to know about this software. See Chapter 4.
- *demonstrates* easy-to-use ways to streamline the production of construction documents. See Chapter 5.
- *reveals* advanced techniques for using word processing software to create the best master specifications available—your own. See Chapter 5.
- *offers* a way out of the morass of disorganized storage of drawings and project records. See Chapter 5.
- *examines* how to slash wasted time with job scheduling software. See Chapter 6.
- *pinpoints* a procedure for solving one of the most vexing problems of project management. See Chapter 6.
- *clears up* the confusion of when and how to use prepackaged cost estimating software and when and how to use your own. See Chapter 7.
- *illustrates* tenant-finish estimating as one way to expand your services. See Chapter 7.
- *starts* you on your way to more comprehensive cost evaluations with life-cycle cost analysis. See Chapter 7.
- *describes* the essential components of money-making facility management services using computers. See Chapter 8.

- *provides* a strategy for complementing your services with computer-generated maintenance manuals. See Chapter 8.
- *challenges* outdated methods of library management with powerful relational data base management applications. See Chapter 9.
- *shows* how to develop a vocabulary tailor made to your office's information management needs. See Chapter 9.
- *itemizes* the techniques for controlling and retrieving your collection of product catalogs, samples, books and other reference material. See Chapter 9.
- *explains* how to capture the universe of knowledge contained in commercial data bases. See Chapter 10.
- *presents* the many ways computers can help improve the vital communication links necessary for a successful professional practice. See Chapter 10.

For those applications that require specialized programs, a list of available software is given at the end of the section to get you started on your search for the best program for your needs. Use these only as a starting point, however. The computer software industry is constantly changing, companies come and go, addresses change and new versions of old programs are released in rapid succession. Refer to the latest edition of one of the many directories listed in Appendix C for a current compilation of specific applications software.

In addition, keep in mind the extraordinary rate at which the remainder of the computer industry is changing. The hardware and software requirements and cost variables given in each section are current at the time of this writing and represent *minimums* for the application described. You may find that what is considered an entry-level component (hardware or software) when you buy has much more power than that recommended. Use them only as minimum requirements if you have an existing system or as guidelines for purchasing new hardware or software.

You will find this book helpful regardless of your computer experience. It was written for architects, interior designers, students and others who work in design offices in various capacities. If you have been using computers for some time this *Guide* will show how to get even more from the equipment and software you have. If you are taking your first, tentative steps to computerize, you will find detailed, step-by-step guidelines on how to get started and realize immediate benefits.

There are dozens and dozens of applications described in this *Guide,* but they only begin to suggest the myriad ways you can put your computer to work. You can begin your journey to improved productivity and service by implementing the functions most appropriate for your firm. Then, use this guidebook as a springboard for developing your own specialized applications. However you use this book you will find a wealth of ideas and potent ways to harness the power of the design professional's newest tool.

The following are trademarks used in this book:

AE/CADD: Archsoft, Inc.

AE/db: Halford A/E Systems Corporation

AutoCAD: Autodesk, Inc.

Benchmark: Metasoft Corporation

CADG+FM: The Computer-Aided Design Group

Cadvance: CalComp

dBase III: Ashton-Tate

Displaywriter: IBM

Fames: Decision Graphics, Inc.

The Harvard Total Project Manager: Harvard Software, Inc.

Lotus 1-2-3: Lotus Development Corporation.

MicroCAD: Imagimedia Technologies, Inc.

MICROGRAFX: MICROGRAFX, Inc.

Microsoft Project: Microsoft Corporation

Promis: Strategic Software Planning Corporation

Timeline: Breakthrough Software Corporation

Time-Plan: Mitchell Management Systems, Inc.

Versacad: T & W Systems, Inc.

The following are registered trademarks used in this book:

AEPEX: Timberline Systems

Apple: Apple Computer, Inc.

Cadkey: Micro Control Systems, Inc.

CadPlan: Personal CAD Systems, Inc.

Comet: Computer Corporation of America

DB Master: Stoneware, Inc.

Design Board 3-D: MegaCadd, Inc.

Easylink: Western Union Telegraph Co.

EIES: GTE Telenet Communications

GTE Telenet: The GTE Corporation

IBM: International Business Machines Corporation

IntePert: Schuchardt Software Systems

MCI Mail: MCI Communications Corporation

MicroPERT: Sheppard Software Co.

Milestone: Organic Software Associates

Ontyme II: Tymshare, Inc.

Plan/Trax: Engineering-Science, Inc.

PMS-II: North America MICA, Inc.

power-base: PowerBase Systems, Inc.

Primavera Project Planner and *Primavision:* Primavera Systems, Inc.

Project Manager Workbench: Applied Business Technology Corporation

SuperProject: Computer Associates International, Inc.

Target Task: Comshare, Inc.

Telemail: GTE Telenet Communications

VisiSchedule: Visicorp

WordStar and *MailMerge:* MicroPro International

CFMS is a registered trademark, jointly owned by Harper and Shuman, Inc. and PSAE, a division of the AIA Service Corporation.

The Source is a service mark of Source Telecomputing Corporation, a subsidiary of The Reader's Digest Association, Inc.

Acknowledgments

I would like to thank the many people who helped in the production of this book by giving their advice, sharing experiences and knowledge and providing examples of computer-generated output. Specifically, the following people were especially helpful in the creation of this work: Derwin H. Bass, Dow, Howell, Gilmore Associates, Inc.; William Linton, Tecton Media, Inc.; Jeanne Murphy, Society for Marketing Professional Services; Virgil Carter, Carter/Cody Associates; James M. McManus, Stecker, LaBau, Arneill, McManus Architects Incorporated; Mark D. Estes; Donald J. Haulman, Haulman Associates; C. M. McReynolds; and Paul P. McCain, The Fails Management Institute.

Additionally, I would like to thank Elizabeth Macklin, The American Institute of Architects; Kristine K. Fallin, A. Epstein and Sons International; Clifford D. Stewart, the Stewart Design Group; Crawley Cooper, Jung/Brannen Associates, Inc.; Jeffrey M. Hamer, Computer-Aided Design Group; Annette Gaskin and Jan Vargo with Kaplan/McLaughlin/Diaz; Gary Merideth, RNL and William van Erp, Gensler and Associates/Architects.

Special thanks to David Witzke and Diane Creel with The Earth Technology Corporation, Wendell P. Palmer of Greiner Engineering, and William Tracy, Gensler and Associates/Architects, for their assistance.

Contents

Contents

CHAPTER 1

Generating New Architectural Work with Marketing Information Systems

Using computers for marketing support is a relatively new phenomenon for most design firms. At about the same time organized marketing has become prevalent in architectural and interior design firms, personal computers have come within reach of nearly every office. The firms that can combine the power of computers with strategic marketing plans will have a competitive advantage in the years to come.

Microcomputers can support your marketing effort in several ways. The following list itemizes a few of the possibilities:

lead tracking

assisting with proposals

maintaining a project history data base

maintaining a resumé data base

indexing slides, photographs, correspondence and other marketing support activities

creating visual enhancements, such as making slides, charts and other presentation material

tapping into commercial data bases for marketing research information

preparing fee estimates for proposals

maintaining mailing lists

assisting with preparation of government 254 and 255 forms

keeping track of consultants and joint venture prospects

providing electronic mail for maintaining communication with branch offices or clients

1

In many cases you need to buy specific application software, such as graphics packages, to do specific jobs. Trying to write this kind of program yourself or hiring someone to write it is not cost effective. However, there are many tasks that can be automated using data base management and spreadsheet software and a little of your imagination. Many of the prepackaged marketing programs are simply this type of software customized to serve a specific function.

The following sections outline how to apply microcomputers to some of the more common marketing functions in your office. You will find these loaded with ideas to get you started. Also, refer to Section 2.1 for guidance on maintaining correspondence files, Section 2.2 on keeping personnel records current so resumés can be used for proposals, Section 2.5 for ways to organize consultant information, Section 10.1 for more information on tapping commercial data bases for marketing research, and Section 10.4 for ways to use electronic mail.

1.1

SUCCESSFUL LEAD TRACKING

Using a computer to track leads can improve your chances for success. Even for small firms, the number of contacts that are made every year can run into the hundreds and each of these contacts are in various stages of the marketing cycle; some are just tentative leads, some have requested proposals, and others may be "on hold." If you have a way to organize this information a potentially profitable client won't get lost because you didn't follow up at the appropriate time.

Basic Application Requirements

Much of a design professional's daily marketing effort involves maintaining a record of every lead the firm might have regardless of how likely it is that lead will turn into an actual job. In some cases the lead is very tentative, amounting to only a name, phone number, and general type of project. As you learn more about the prospect and begin to promote your firm, you gain more detailed information about the client, the project and the requirements for making a proposal. The entire process from initial lead to contract signing may take months or even years. A lead tracking system should give you the ability to maintain and update information during this marketing period and summarize the status of your office's marketing efforts at any given time.

In addition to the basic data of name, address, phone number and so forth, your records should contain the scope of work of the lead, its schedule, its profit potential and the probability you will get the work. This information is vital to a good marketing program because it allows you to make strategic marketing and

2

business decisions based on existing and likely future workload. The data can then be used to provide management with revenue and sales forecasts. This is one of the most important uses of a lead tracking system on a microcomputer—one that is usually too difficult to accomplish manually.

For example, based on a report from your lead tracking system, you would want to concentrate your firm's resources on those prospects that have the highest probability of becoming jobs and those with the greatest profit potential.

Other kinds of reports should not only give you current status of sales efforts but also provide you with a "tickler file" so you know when to follow up leads. In each case, you should be able to sort the reports by project type, status, geographical location, expected start date of design, probability, the person making the contact, project name or any other useful data field.

Additional Application Requirements

For a simple application, lead tracking can be accomplished with a single-file data base management program. For a more sophisticated system you can use a relational data base management system and maintain separate files for leads, client information, project history, resumés and other marketing data. Refer to Section 1.4 for an application of this type.

Requirements of Software

A file management system (FMS) type of data base management software with the following features is required for this application. If you want to separate your data into different files you will need a relational system. Refer to the Appendix on Fundamentals of Database Management Systems for a complete description of these and other criteria for selecting a DBMS.

1. The program should allow at least 30 fields per record.
2. You should be able to index on at least ten data fields.
3. The software should allow you to sort on several key fields together instead of just one alone.
4. In addition to numeric and alphanumeric field types, the software should have field formats for dates since reference and sorting according to time is a critical function of this application.
5. Security features, such as password protection, should be available to limit file access to only those authorized.
6. Since this application can become complex and each record lengthy, the program should allow more than one "screenfull" of information per record.

3

7. The program must have flexible methods of querying the data base, both on screen and in printed reports. This includes relational queries, Boolean logic searches and partial string searches.

8. The program must have a flexible report generator since you will want to print out results in various ways.

9. The program must have basic four-function arithmetic calculation capability for performing revenue forecasts.

Requirements of Hardware

RAM.   Many file management systems will work with as little as 48K of RAM, but you should consider at least 128K.

Disks.   You should have, at a minimum, two disk drives, one for the program and one for your data. Since many data base management applications require a great deal of storage you should estimate your needs prior to buying a system. Hard disks have the advantages of providing some storage space and faster access time.

Printer.   A dot-matrix printer is the minimum requirement for this application. Since you will want reports produced quickly in-house you should have some type of high-speed printer even if you have a slower, letter-quality printer.

Cost Variables

Hardware.   A complete set up with two disk drives and a dot-matrix printer can be purchased for as little as $2,000 or less. A ten-megabyte hard disk drive will add about $800 to $1,300.

Software.   Simple file management programs range from $100 to $400, with a few costing more than $400.

Setup.   Setup costs depend on the complexity of your application. You will need from one to two hours to set up a simple file management system while a more complex RDBMS will take from eight to twenty hours. Keep in mind that much of this setup time will include thinking through your method of tracking leads and the kinds of reports you want.

Data entry.   Data entry can be performed by the marketing person or by a secretary or marketing coordinator working from printed reports provided by others.

Implementation Procedures

1. Decide on what kinds of information you want to track and the kinds of reports that will be most useful to your office. This will help determine the data fields, the kind of data base management system you will need, the storage capabilities of your hardware and the specific requirements of software.

2. Develop standard information-gathering forms. Paper forms make data entry by clerical staff easier and they force the people doing the marketing to collect data that might normally be forgotten.

3. Decide on the data fields for your system. Your specific needs will determine exactly what information you maintain. Use the following list as a starting point for setting up your own record format. If you decide to use a relational data base management system, some of these will be in separate files. For example, you may want to put all project information in one file so it can be used for other purposes in addition to marketing.

Possible data fields

contact organization name

contact number

contact name

contact title

project title

address

city

state

zip code

telephone

contacted by

date of contact

type of contact (for example, cold call, referral, request for proposal, etc.)

method of contact (phone call, visit, etc.)

type of project (office building, remodel, programming, etc. You should set up a list of the types of work your office does and assign them code numbers to make data entry easier.)

scope of services

project budget

expected design start date

expected construction start date

expected completion date

client type (private, local government, state government, etc.)

result of contact (follow up later, submit proposal, do not follow up, interview set up, etc.)

follow-up date

5

remarks

project location

project size

estimated fee revenue

percent probability of project proceeding

percent probability of winning job

4. Following the instructions of your data base management software, set up the data entry forms, indexes, report formats, and other components.

5. Establish an office policy of when reports are to be printed, who sees them, and how they are to be used. Also, establish an office policy and procedures for entering data and keeping it up to date. This responsibility may be given to a secretary, marketing coordinator or, if your office is small, to the principal responsible for marketing.

6. Keep track of your leads through your fiscal year. This should include awarded contracts as well as projects that you lost or that were cancelled. At the end of the year you can print out a summary of won and lost jobs, giving you a valuable set of data with which to evaluate your marketing efforts and to plan for the next year.

7. If you are using a floppy disk system, start a new disk for each fiscal year, transferring those leads still active to the new disk. If you have enough room on a hard disk system you may not need (or want) to do this.

Case in Point

Greiner Engineering in Denver, Colorado, uses two programs for tracking leads; one focuses on potential *projects* while the other organizes *sales calls*. Wendell Palmer, Executive Vice President of the Rocky Mountain Division developed the systems. The lead-tracking program runs on an Apple microcomputer and keeps track of marketing contacts for Greiner Engineering's staff in four different offices around the region.

A project entry starts with *any* kind of lead, no matter how small or how little information is known about it. The Greiner organization has about 150 new contacts and leads per month. In addition to the usual background information concerning project name, project type, address and so on, the program maintains data on the type of market, the estimated fee, the likely fee, estimated starting date, length of job and the probability of getting the job. This information is used for revenue and sales forecasts, assisting Greiner management in making long-range marketing and business plans.

One of its biggest advantages is providing information that is used for planning marketing strategies and suggesting where to spend the marketing dollar. Greiner

REPORT FOR--MAIN OFFICE

CLIENT# PROJ.# REP	CLIENT PROJECT DATE ENTERED	DATE UPDATE	MARKET CLIENT TYPE STATUS	OFFICE DEPARTMENT	EST. FEE (000)	ZJOB	ICOMP	FORECAST (000)	NTP DATE
101 1 GLK	A.B.C MANUFACTURING PLANT #1 ADDITION 2-26-84	8/22/84	INDUSTRIAL PRIVATE SHORTLISTED	MAIN OFFICE GEN'L ENGRING PROJECT LENGTH-8 MONTHS	125	.9	.6	67.5	6/84
289 1 ETV	HI-TECH MANUFACTURING NEW LABORATORY 2-26-84		INDUSTRIAL PRIVATE PRICE PROPOSAL	MAIN OFFICE ARCHITECTURE PROJECT LENGTH-14 MONTHS	380	1	.5	190	7/84
101 2 GLK	A.B.C MANUFACTURING NEW SUBSTATION 2-26-84		INDUSTRIAL PRIVATE SELECTED	MAIN OFFICE MECH./ELEC. PROJECT LENGTH-4 MONTHS	30	1	1	30	3/84
289 2 ETV	HI-TECH MANUFACTURING NEW HVAC SYSTEM 2-26-84		INDUSTRIAL PRIVATE PRICE PROPOSAL	MAIN OFFICE MECH./ELEC. PROJECT LENGTH-3 MONTHS	15	.8	.8	9.6	3/84
482 1 ETV	SMITH MEMORIAL HOSPITAL NEW INTENSIVE CARE UNIT 2-26-84		HEALTH CARE PRIVATE PRICE PROPOSAL	MAIN OFFICE ARCHITECTURE PROJECT LENGTH-6 MONTHS	30	1	.8	24	5/84

321.1

Figure 1.1-1
Marketing Report

7

also uses this data in a spreadsheet program to develop detailed marketing budgets as well as monthly sales information.

The sales call program runs on a VAX mainframe although the same application could be implemented on a micro. The system was originally developed using the computer they used for other engineering work.

This application keeps track of who called on who since there are several representatives in many offices around the country. The program is user friendly in that it prompts for the required information. Data recorded includes the client name and number, address and phone, the date the marketing call was made, whether it was a phone call or personal visit, when to call again and who the Greiner representative is. The computer can then produce reports sorted by representative, types of client, office, department, and project status for periodic review by management. It is also used to produce mailing labels from the entire list or from selected names based on any criteria desired. Normally, reports are printed monthly, but the interactive nature of the system allows a query at any time.

All past client contacts are maintained in the system with their records "tagged" so they are not active on a daily basis but are able to be searched and recalled if necessary.

Figure 1.1-1 shows one of the marketing reports produced by the system.

Additional Tips

- The system must be user friendly or it will not be used. This is especially important if there are several people using the same system. You want your marketing people to concentrate on marketing, not programming.

- If your time or disk space is limited consider entering only those leads that have a *reasonable* chance of becoming viable marketing prospects. For example, you might not want to enter an entire "cold call" list, only those names who responded to your call.

Sources for More Information

Seminars

SMPS holds seminars on the use of computers in marketing in various locations around the country from time to time. These seminars are open to both members and nonmembers. Write to them for a current schedule.

Society for Marketing Professional Services
801 North Fairfax Street Suite 215
Alexandria, VA 22314

Partial List of Application Software for Design Marketing

AMS-1
Society for Marketing Professional Services
801 North Fairfax Street Suite 215
Alexandria, VA 22314

Construction Marketer
Tecton Media, Inc.
350 Madison Avenue
New York, NY 10017

Architect's DB Master Templates
Client Marketing Directory
Top-Ten Software
103 East 84th Street
New York, NY 10028

(This program requires DB Master software.)

1.2

MAINTAINING PROJECT HISTORIES

Complete, concise records of your past projects are invaluable to your marketing efforts. Not only do they provide the basis for presenting your qualifications to potential clients but they also allow you to analyze your past fee structures so you can give competitive, but profitable, fee estimates. With the proper report formatting, the same information can be used to produce 254 forms for government proposals.

A well-structured project history application can form the basis of an integrated marketing information system and provide useful data for other management tasks. With a detailed project history data base you can extract data for use with other applications such as estimating fees (Section 1.6), maintaining information on clients for possible future work (Section 1.4), doing preliminary cost estimates (Section 7.1), and assisting with man-hour projections for project management (Section 6.1). If a project history data base is set up correctly, you can either transfer portions of the information to other application programs or set up a relational data base management system so all applications share the same common data.

This section will describe how to set up systems for maintaining a project history data base either as a stand-alone application or as part of a relational system integrated with fee histories (Section 1.6) and client information (Section

9

1.4). Refer to Appendix A, "Fundamentals of Data Base Management Systems," for a complete description of this type of software. Section 1.4 tells how to set up a complete integrated system.

Basic Application Requirements

Date base management software is required for project histories since the same type of information is recorded for each job with some of it being selectively recalled and sorted. For example, from your file of project histories, you may want to look at all the school projects you have done in the past three years where construction cost was over $1,000,000. With this information you could list your educational facility experience in a job proposal and also see if your past fee estimates were profitable.

For setting up a computerized project history system you need the following basic capabilities in a data base management system:

1. the ability to define a form on the screen for data entry
2. the ability to search through your data base for selective information
3. the ability to sort the records in your data base
4. the ability to print out reports based on your selection and sort criteria
5. the ability to easily add, edit and delete records in the data base

Additional Application Requirements

If you choose to keep a project history data base as an isolated application to support your marketing efforts a simple file management type of data base management system (DBMS) will serve your needs and meet the basic application requirements listed above. However, if you want a more comprehensive system you will need relational data base management software.

Information about a project can be separated into three major areas that should form the basis of a relational data base management system. This information concerns fees, a project description (including construction costs), and the client. (See Figure 1.2-1.) Separating these blocks of information (files) gives you more flexibility in using the data they contain. For example, with fee histories you can estimate more accurately your costs to do a job based on selected criteria, analyze your office's overall fee history, or establish preliminary man-hour projections for managing a new project. Any of these tasks may take place separate from your marketing efforts, but the data is still available for writing proposals when it is required. Trying to include all this information with other marketing data in one large file would be cumbersome and slow.

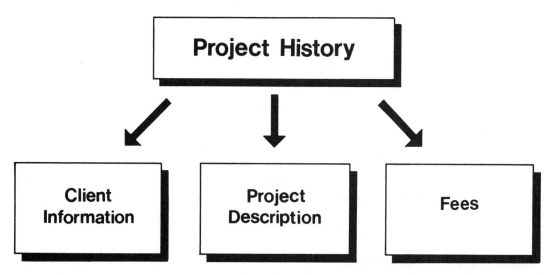

Figure 1.2-1
Relational Data Base Format for Project Histories

Requirements of Software

In addition to the basic selection criteria mentioned in the Appendix on data base management systems, your program for a file management system should have the following minimum capabilities:

1. You should be able to index on a minimum of five fields. This gives you basic access to some of the more important fields in your data base. Ideally, you should be able to index on any of the fields in the record.

2. Your program should allow you to sort on one or more key fields so you can organize your project histories according to any criteria the situation might demand. Many of the less expensive file management programs allow sorting on only one key field.

3. If your computer and program are available to anyone in the office, you will want the software to provide some type of password security so that confidential fee information is not available to everyone.

4. Since some project histories can be lengthy, the software should allow more than one screenfull of data per record.

5. The DBMS should have the full range of query functions including relational and Boolean conditions. (See the Appendix on Fundamentals of Data Base Management Systems for a complete discussion of these features.)

Your program for a *relational* DBMS should have the following additional capabilities:

1. It should allow at least three files to be open at once although more are useful if you want to have look-up files.

2. You should be able to set up custom menus to make it easy for anyone in the office to use the system without having to know the program's commands.

3. You should be able to transfer information to other programs such as a spreadsheet for more extensive data manipulation or a word processing program for proposal preparation.

4. It should allow you to easily add data fields as your needs change.

Requirements of Hardware

RAM.   Most file management systems will work with as little as 64K of RAM. More sophisticated relational data base management systems and integrated packages will need 128K or more.

Disks.   Depending on the capacity of the system, floppy disks will work for most applications. However, if you decide to set up a complex relational data base management system and your office is large, you will quickly outgrow floppy disks. You should consider a ten- or twenty-megabyte hard disk.

Printer.   For quick, in-house reports a dot-matrix is sufficient. For proposals you will want a letter-quality printer. This can be a daisywheel or laser printer that combines the speed of a dot-matrix printer with the appearance and choice of type styles of a daisywheel.

Plotter.   A plotter is only necessary if you will be producing extensive graphics from your data base.

Cost Variables

Hardware.   A complete setup with two disk drives and a letter-quality printer can be purchased for as little as $3,000 or less. A ten-megabyte hard disk drive will add about $800 to $1,300.

Software.   Simple file management programs range from under $100 to $400, with a few costing more than $400. Relational data base management programs range from about $400 to over $1,000, but with many very good programs under $800.

Setup.   Setup costs depend on the complexity of your application. A simple screen form for a file management system can be set up in less than 15 minutes with some programs. Working out a complex relational data base management system may take from several hours to more than a day if you do custom programming.

Data entry. Data entry can be done directly by the project manager when the job is complete without the need to fill out a form that is then entered by clerical staff. This may take just a matter of minutes to an hour or more if all the necessary information is not at hand.

Output. Screen-related output is very cost efficient for any data base management system that has a good query language or menu-driven commands. For more complete printed reports it may take more time to first set up a report format. However, once this is done it can be reused without additional work.

Implementation Procedures

1. Decide on the type of information you want to keep on each project your offices does. The big variable here is to whether you are going to make a major commitment to designing a relational DBMS to include other marketing applications, cost estimating and project management or whether you are going to limit yourself to simple project histories to use in a "job experience data base."

Since you will want to establish your own unique set of data, there is no one set of data fields that can be used for recording project histories. You may want to use the following list as a starting point for developing your own data entry forms (either on paper or terminal) for a file management type of data base.

project name

project number

date information entered

project location

job type (for example, architecture, interiors, programming)

building type

square footage

construction start date

construction completion date

project description (This data field could be one long text field or several individual data fields such as number of floors, exterior material, structural system, etc. If it is a free text field, you may want to consider using a relational data base management system and simply have a number in this field that relates to a corresponding record in another file.)

project manager

project designer

cost estimate

original bid

final total construction cost

cost per square foot

other costs (such as furnishings, site work, etc.)

budgeted hours and fees by phases with percent of total

actual hours and fees by phases with percent of total

reimbursable expenses and nonbillable direct expenses

consultant fees—total, per square foot and percent of total

consultant names and contact person

brief project evaluation (Again, if this was a lengthy text field you may want to use a RDBMS and place this field in another file.)

2. Determine if you need a relational data base management system or a simple file management system.

3. Calculate the amount of storage you will most likely need. Determine the bytes required for each record and multiply by the estimated number of records. Allow for growth in the data base. This calculation will help you determine if you need hard disk storage or if you can use floppy disks.

4. Set up the data entry forms, report formats and other portions of the program as required by your software.

5. Determine if you want the project manager or some other person to enter information directly into the computer or whether you want a project history form filled out first so the data can be checked before input. Having an intermediate paper form is probably the best method since it can easily be checked by several people before being committed to computer memory. If your program has the capability, the screen entry form can be set up to resemble the paper form to make data entry easier and faster.

Examples

Dow, Howell, Gilmore Associates, Inc. uses the Condor Data Base Management System for several marketing applications. They use two files to maintain project histories—a "Past Projects Information" file and an "Additional Information" file. These are shown in Figures 1.2-2 and 1.2-3. Among other uses, they can select the proper PROFILE code to search for projects that best suit the requirements of a government client. With a report function, the information from the selected records can then be printed directly on standard 254 forms.

For estimating fees on proposed work, they combine information from both forms to produce a report that gives comparisons of fees of similar past jobs.

```
: : : : : : : : : : : : : : : : : : : : : : : : : : : : : : : : : : : : : : : : : : : : : : : : : : :
:                                                                                  :
:  PAST PROJECTS INFORMATION                        DATA BASE MANAGEMENT  :
:                                                                                  :
:  PROJECT IDENTIFICATION:                                                         :
:  [NAME] _____  TYPE [PROFILE] ___   :
:  [PROJ.NO] _____  [LOCATION] _____   :
:                                                                                  :
:  [CLIENT] _____     [PROJ.MGR] ___   :
:  [ADDR1] _____  [ADDR2] _____   :
:  [CITY] _____  [ST] __  [ZIP] _____   :
:  [PHONE1] _____  [PHONE2] _____  [DATE] _____   :
:  [CONTACT] _____  [TITLE] _____   :
:  [BUS.TYP] _____      [SIC] ____   :
:                                                                                  :
:  PROJECT DESCRIPTION & DATA:                                                     :
:  [DESCRIPT] _____   :
:  [GROSS] AREA _____ SF [NET] AREA _____ SF [FLRS] ____   :
:  [SITE] _____ ACRES                                           :
:                                                                                  :
:  BIDDING PROCESS, DATE & SUCCESSFUL PRIME CONTRACTOR:                     :
:  [PROC] __  (1 - Competitive; 2 - Negotiated; 3 - Constr. Mgmt.)   :
:  [BID.DATE] _____  [INDEX] _____  [COMPLETION] _____   :
:  [CONTR] _____  [CSZ] _____   :
:                                                                                  :
:  PROJECT COST SUMMARY:                                                           :
:  [BUDGET] _____  [BID] _____  [ACTUAL] _____   :
:                                                                                  :
: : : : : : : : : : : : : : : : : : : : : : : : : : : : : : : : : : : : : : : : : : : : : : : : : : : :
```

Figure 1.2-2
Past Projects Information Record

```
: : : : : : : : : : : : : : : : : : : : : : : : : : : : : : : : : : : : : : : : : : : : : : : : : : :
:                                                                                  :
:  ADDITIONAL INFORMATION                          DATA BASE MANAGEMENT  :
:                                                                                  :
:  PROJECT IDENTIFICATION:                                                         :
:  [NAME] _____  TYPE [PROFILE] ___   :
:  [PROJ.NO] _____  [LOCATION] _____   :
:                                                                                  :
:  [CLIENT] _____     [PROJ.MGR] ___   :
:                                                                                  :
:  PROJECT COST SUMMARY:                                                           :
:  [BUDGET] _____  [BID] _____  [ACTUAL] _____   :
:                                                                                  :
:  BID BREAK-DOWN:                                                                 :
:  [GENERAL] _____  [MECH] _____  [ELECT] _____   :
:  [SITE] _____  [SPEC.EQ] _____  [FF&E] _____   :
:                                                                                  :
:  TOTAL OF ALL CHANGE ORDERS:  [CHG.ORD] _____   :
:                                                                                  :
:  PROFESSIONAL FEES:                                                              :
:  [FEE.BUDGET] _____  [FEE.ACTUAL] _____  [PROFIT] ___ %   :
:                                                                                  :
: : : : : : : : : : : : : : : : : : : : : : : : : : : : : : : : : : : : : : : : : : : : : : : : : : : :
```

Figure 1.2-3
Additional Information Record

15

Maintaining Project Histories

The past projects information also provides a complete listing of former clients for references, mailing lists and follow-up contacts for leads to new jobs.

These forms are only part of the Dow, Howell, Gilmore system. Their leads information form and potential projects form are shown in Figures 1.2-4 and 1.2-5.

Additional Tips

- Set up data fields in your individual record forms to correspond to the type of work you do and how you market. For example, a firm that does interior design as well as architecture will want extra data fields so furnishings costs can be recorded in addition to construction costs. Cost per square foot of *rentable* area as well as cost per gross square foot is a good statistic to have as well. If your firm does a lot of government work include data fields that correspond to those included as part of 254 and 255 forms.

- Make building type fields as specific as required for your marketing efforts. Firms that do a lot of educational work will want to include specific types such as "elementary schools," "secondary schools," "preschools" and "universities" instead of just "schools."

```
LEADS INFORMATION FORM                     DATA BASE MANAGEMENT

[CLIENT] _____   [LEAD.NO] _____
[ADDR1] _____  [ADDR2] _____
[CITY] _____  [ST] __  [ZIP] _____
[PHONE1] _____ [PHONE2] _____  [DATE] _____
[CONTACT] _____  [TITLE] _____
[BUS.TYP] _____  [SIC] _____
[SOURCE] _____  [RESP] _____

                SUMMARY LOG OF CONTACTS
                -----------------------

CONTACT       DATE      COMMENTS
[1ST.CALL]  _____   [1] _____
[2ND.CALL]  _____   [2] _____
[3RD.CALL]  _____   [3] _____
[INTRO.LTR] _____   [I] _____
[BROCHURE]  _____   [B] _____
[PROPOSAL]  _____   [P] _____
[OTHER.X]   _____   [X] _____
[OTHER.Y]   _____   [Y] _____
[OTHER.Z]   _____   [Z] _____
```

Figure 1.2-4
Leads Information Record

16

```
::::::::::::::::::::::::::::::::::::::::::::::::::::::::::::::::::::::
:                                                                :
:  POTENTIAL PROJECTS FILE              DATA BASE MANAGEMENT  :
:                                                                :
:  [CLIENT] _____  [LEAD.NO] _____       :
:  [ADDR1] _____ [ADDR2] _____         :
:  [CITY] _____ [ST] __ [ZIP] _____           :
:  [PHONE1] _____ [PHONE2] _____ [DATE] _____       :
:  [CONTACT] _____ [TITLE] _____              :
:  [BUS.TYP] _____ [SIC] _____         :
:  [SOURCE] _____ [RESP] ___            :
:                                                                :
:  PROJECT DATA:                                             :
:  [NAME] _____ TYPE [PROFILE] ___      :
:  [SCOPE] _____ [BUDGET] _____       :
:                                                                :
:  SELECTION SCHEDULE DATES:                                 :
:  [PROPOSAL] _____ [INTERVIEW] _____ [SELECT] _____  :
:                                                                :
:  COMPETITION:                                              :
:  [1] _____              :
:  [2] _____              :
:  [3] _____              :
:  [4] _____              :
:  [5] _____              :
:                                                                :
:  [PERCENT] ___ CHANCE OF SUCCESS                           :
:                                                                :
::::::::::::::::::::::::::::::::::::::::::::::::::::::::::::::::::::::
```

Figure 1.2-5
Potential Projects Record

- Set up report formats that can give you periodic statistical information about your past jobs. For example, from your data base you could extract such information as average fees per square foot, which building types were the most profitable, and so forth. The ability to make more of the information in a data base that is simply listed is one of the greatest advantages of a computerized system—use it!

- Be sure to back up your information on a regular basis. Data on past projects constitute a storehouse of unique, valuable knowledge that shouldn't be lost through accidental disk damage or a hardware malfunction.

1.3

FAST PROPOSAL PREPARATION

For small firms with limited budgets and no separate marketing staff, preparing proposals is a time-consuming process that is rushed through at the last minute, often resulting in errors and incomplete submissions. Although most firms are now using word processing, the full capabilities of these programs are frequently not utilized. This section describes how you can make the best use of word processing programs on your microcomputer to maintain marketing information, improve your proposals, and decrease preparation time.

Basic Application Requirements

Using word processing should not be viewed as a substitute for preprinted promotional material. You should still have some type of office brochure describing your firm, its experience, photographs of past work, and other general information. In addition, you may have specific market brochures, individual, preprinted project descriptions and other material. These are all valuable when submitting preliminary qualification packages or as things to leave behind when making sales calls. However, when a potential client requests a proposal for a specific project you need to tailor your submittal to *their* needs and interests.

Much of the proposal will be custom written to explain such things as your approach to the problem, your fees, schedule and the like. Still, a great deal of it will be standard descriptions of your design philosophy, methods of working with clients, past experience in a particular project type, brief resumés of the staff you will assign to the job and other "boilerplate."

The application described in this section can serve two functions for the small design firm: It can maintain marketing information such as project histories, client lists, and resumés and it can assist in the production of proposals. In this sense it is a simpler, streamlined method for those applications described in Sections 1.2 and 1.4.

For this application you need to be able to set up standard files on your word processor that you can recall when needed to insert into your proposal. If you don't already have one, you will want to purchase word processing software that has a "merge" capability so that one file can call data from another file.

Additional Application Requirements

You may also want to purchase software that is designed to help outline, spelling checkers to avoid those embarrassing mistakes in the final copy, and style checkers to help suggest improvements in grammar and writing style.

One valuable addition to consider when purchasing software is its ability to import data from other programs. The ability to include spreadsheet information or data from a data base management program adds a great deal of flexibility to your method of assembling proposals.

Requirements of Software

In addition to the basic editing features of any word processing program, your software should also have the following features:

1. the ability to merge data from one file or files into the calling file
2. manual "file-read" ability so you can read another file into the file you are working on when desired
3. on-screen page formatting so you see on the screen exactly what the printed text will look like
4. the ability to print boldface and underline
5. the ability to vary line spacing and character pitch so you can use different print styles (You will also need a printer capable of doing this.)
6. a column mode so you can move columns and perform other editing on columns rather than being limited to only the full page width
7. a search and replace function so you can look for a particular word or series of words and have the program replace them with another string
8. the ability to include headers and footers on each page

Requirements of Hardware

RAM.   With the hardware available today, available RAM usually isn't a problem. Most programs only need 64K of memory, some 128K. Word processing programs that are part of an integrated package may need more, however.

Disks.   You should have at least two floppy disks, one for the program and one for your proposal files. With a hard disk system, of course, all the data can be on one disk.

Printer.   You will need a letter-quality printer, either an impact type such as a daisywheel printer or a laser printer that can produce correspondence-quality copy. The printer and software should be capable of varying pitch and line spacing so you can adjust the amount of copy in a given page area.

Screen.   An 80-character screen is best so you can see the full width of a "page."

Cost Variables

Hardware.   A minimum configuration with two disk drives and a letter-quality printer can be purchased for as little as $3,000 or less. A ten-megabyte hard disk drive will add about $800 to $1,300.

Software.   Word processing programs range from under $100 to $500 depending on their complexity. Spelling checkers, indexing programs and other add-ons to word processing are in addition to this price.

Setup.   Setup costs depend on the time it takes you to establish your standard proposal formats and enter the data you will be using repeatedly such as resumés, project experience, and the like.

Implementation Procedures

1. Develop a style guide. This is a standard format for how all your proposals will look when they are completed. You should decide on such things as the sequence the information will be presented, how paragraphs will be indented, spacing, where titles will go and all the other compositional details of your final piece.

2. Develop project descriptions for your past jobs using a consistent format and writing style. As you do this assign a project type code to each. This will be invaluable for indexing your projects for later recall when you are assembling a proposal for a specific job category. The types of codes and their specificity will, of course, depend on the kind of work your firm does. For example, an office that specializes in schools may divide them into elementary schools, schools for the disabled, secondary schools, private schools and the like while another firm may simply assign a general category of "schools" to that type of work. Keep in mind that you will also want to use the same categories when indexing your staff's experience.

3. Write resumés for all office staff using a consistent format and writing style. Use the "pyramid" style so the most important information comes first and the more detailed personnel history is elaborated later. This way you can edit from the back forward if the proposal request doesn't require a great deal of detail.

4. Write other standard paragraphs that you think you will be using repeatedly. These may include such things as your office's design philosophy, how you develop fees and schedules, your method of working with clients and similar office procedures.

5. Develop a standard file-naming convention for all your information. This will make the process of assembling the final proposal much easier and provide you with guidelines for naming new files as you expand your system. Since most firms using this application will be small, you might consider using a simple three-letter prefix for job experience followed by a sequential number. For example, a file describing a retail project would be named RET-5 for the fifth retail project the firm did. You could also add date information such as RET/85/5 for the fifth retail project the firm did in 1985.

Naming resumé files is best done with the last name of the person described in the resumé. Once again, for small firms using this application, the simplest approach is the best. If you want to index resumés based on project experience, you can use the same categories developed for job descriptions, place these on index cards and list the staff names that have worked on these types of jobs.

If you have a lot of employees with a wide variety of experience, you will want to use a data base management program similar to the one described in Section 1.4.

6. Print out copies of each of the standard files you have developed. Assemble these in a loose-leaf notebook as a reference. Whoever is putting together the proposal can easily see what is included in each file and simply list those files by name in the order in which they are to appear. A secretary can then do the final editing and assembly of the proposal.

Additional Tips

- Develop one proposal style and stick with it. This way you can spend your time working on the proposal, not how it should look on the printed page.
- Write both a short form and a long form of project descriptions. Some proposal requests ask for very detailed information on your past projects while others just want a brief summary.

Sources for More Information

If you are just starting a marketing program or want to improve the proposals you now submit to clients, the following books and newsletters will help you organize your efforts and the format of your proposals.

Books

Coxe, Weld. *Marketing Architectural and Engineering Services, 2nd ed.* New York: Van Nostrand Reinhold, 1983.

Jones, Gerre. *How to Market Professional Design Services, 2nd ed.* New York: McGraw-Hill Book Company, 1983.

Morgan, Jim. *Marketing for the Small Design Firm.* New York: Whitney Library of Design, 1984.

Newsletters

A/E Marketing Journal. P.O. Box 11316, Newington, CT 06111.

Professional Marketing Report. P.O. Box 32387, Washington, DC 20007.

Small Computers in Practice. EMA Management Associates, Inc., 1145 Gaskings Road, Richmond, VA 23233.

Other

The Computer vs. Preprints. Diane C. Creel; William W. Young.

Society for Marketing Professional Services, 1983. Available from:

SMPS
1437 Powhatan Street
Alexandria, VA 22314

1.4

INTEGRATED MARKETING INFORMATION SYSTEMS

If you are just starting to use microcomputers to assist with your marketing, the kinds of specific applications discussed in Sections 1.1, 1.2 and 1.3 may be the best direction for you to take. These are easy to set up, convenient to use, and simple to maintain. However, if you are ready to move into a more sophisticated system or want all of your marketing information in one data base you should consider an integrated system. In this kind of system all data relating to lead tracking, project histories, resumés, and revenue forecasting is included in one relational data base management system giving you great flexibility in maintaining and selecting the information to meet various marketing needs.

This section describes the basic requirements of setting up an integrated marketing information system. It is based on the Marketing Information Retrieval System (MIRS) devised by The Earth Technology Corporation, Long Beach, California. I would like to extend special thanks to David Witzke and Diane Creel for their assistance.

Basic Application Requirements

This application requires a system that contains the multitude of interrelated information required for a thorough marketing program, but that is easy to use without the need for complicated computer commands. It also needs to be flexible enough to accommodate changes as your needs change and your firm grows.

Requirements of Software

This application requires the use of a relational data base management system (RDBMS). If you are unfamiliar with this type of software refer to the Appendix on Fundamentals of Data Base Management Systems for a complete description.

The following are some of the specific software requirements you will need to successfully implement this application.

1. You will need at least five files open at one time.

2. The system must provide for multifield indexing.

3. The software should allow you to sort on several key fields together instead of just one.

4. In addition to numeric and alphanumeric field types the software should have data field and logical field types. A text field type (like dBase III's "memo" file) is very useful to store long, variable-length descriptions of things like notes, resumé experience, and the like.

5. Security features should be available to limit access to the data to only those authorized.

6. Fields should allow at least 132 characters.

7. Since this application can become complex and each record lengthy, the program should allow more than one "screenfull" of information per record.

8. The program must have flexible methods of querying the data base, both on screen and in printed reports. This includes relational queries, Boolean searches, and partial string searches.

9. The program must have a flexible report generator since you will want to print out results in various ways. For a relational data base management system this includes being able to access more than one file at a time for report generation.

10. The program must have at least basic four-function arithmetic calculation capability. In addition, it is helpful for this application to be able to perform counts on the number of records meeting certain criteria or to perform averaging.

11. You should be able to modify the structure of existing files or add fields without loss of data.

Requirements of Hardware

RAM.   A minimum of 256K is required.

Disks.   You need a minimum of two disk drives, one for the program and one for your data, or one disk drive and one hard disk. An integrated marketing information system requires a great deal of storage so you should seriously consider a hard disk. In any case, be sure to estimate your needs prior to buying a system.

Printer.   Since you will want reports produced quickly in-house, but will also want letter-quality output for reports and client use, you should consider having both a dot-matrix printer and impact printer, or a laser or ink-jet printer.

Cost Variables

Hardware.   A complete setup with one disk drive and one 20-megabyte hard disk and a letter-quality printer can be purchased for as little as $4,500 or less.

Software.   Relational database management programs range from about $400 to over $1,000, but with many very good programs under $800.

Setup.   Setup costs depend on the complexity of your application. In the case of an integrated system described in this section you should plan for the time to analyze your needs and program for your special requirements. Actual setup and programming time may take several days while the testing and "shake-down" period may take several months.

Data entry. If preprinted forms are used, data entry can be done by your marketing coordinator, secretary or other clerical help.

Implementation Procedures

1. Analyze and define your firm's needs. This includes the information you need to have in the system, the reports and on-screen queries that will be required, how the different files of information will be related, and what security you will want built into the system.

2. Based on this analysis, develop data collection forms to provide a standard format for everyone who markets. See Figures 1.4-1 and 1.4-2.

3. Research and select the relational data base management software most appropriate to the needs identified in step 1. Use the "Requirements of Software" listed above and in the Appendix to help make your selection.

4. If you do not already have a microcomputer, identify the hardware needs required by the software and any other applications you may have for the computer. If your firm is a medium-to-large office you may want to consider having a separate system just for the marketing department. A small office, of course, will want to use one machine for several applications.

5. Following the instructions of your software, set up the required data files, indexes, report formats, and other special programming required by your application. Use a data base management program that allows you to define custom menu screens rather than requiring cryptic commands. This requires extra time in programming but is absolutely necessary if the system is to be easy to use.

6. Determine a policy for how the system is to be maintained. This should include who is responsible for file maintenance and updating, how often the files will be updated and the procedures for office staff to provide the necessary data for updating.

Examples

The Earth Technology Corporation, a geotechnical and earth sciences engineering firm based in Long Beach, California uses a comprehensive, integrated Marketing Information Retrieval System (MIRS) for their firm. Their system was planned for use by more than 250 employees in six offices throughout the United States. They used the dBase III data base management software program by Ashton-Tate to custom design a menu-driven application program. In addition, a user's manual was prepared that simply and clearly explains to the staff how to use the program.

The data base is organized around four components: a client contact system,

The Earth Technology Corporation

CLIENT CONTACT INFORMATION

☐ NEW CONTACT   ☐ FOLLOW-UP
☐ CHANGE   ☐ DELETE

ORGANIZATION NAME: _____

CONTACT NAME: _____   TITLE: _____

ADDRESS: _____   TYPE OF CONTACT: ☐ COLD CALL
                                                              ☐ REFERRAL
CITY: _____   ☐ MAINTENANCE MARKETING CALL
                                                              ☐ SOQ/PROPOSAL
STATE: _____ ZIP: _____   ☐ PRESENTATION
                                                              ☐ POST MORTEM
CONTACT TELEPHONE NUMBER: (____) _____ – _____   ☐ OTHER: _____

DATE CONTACTED (MM/DD/YY): _____/_____/_____   _____

METHOD: ☐ PHONE CALL   ☐ PERSONAL VISIT
                                             CONTACTED BY: _____ / _____
MARKET TYPE: NAME   OFFICE

☐ FEDERAL GOVERNMENT   ☐ LOCAL GOVERNMENT   ☐ UTILITIES   ☐ CONSTRUCTION AND A/E
☐ STATE GOVERNMENT   ☐ INDUSTRIES   ☐ OIL AND GAS ☐ MINING
☐ OTHER: _____

NAME OF PROJECT(S) DISCUSSED (INCLUDING LOCATION AND SCOPE OF SERVICES): _____
_____
_____

AREA OF CLIENT INTEREST: (CHECK THE ONE MOST APPROPRIATE)

☐ OFFSHORE   ☐ COLD REGION TECHNOLOGY   ☐ GEOPHYSICS   ☐ PIPELINES
☐ HIGH-LEVEL WASTE   ☐ ADVANCED TECHNOLOGY   ☐ ENVIRONMENTAL ☐ CRITICAL SITING
☐ LOW-LEVEL WASTE   ☐ HAZARDOUS WASTE   ☐ SOLID WASTE   ☐ TESTING SERVICES
☐ GEOTECHNICAL   ☐ RESEARCH & DEVELOPMENT   ☐ MINING   ☐ WATER RESOURCES
☐ OTHER: _____

RESULT OF CONTACT:

☐ OPPORTUNITY IDENTIFIED   ☐ RFP   ☐ RFQ   ☐ SOQ
☐ PROPOSAL   ☐ INTERVIEW (FOLLOWING PROPOSAL)   ☐ WON JOB (EXPLAIN BELOW)
☐ WILL NOT RESPOND TO RFQ/RFP ☐ LOST JOB (EXPLAIN BELOW)   ☐ OTHER (EXPLAIN BELOW)

NOTES: _____
_____
_____
_____
_____
_____
_____
_____
_____
_____
_____
_____
_____
                                                         (CONTINUED ON BACK)

FOLLOW-UP: ☐ 30 DAYS   ☐ 60 DAYS   ☐ 90 DAYS   ☐ OTHER _____
             ACTION ITEMS   DEADLINE   RESPONSIBILITY

_____   _____   _____
_____   _____   _____
_____   _____   _____

DISTRIBUTION: CORP. MKTG., _____

Figure 1.4-1
Client Contact Data Form

 **The Earth Technology Corporation**

REVENUE FORECAST DATA FORM

PROSPECT NUMBER _____
(LEAVE BLANK)

ORGANIZATION NAME: _____

PROJECT NAME: _____

PROJECT DESCRIPTION (INCLUDING LOCATION): _____

_____

_____

SERVICES TO BE PROVIDED: _____

_____

_____

STATUS: (DUE DATES IN MM/DD/YY)

☐ OPPORTUNITY IDENTIFIED   ☐ RFQ/RFP; DUE DATE: _____   ☐ SOQ; DUE DATE: _____   ☐ PROPOSAL; DUE DATE: _____
☐ SHORT LISTED   ☐ INTERVIEW; DATE: _____   ☐ SELECTED   ☐ CONTRACT SIGNED; NTP DATE: _____
☐ PROJECT LOST (EXPLAIN BELOW)   ☐ PROJECT CANCELLED (EXPLAIN BELOW)   ☐ PROJECT POSTPONED (EXPLAIN BELOW)

MARKET TYPE:

☐ FEDERAL GOVERNMENT   ☐ LOCAL GOVERNMENT   ☐ UTILITIES   ☐ CONSTRUCTION AND A/E
☐ STATE GOVERNMENT   ☐ INDUSTRIES   ☐ OIL & GAS   ☐ MINING

PROBABILITY:

_____ % JOB WILL PROCEED   _____ % COMPETITION   ESTIMATED REVENUE TO EARTH TECHNOLOGY ($000) _____

FIRST ETC CONTACT: _____   SECOND ETC CONTACT: _____

ESTIMATED NOTICE TO PROCEED DATE: _____   ESTIMATED PROJECT LENGTH: _____ MONTHS

OFFICE: _____   OTHER OFFICES INVOLVED: _____

MARKET ACTIVITY:

☐ OFFSHORE/CRT   ☐ PIPELINES   ☐ GEOTECHNICAL
☐ GEOPHYSICS   ☐ ADVANCED TECHNOLOGY (WESTERN ONLY)   ☐ HAZARDOUS WASTE/SOLID WASTE
☐ HIGH-/LOW-LEVEL WASTE   ☐ ENVIRONMENTAL   ☐ TESTING SERVICES (WESTERN ONLY)
☐ WATER RESOURCES   ☐ CRITICAL SITING

REMARKS: _____

_____

_____

DATE: _____   _____
                                          SIGNATURE OF ACTIVITY GROUP LEADER

Figure 1.4-2
Revenue Forecast Data Form

26

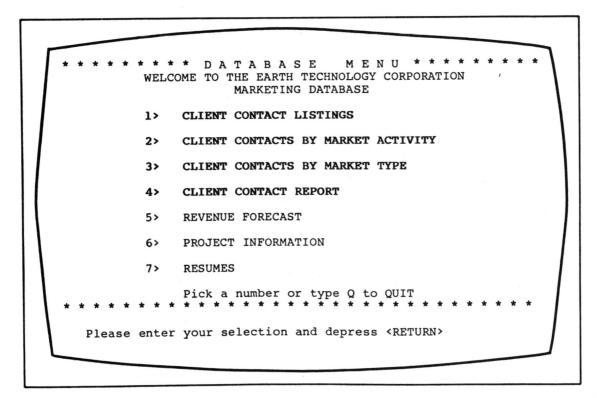

```
* * * * * * * * *  D A T A B A S E    M E N U  * * * * * * * * *
             WELCOME TO THE EARTH TECHNOLOGY CORPORATION
                        MARKETING DATABASE

        1>    CLIENT CONTACT LISTINGS

        2>    CLIENT CONTACTS BY MARKET ACTIVITY

        3>    CLIENT CONTACTS BY MARKET TYPE

        4>    CLIENT CONTACT REPORT

        5>    REVENUE FORECAST

        6>    PROJECT INFORMATION

        7>    RESUMES

              Pick a number or type Q to QUIT
* * * * * * * * * * * * * * * * * * * * * * * * * * * * * * * *

        Please enter your selection and depress <RETURN>
```

Figure 1.4-3
MIRS Main Menu

project information system, resumé system and a revenue forecast system. When a user accesses the system he or she is presented with a preliminary screen menu giving the preliminary choices to enter the four components of the system. See Figure 1.4-3. Any selection from this menu gives another menu of further choices making it very easy for the user to find the information needed quickly and accurately.

The amount of data contained in the system is extensive. Figure 1.4-4 shows the data fields in the project information file. One of the reports produced from information in this file is shown in Figure 1.4-5 including the use of the "memo" field type provided by the dBase III software. The "Project Description" field (Field 6 in Figure 1.4-4) consists of only a ten-character field but calls up a lengthy text description that is stored in a separate file.

A multitude of reports can be generated from the information in the system sorted in a variety of ways. Thus, someone can review the current status of all contacts in the oil and gas market or what contacts have been made to a specific company.

Special query commands are also possible. For example, someone can ask

```
Structure for database : C:PROJECTS.dbf
Number of data records :    161
Date of last update    : 05/06/85
Field  Field name  Type        Width   Dec
    1  ORGAN_NAME  Character      35
    2  PROJ_NAME   Character      70
    3  PROJ_LOC    Character      25
    4  OWNER       Character      35
    5  PROJ_TYPE   Character     132
    6  DESCRIPT    Memo           10
    7  ADDRESS_1   Character      35
    8  ADDRESS_2   Character      35
    9  CITY        Character      20
   10  STATE       Character       2
   11  ZIP         Numeric         5
   12  REFER       Character      35
   13  REFER_PHON  Character      13
   14  ADMIN_CONT  Character      35
   15  ADMIN_PHON  Character      13
   16  TECH_CONT   Character      35
Press any key to continue...
   17  TECH_PHON   Character      13
   18  START_DATE  Date            8
   19  EST_COMP    Date            8
   20  ACTL_COMP   Date            8
   21  EARLY_LATE  Character     132
   22  EST_AMOUNT  Numeric         9
   23  ACTL_AMOUN  Numeric         9
   24  OVER_UNDER  Character     132
   25  CNTRCT_TYP  Character      35
   26  CNTRCT_REL  Character      35
   27  CNTRCT_NRP  Character      10
   28  CNTRCT_NRS  Character      10
   29  ERTEC_NR    Character      10
   30  PROJ_MGR    Character      35
   31  SUB_NAME    Character      35
   32  ADDRS_1     Character      35
Press any key to continue...
   33  ADDRS_2     Character      35
   34  SUB_AMOUNT  Numeric         9
   35  SUB_NUMBER  Character      10
   36  SUB_SERVCS  Character     132
   37  DATE_ENTER  Date            8
   38  PREPD_BY    Character      25
** Total **                    1279
```

Figure 1.4-4
Data Base File Structure

the system to display or print all records for contacts that were made by (1) either of two people in the firm, (2) in the state of California, and (3) where the market type was the federal government.

For proposal preparation, the system is just as powerful. The resumé system is built around five separate files related by personnel name. There is a personnel

```
RECORD NUMBER:              1
PROJECT NAME:              VIRGIL C SUMMER NUCLEAR STATION
PROJECT LOCATION:          S CAROLINA
PROJECT TYPE:              SEISMIC/GEOTECHNICAL/INSTRUMENTATION/LICENSING
PROJECT OWNER:             SOUTH CAROLINA ELECTRIC & GAS CO
CLIENT NAME:               S CAROLINA ELECTRIC & GAS CO
CLIENT ADDRESS:            PO BOX 8
                           JENKINSVILLE SC 29065
REFERENCE:                 MR H E BOLING
PROJECT DESCRIPTION:       Professional services and instrumentation were
                           provided as required by SCE&G to support Nuclear
                           Engineering & Licensing (NEL) for the Virgil C.
                           Summer Nuclear Station.  This work included the
                           preparation and performance of experimental field
                           testing, preparation of reports for submittal to
                           the NRC in order to satisfy the ASLB license
                           conditions, and providing the necessary
                           professional expertise in resolving these and
                           associated matters with the NRC.  All work was
                           performed under the direction of SCE&G/NEL.
                           Instrumentation used in the experimental field
                           testing was appropriately calibrated with NBS
                           traceability.


CONTRACT NUMBER:
PROJECT START DATE:        09/10/82
EST. COMPLETE DATE:        01/10/83
ACTUAL COMPLETE DATE:      03/01/84
ESTIMATED FEES: ($000)          140
ACTUAL FEES:    ($000)          200
PROJECT MANAGER:           C. CROUSE
PRIME OR SUB?              SUB
SUBCONTRACTORS:
ETC PROJECT NUMBER:        83-164
```

Figure 1.4-5
Project Information Report

data file, education file, registration file, experience file, and professional organization file. This structure allows for flexibility in searching for specific job experience members of the firm have as well as printing out listings for proposals. The resumé system also makes extensive use of memo files so a staff member with a long resumé can be accommodated as easily as someone with a brief employment history.

Additional Tips

- If several people in your office will be using the system, do not release it until thoroughly tested and there is enough data to make it effective and easy to use.

- When shopping for a RDBMS, limit yourself to a few choices that are regarded as the best, then study these in detail.

- Make it clear to the users of the system that some problems will occur while any "bugs" in the application are worked out. You should encourage the users to report any problems and make suggestions for improvement.

- Update the data base frequently. This will ensure that the data are current and will promote user confidence in the system.

1.5

TURNING YOUR COMPUTER
INTO A GRAPHICS DEPARTMENT

One of the most recent developments in microcomputer hardware and software is the capability to produce high-quality graphic images at a fairly low cost. Using other hardware designed to work with the microcomputer, you can produce graphics for your proposals, printed marketing material and presentations. You can easily and quickly make charts, graphs, slides, overhead transparencies and color prints of many types of graphic images.

Basic Application Requirements

This is a rather specialized application for your microcomputer and you have many choices as to what final output you can achieve. On the low end, some hardware and software configurations will only produce simple graphics such as bar charts, line charts, pie charts and the like on a dot-matrix printer or simple color plotter. More sophisticated configurations can provide you with high-resolution color slides of almost any kind of image.

If you want to implement this application, your first task will be to decide on what final output you want. This section will briefly describe some of the possibilities to give you a place to start in your evaluation of the right setup for your office's needs.

Graphic aids for marketing (or "visual enhancements" as they are sometimes called) fall into three broad categories: pictures, graphics and typesetting. All three are possible for a design firm to implement now, but typesetting is still expensive and time consuming to do in-house. If you are just beginning to implement this application, start with simple graphics production and move into more sophisticated picture generation later.

Producing graphics on a microcomputer involves two major components, the software to actually create the graphics on the computer screen and some method of transforming the digital data into a usable form. The most common method of changing what you see on the screen into another form is a dot-matrix printer or plotter of some sort. The hard copy can then be used as part of a proposal or, in the case of a color plotter, used to make a color overhead transparency using a copy machine.

Another method is to use a camera to simply photograph the image on the screen. There are hoods that are designed to fit over standard-size computer screens and that accommodate either 35 mm cameras or larger-format cameras using instant development film.

More sophisticated systems have a self-contained camera and high-resolution screen built into a unit that takes the digital signals from your computer and redisplays an image so it can be photographed. You have the option of selecting whatever color you want for the various parts of the image. Automatic exposure of the film as well as other features are also possible. In addition, you have the option of making 35 mm slides, overhead transparencies or color prints.

Finally, there is one system that lets you create a series of "slides" on your screen, store them on disk and play them back in a variety of ways in whatever sequence you want. They can be played back directly on a color monitor for small audiences or shown through a projection television system (*Videoshow*, available though Riddick Communications Corporation, Richmond, VA).

Requirements of Software

Since there are so many different types of graphics software designed to do different jobs there is no one set of requirements. Most of the programs will produce bar charts, line charts and pie charts, but no others. Some will also generate scatter graphs, 3-D graphs, organizational charts and network diagrams (such as CPM charts). There is also a wide variation in other features such as the number and types of text fonts each will produce, how many colors can be generated and what kind of hardware they can drive.

This last point is most important. Because there are hundreds of possible combinations of software and hardware components available, the software must be capable of supporting the output you want. This is one instance where you should not shop for software first, then hardware; rather, you must shop for both together.

Requirements of Hardware

RAM. RAM requirements are quite variable depending on the software package. A few of the simpler ones only need 64K of memory but most need at least 128K. Some need as much as 320K.

Disks. Again, some programs will require only the minimum of one disk, others need two. Practically all will support a hard disk.

Printer/Plotter. For simple charts and crude originals used in making overhead transparencies, a dot-matrix printer is usable. However, if you are serious about using this application for marketing you should consider an ink-jet printer, laser printer or color plotter for the best quality.

Screen. If you intend to photograph images directly off your screen, get the highest-resolution color monitor you can afford. The standard 560 × 240 pixel resolution of most screens will give you grainy reproductions.

Cost Variables

It is impossible to give any exact figures for hardware or software because of the wide range of possible configurations for graphics applications. However, the following list should help you decide if you want to pursue using microcomputers for this application. In the volatile field of computer equipment, prices change weekly so use these prices only as guidelines.

Hardware. Simple "hoods" with camera attachments for direct photography from the screen run between $200 and $900 depending on what system you choose and whether a camera comes with it.

The *Polaroid* "Palette Computer Image Recorder," which includes a camera and separate screen with the ability to custom mix colors, was about $1800 at the time of this writing.

Instant slide development film units and slide mounters are extra but give you the capability to create your own presentation slides in minutes. These may add several hundred dollars more to your setup.

The cost of output devices range from several hundred dollars for a simple dot-matrix printer to thousands of dollars for large, multicolor pen plotters.

Color graphics boards may range from about $200 to several thousand dollars for the more sophisticated models.

Software. Most graphic software for microcomputers that produce bar charts, pie charts and others cost between $200 and $700. A few are available for less money but are limited in what they can do.

Additional Tips

- Your first task is to decide what *you* need in the way of graphic presentation and shop for the right kind of software along with the appropriate hardware. For occasional needs, check to see if there is a company in your city that offers computer-generated slide production and similar graphic services.

- Some graphics software comes as part of an integrated package. This makes it easy to take data from a spreadsheet and turn it into a graph, but remember that stand-alone programs will give you more graph styles, color ranges, type styles and other options that may make them more appropriate for your use.

- Be alert to new developments in optical laser-disk technology. As this is developed and prices drop, it may completely change the way architects and interior designers make presentations and market their services.

Sources for More Information*

Hood and camera systems for photographing monitors

Screenshooter
NPC Photo Division
1238 Chestnut Street
Newton, MA 02164

Instagraphic CRT Slide Imager
Eastman Kodak Company
Department 620
343 State Street
Rochester, NY 14650

DATACAM I and DATACAM 35
Photographic Sciences Corporation
770 Basket Road
P.O. Box 338
Webster, NY 14580

Direct slide production

Polaroid Palette Computer Image Recorder
Polaroid Corporation
784 Memorial Drive—3
Cambridge, MA 02139

1.6
PROFITABLE FEE ESTIMATES FOR PROPOSALS

In today's competitive professional services marketing environment, architects are often asked to give fee quotes or estimates very early in contract negotiations or as part of a competitive selection process. Often the full scope of the project

---

* Note: These are current at the time of this writing. Check with your local computer supplier or photographic supply store for additional systems that may be on the market.

is not known, so you can't (or don't have time to) do a detailed estimate as discussed in Section 2.3. Instead, you must make your "best guess" of the fees required to do a job that may last a year or more. One way to do this without committing yourself to an unprofitable quote is to review the fees you charged on similar jobs in the past and the only way to do this is to have complete and organized data on past jobs. However, remember that this application is only for preliminary estimates if you don't have time to do a complete fee estimate as described in Section 2.3, or if you want to double check a detailed fee estimate.

Basic Application Requirements

A record of fees charged on a past project is a subset of that job's total project history. (See Section 1.2.) You can computerize this aspect of office management as a separate application or integrate it into a relational data base management system (RDBMS) as discussed in Section 1.2. This section will show how to make it a part of a RDBMS to work with the applications discussed in Sections 1.2 and 1.4. If you choose to keep it separate, the only difference is that each record must contain more basic data about the client and the project. In a RDBMS, client and project information is available (related) from other files. Figure 1.6-1 shows this relationship diagrammatically.

In order for a history of fees to be useful it must allow you to relate the dependent variable (fees) to an independent variable that can be used to predict the money required to do a job. Some of the common independent variables

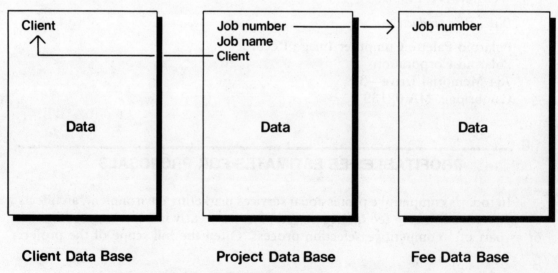

Client Data Base   Project Data Base   Fee Data Base

Figure 1.6-1
Fee History in Relation to Other Project Data

34

are construction cost (fees figured as a percentage of this), square footage, planning unit (fees per hotel room or apartment) or some combination of these. Each office develops "rules of thumb" for estimating fees, but these often become dated or inaccurate as production techniques and client demands change. Maintaining fee histories that include the critical independent variables for *your* office's work will help you more accurately estimate fees using these methods.

To make full use of this application you should be able to accomplish the following:

1. Develop a list of fees charged on past projects that are similar to the one you are estimating. You should be able to select the projects on whatever criteria seem appropriate such as a square-footage range, number of stories, type of construction, building type, and so forth.

2. The list should include both your original fee estimate as well as the *actual* fees spent to do the job and the percentage of profit (or loss).

3. The list should also include consultant fees and expenses.

4. The list should be categorized by job phases with both estimated and actual costs so you can see in what phase you made or lost money.

Notice that much of this information is (or should be) documented in your project accounting system. If your job-cost accounting software allows you to selectively summarize and review this kind of information your task will be a little easier. However, you still need this kind of fee summary because accounting systems do not relate fees to the kinds of dependent variables mentioned above. The power of this application is that it can provide analysis of fees as a function of the kind of work on which they were spent to accomplish.

This application could be implemented with a spreadsheet program although it would not be as flexible. Each project type would have its own template in which you entered data about projects as they were completed. The program would easily do the calculations for you and keep a running average of the numbers as you completed jobs. Once you set up one template it could be copied as many times as the number of project types you wanted to keep track of.

Additional Application Requirements

However, instead of using a spreadsheet, this section assumes that this application will be integrated with other marketing functions as part of a RDBMS. As such, it must have one or more data fields that can be used to relate it to other files in your system. A project number is the easiest and most likely candidate since it is unique and short. If you were preparing a report on fees of a select list of past jobs, the project number could be used to identify records in the project description file so you would have a more complete summary of each project. Similarly, client information for each of those jobs could also be recalled if needed.

Requirements of Software

All of the requirements mentioned in Section 1.2 apply to this application as well. In addition, having software that has more extensive arithmetic capabilities is useful. As you select records for processing, the program can peform the mathematics critical for fee analysis. If your program does not have this ability it is even more important that data can be transferred to other types of programs such as a spreadsheet. Refer to the Appendix on "Fundamentals of Data Base Management Systems" if you are unfamiliar with this type of software.

Requirements of Hardware and Cost Variables

Hardware requirements and cost variables are the same as listed in Section 1.2 except that more time will be necessary to set up the mathematical analysis portion of the data base (or spreadsheet program if you use one).

Implementation Procedures

1. Determine the basis on which you want to be able to estimate fees. Will it be dollars per gross square foot, net square foot or some other unit?
2. Decide how much detail you need for this kind of preliminary estimating. Some offices will want a breakdown by design phases; others will simply need an overall cost per square foot.
3. Determine the data fields you need. The exact fields you establish will depend on your requirements, but consider the following ones as a starting point. Some of the fields may not be necessary if your program can perform arithmetic calculations or if you intend to export data to a spreadsheet program for calculation. For example, if your software has limited math capabilities, you may need to calculate "fees per square foot" as part of the project history data entry instead of having the computer do it for you.

project name
project number
construction cost
budgeted fees (may be lump sum or divided by job phases)
actual fees billed
actual fees spent (true cost of doing the job)
square feet

consultant fees—structural, mechanical, electrical, other

percent profit (or loss)

fee per square foot (based on actual fees spent)

fee as percent of construction cost (based on actual fees spent)

remarks (useful for recording any unusual circumstances of the job that affected fees)

4. Following the instructions of your software, set up the data entry screens, indexes, report formats and other files as required by the program. As with any relational data base system, include only those data fields that are unique to *fees*. Other data will be extracted from the other files in the system.

Additional Tips

- Don't try to be *too* detailed in your information. Remember that this kind of cost estimating should only be a preliminary budget or as a double check to a more detailed cost-based estimate discussed in Section 2.3.

- Restrict access to the "Fees File" with password protection. This controls the fee data, but doesn't restrict someone from gathering other project information for marketing purposes.

CHAPTER 2

Practical Steps to Help
Streamline Your
Business Management Needs

Most design professionals first use computers for word processing and accounting. These applications are usually the easiest to begin with and provide the most immediate benefits. However, there are many other aspects of business management for which automation is ideally suited. This chapter explores some of these and provides you with guidance on how to get started immediately. You can then use the ideas in this chapter as a springboard for developing other applications unique to your firm's needs.

If you are not yet using a computer for your financial management, Section 2.4 describes the basics of this type of software. Use it as a starting point for determining your needs and reviewing existing financial management packages. Although many business applications can be run on machines with floppy disks, you should seriously consider spending a little more money for a hard disk. Capacities of hard disks for micros are increasing while their costs are decreasing so if you are purchasing a new system buy one with a hard disk and a method for easy backup such as a tape-streamer.

2.1
TIME-SAVING RECORDS MANAGEMENT

Records management in architectural and interior design offices has always been a problem because of the requirement for multiple access points for the same document. For example, you may want to retrieve a letter at one time based on the person who sent it, at another because of some topic it discusses and at a third time to know if someone else got a copy. Many offices try to solve the problem by making copies of the same document and filing them in different places: in the job file, a chronological file, a correspondence-sent file and so forth. This is awkward at best and incomplete at its worst. If you are trying to reconstruct a job for a legal defense, for instance, how can you be sure you have retrieved *all* the documents related to the subject at hand without reading through every piece of paper in your files?

This section describes how you can set up a simple indexing system to gain control of the diverse types of records you have, and improve access to the vital information they contain.

Basic Application Requirements

Records serve five primary functions in a design office, either singularly or in combination. They serve as a communication tool, a legal document, a reminder for later action, a historical account of some action and as a temporary "information holder" to bridge from one phase of a project to another. Some of these are best accommodated with a records management system while others are better handled by a project management system. For example, design checklists kept by a project manager are a better way of maintaining continuity from one design phase to another than by cluttering the job files with them.

You should decide which documents you need to include in a records management system and which are best included in a project management system. Refer to Chapter 6 for a description of several applications directly related to project management. Refer to Section 5.4 for a discussion of how to index drawings and other project documents.

A successful implementation of this application should allow you to access your records in the following ways:

by date

by people involved including the originator of the record, the receiver of the record, those mentioned in the record and those receiving copies (You may also want to include the firms these people work for.)

by subject or subjects

by phase of service

by record type such as meeting minutes, letter, field report, etc.

by reference to other documents

by record identifying number (if used)

You may not need to access your office's records by all of these headings, but the more you include the more flexibility you will have. Keep in mind that this application is not a way of *physically storing* the record (although this is possible), but simply a way of indexing and managing them.

Requirements of Software

You will need a file management type of data base management system to implement this application. The following are some of the specific software requirements you will need. Refer to Appendix A, Fundamentals of Data Base Management Systems, for a complete description of these and other criteria for selecting a DBMS.

1. The program should allow at least ten fields per record.
2. You should be able to index on all the data fields.
3. The software should allow you to sort on several key fields together instead of just one alone.
4. You may want to consider security features that would limit access to the data to only those authorized.
5. The program must have flexible methods of querying the data base, both on screen and in printed reports. This includes relational queries, Boolean searches and partial string searches. For example, you may want to find all records where the subject is exterior masonry wall *and* involved either Mr. Smith *or* Mr. Jones.

Requirements of Hardware

RAM. Many file management systems will work with as little as 48K of RAM. The ones that are part of an integrated package require more, usually 128K or greater.

Disks. You should have at a minimum two disk drives, one for the program and one for your data. For a records management application you may want to consider dedicating one disk per job with an additional disk for general office files. Even if you have a hard disk system, this keeps storage space free for other applications. When a job is complete, you can then archive the disk with the other job files.

Printer. A dot-matrix printer is the minimum requirement for this application.

Cost Variables

Hardware. A complete setup with two disk drives and a dot-matrix printer can be purchased for as little as $2,000 or less.

Software. Simple file management programs range from under $100 to $400 with a few costing more than $400.

Setup. Setup costs depend on the complexity of your application. You may need from one to two hours to set up a simple file management system after you have decided how to organize your records.

Data entry.   Since a great deal of paper works its way through an architectural office, data entry time can be significant. However, once a standard procedure has been established and clerical staff has been trained in how to enter data, the small amount of extra time required will more than offset the wasted time trying to find documents later on.

Implementation Procedures

1. Decide on the requirements of a records management system for your office. Some of the considerations include the following:

- What kinds of records do you want to manage? Are these accounting records, general correspondence, marketing correspondence, job files, etc?
- What kind of access is usually required? How are records accessed now?
- What are the variations caused by the scope and type of work that the office performs?
- What clerical help is available or likely to be available?
- How much time and money will be devoted to records management? How important is it to the firm?

2. Decide on subject headings you will use to classify the subject content of your records. These should reflect enough detail to allow you to retrieve exactly what you want, but not so elaborate as to make it difficult to classify a record. Refer to Section 9.3 for guidance on developing your own classification system.

3. Determine how you want to physically file the records you are classifying. Some possibilities include chronologically, by job number, by arbitrarily assigned accession numbers or some combination of these. It really doesn't matter as long as you are consistent with your method and your indexing is complete. However, the best approach is to file according to the way you access the records *most often*. In the majority of offices this would be by job name or number and then by phase.

Regardless of the method you use, each record must have a unique identifying number so you can find the hard copy after referring to your computer index. This identifying number becomes the "key" field when setting up your data base management system. If you want to keep job records separate, one method is to use the job number as the first part of the identifying number and the date and accession number as the second part. Your number might then look something like this: 8615/860212/4.

The job number is 8615, the date of the document is February 12, 1986 (860212), and this is the fourth document of job number 8615 indexed that day. The "key" could also consist of two or three fields that together would uniquely identify the document. Thus, the first field of the key could be the project number, the second the date, and the third the accession number for that date. This method has the advantage of allowing you to search on any one of the key fields—for example, you could ask the computer to list all the documents for a particular job number that were generated between two given dates.

4. Following the instructions of your data base management system, set up the file definitions, data files, indexes, report formats and other files required by your software.

5. Establish a set policy on how records are to flow through your office, who will enter the information into the computer, how often and how the hard copies will be filed. If your office is organized around a strong project manager type of project team, this person should be the interface between job records and the secretarial staff who maintain these records.

Examples

Figure 2.1-1 shows what a typical data record would look like after a document had been entered into the system.

Additional Tips

- In order to minimize data entry time and assure that the data going into the system is complete, the project manager should be responsible for marking each document with the keywords that should be included in the subjects field. A secretary can then easily enter the required data into the system before filing the hard copy.

```
 1. Project number    8615
 2. Date (YYMMDD)     86/02/12
 3. Accession number  04
 4. Document type     Letter
 5. Service phase     DD
 6. Subject 1         Window flashing
 7. Subject 2         Window sealant
 8. Subject 3
 9. Comments          Advised against system recommended by contractor
10. Originator        F. Dawson
11. Receiver          P. Adams
12. Copies to         W. Smith, B. Evans
```

Figure 2.1-1
Records Management Entry for Correspondence File

Sources for More Information

Architectural Records Management.
Available from:

The American Institute of Architects Foundation
1735 New York Avenue, N.W.
Washington, DC 20006

Aschner, Katherine, ed. *Taking Control of Your Office Records: A Manager's Guide.*
White Plains, NY: Knowledge Industry Publications, Inc., 1983.

Diamond, Susan Z. *Records Management, A Practical Guide.* New York: American
Management Associations, 1983.

2.2

GETTING DOUBLE DUTY FROM PERSONNEL RECORDS

Personnel records are maintained for two primary purposes: to provide information for proposal preparation and to satisfy legal and accounting requirements such as salary and benefits data, accrued vacation time and tax data. Keeping track of an employee's professional experience to use in proposal preparation was discussed in Section 1.4. Although additional information is required for accounting and employment records there is no reason why you cannot combine the two in order to minimize data entry and reduce the possibility of errors that can occur when you maintain duplicate records.

Since personnel information is maintained for several different, but related, purposes you can streamline this aspect of office record keeping by using a relational data base management system (RDBMS). If you have a very small office (less than ten employees) you may want to consider setting up several separate data bases using a simple file management system since the small amount of data redundancy probably will not cause many problems. This section will discuss how to use a RDBMS for organizing employee records of larger firms.

Basic Application Requirements

Personnel records require that you maintain several "groups" of data on employees. There is basic information such as address, phone number, social security number and so forth, salary and benefits data, experience data and employment history data including employment date, promotions and raises. How you group all of this information depends on your needs, but some *should* be segregated such as salary and benefits data. It is very unlikely that people needing information on an employee's experience will ever need to see salary data. Because of this, there must be a password security feature built into this application so you can control who is able to read and change certain files.

You must also be able to print out several types of reports for such things as proposals, salary and promotion review, benefits review and the like. Your system must have the flexibility to do this.

Additional Application Requirements

A slightly more complex use of this application involves maintaining an ongoing tally of cumulated vacation time, sick leave and compensatory time. In this case, the program you use must be able to perform basic arithmetic functions.

Requirements of Software

The following are some of the specific software requirements you will need to successfully implement this application. Refer to Appendix A, Fundamentals of Data Base Management Systems, for a complete description of these and other criteria for selecting a DBMS.

1. For a relational data base management system you will need at least four files open at one time; more if you decide to break down the data into smaller groupings.

2. You should be able to index on at least six data fields. It is preferable to have the ability to index on a larger number.

3. The software should allow you to sort on several key fields together instead of just one alone.

4. In addition to numeric and alphanumeric field types you may find it useful to have a social security and date field type. Another very useful format is a text field similar to dBase III's "memo" field. This allows you to have a variable length field as part of a separate file that can be easily called up when needed. This is particularly useful for holding information related to salary history and experience data since newly hired employees will have a "smaller" file in these areas that people who have been with the firm for many years. If you try to keep this data in fixed-length fields you end up wasting a lot of storage space.

5. Security features must be available to limit access to the data to only those authorized.

6. For this application, it is very useful if your data base management system is compatible with other programs. If it is, you can easily send employee experience text to your word processing program for writing a proposal.

7. Since this application can become complex and each record lengthy, the

program should allow more than one "screenfull" of information per record.

8. The program must have flexible methods of querying the data base, both on screen and in printed reports. This includes relational queries, Boolean searches, and partial string searches.

9. The program must have a flexible report generator since you will want to print out results in various ways. For a relational data base management system, this includes being able to access more than one file at a time for report generation.

10. If you require it, the program must have at least basic four-function arithmetic calculation capability.

Requirements of Hardware

RAM. Some relational data base management programs operate with as little as 64K of RAM with the more sophisticated ones requiring 128K or more.

Disks. You should have at a minimum two disk drives, one for the program and one for your data. Since many data base management applications require a great deal of storage you should estimate your needs prior to buying a system. For most medium-size offices, however, there will not be enough employees to create a storage problem.

Printer. A dot-matrix printer is the minimum requirement for this application.

Cost Variables

Hardware. A complete setup with two disk drives and a dot-matrix printer can be purchased for as little as $2,000 or less.

Software. Simple file management programs range from under $100 to $400 with a few costing more than $400. Relational data base management programs range from about $400 to over $1,000, but with many very good programs under $800.

Setup. Setup costs depend on the complexity of your application. A fairly complex RDBMS such as described here may take from eight to twenty hours.

Data entry. Initial data entry can be time consuming since you will need to take all your employment information now on paper and keyboard it into your system.

Maintenance. Personnel files must be kept current. You must plan on having someone update the data base at regular intervals. How often this occurs and how much time it takes depends on the number of employees you have and the amount of changing data you maintain.

Implementation Procedures

1. Decide whether you really need to implement this application. For small firms, an accountant or part-time bookkeeper can easily maintain salary, benefits and vacation time data manually. Some banks can also do this as part of their payroll services. If you have over 40 employees or spend over 40 hours per month maintaining personnel records the chances are good that automating this application will yield benefits.

2. Decide what kinds of data you must maintain and the types of reports that are of most use to you in managing the firm. Check with your accountant and attorney for the exact kinds of personnel data your local and state government requires employers to maintain. Also verify current federal records requirements. For example, Equal Employment Opportunity reports only apply to firms with 50 or more employees and $50,000 or more in government contracts.

3. Establish the data fields you will need and what "groups" to put them in so you can set up the files of your relational data base management program. At a minimum you should consider four files: basic data, background, employment history and experience. The experience file will be similar to that described in Sections 1.3 and 1.4.

Use the following list of possible data fields as a starting point to develop your own data base structure:

Basic Data
full name (last, first)
employee number
social security number
address
city
state
zip code
telephone
who to contact in emergency
equal employment opportunity data fields if required

Background Data
registration
state(s) in which registered
year(s) of registration
registration number(s)

47

NCARB certification

educational degree(s)

year(s) graduated

school(s)

professional organization memberships

Employment History

date hired

termination date

title or job classification

starting salary

salary increases and dates (This could be a "memo" type of file or several data fields.)

bonuses

exemptions claimed

insurance data

current billing rate

current salary

vacation time

personal time off

sick leave

compensatory time (if used)

Experience

Refer to Sections 1.3 and 1.4 for a more complete description of how to set up this type of information. At a minimum, you would want a list of project types the employee has had experience with as well as an ongoing list of projects worked on while with the firm.

4. Following the directions of your software, set up the data definition files, indexes, report formats and other files as required by your RDBMS. The data field that will relate all the files will probably be the employee's name although you can use an employee number or a social security number. Using an employee number is a little easier and helps avoid errors in entering a request.

5. Set up paper forms for new employees to use when hired. These should correspond to your data base organization to make data entry easy.

6. Decide on a policy for updating the files. If you don't keep track of vacation time or sick leave, you may only need to update when people are hired or leave,

or when salary adjustments are made. In other cases, a weekly revision may be necessary.

Additional Tips

- Avoid making your data base more elaborate than it needs to be. Employees resist having to spend too much time updating their files and entering data that is never used.

- Be diligent about keeping the data base current. Even if you want to accumulate paper forms, notes and the like before "turning on" the system, set up a special file or "in basket" to hold this information prior to entering it so you don't lose track of small, but important, changes.

2.3

ACCURATE FEE ESTIMATES WITH A MICRO

Estimating fees accurately is critical to the financial success of your practice. Not only does a fee estimate often limit your total ultimate billing potential, but it is also critical to getting the job in the first place. In today's competitive marketplace, early fee quotes are often one of the deciding factors in being selected for a job.

The method of estimating discussed in this section should be used *in conjunction* with the method described in Section 1.6. That method is useful for *preliminary* estimating based on variables inherent in the project type under consideration. The method described here is much more detailed and is based on the *tasks* required to complete a project. The two should be done separately and then compared as a check against each other.

Basic Application Requirements

The application described here is a cost-based method of setting fees. This is one of the best ways to begin the fee-estimating process because it establishes the minimum level of compensation you need to break even to do various phases of the work. Once this level is established you can set your desired profit level, nonreimbursable direct expenses and consultant's charges then and adjust your fee quote up or down as you think necessary. This adjustment may be desirable to take into account the variables of the marketplace: what the competition is charging, what clients are willing to pay, extra value that you place on your reputation or special expertise, a better time schedule that you can offer and similar factors.

If, after you have estimated the fee and given it to the client, the client wants a lower fee, the information you have by using this method allows you to negotiate *services*, not fee, to reduce the total cost to the client without having you suffer.

A spreadsheet is the best type of software to use for this application since it is all "number crunching" and the ability to see how changes in hours, dollars and scope of work affect the bottom line fee is necessary.

Additional Application Requirements

You can set up several separate, but related, spreadsheets to help you estimate your fees in a very detailed way with one template taking information from another to use in its calculations. If you have not yet purchased software you may want to look for this feature. However, it is not essential for implementation of this application.

Having a spreadsheet as part of an integrated software package may be of some use if you want to graph numbers or easily transfer some portions to a proposal being generated with a word processing program. In most cases, however, you will simply want to "add up the numbers" and be able to perform "what if" calculations.

Requirements of Software

The spreadsheet program you select for this application should have the following minimum characteristics:

1. the standard mathematical functions
2. the ability to vary column widths
3. the ability to add rows and columns at the end and in the middle of the matrix
4. a column formatting capability to allow right justification, decimal point location, comma location and percentages
5. the ability to print only selected portions of the matrix

As mentioned above, you may also want the ability to retrieve data from other files so a summary spreadsheet can call data from other "worksheet" spreadsheet files.

Requirements of Hardware

RAM. Many stand-alone spreadsheet programs can operate on hardware with a minimum amount of RAM (64K or less), but if you want integrated software you will need 128K, 256K or more depending on the program.

Disks. For many programs, a single disk drive is sufficient, but you will most likely want at least two. A hard disk is desirable for faster operation of some of the integrated software packages.

Printer. A dot-matrix printer is the minimum requirement. For speed of operation a dot-matrix, laser, or ink-jet printer is the best choice.

Cost Variables

Hardware. A complete setup with two disk drives and a dot-matrix printer can be purchased for as little as $2,000 or less. A ten-megabyte hard disk drive will add about $800 to $1,300.

Software. Spreadsheet programs may range from about $100 to $400.

Setup. Depending on the complexity of the template you want for this application, setup time may range from four to twelve hours.

Implementation Procedures

1. Since this is a cost-based method of calculating fees, you first need to determine the phases and tasks on which estimates will be made. Each office will be a little different based on the type of work it does and how it categorizes time. You may want to follow the detailed list published in the AIA documents or develop your own. Whatever system you use should act as a checklist to remind you of the various detailed tasks required by *your* office to do the majority of its work. It should include spaces to add extra tasks that may be unique to the job you are calculating.

Figure 2.3-1 shows one page from a set of forms developed for an interior design firm. The entire set of forms is divided into the normal phases of Programming, Schematic Design and so forth. Within each phase are subphases and individual tasks for each of those. Of course, not every task is appropriate for every job, but they do serve as a reminder of the multitude of work tasks required for most projects.

2. Using the a worksheet developed in the first step, estimate the time each task for each phase will require. These will be based on the scope of work as defined by the client as well as your expected work requirements. There is no need to use a computer at this point since much of this effort is thinking through the job to decide what is involved.

You can make notes as appropriate to show how you estimated the hours and include the initials of the staff members that will be assigned to the task if you like. This will be useful for deciding on what hourly rate to use in the next step.

3. Add up the hours to arrive at the total number of hours you estimate

WORK TASK CHECKLIST

Project: ABC CORPORATION   Job #: 8627

Completed by: RTS   Project manager: RTS   Date: 4/15/86

Work task	Notes	Est. Hrs.	Staff
Programming			
101 PROJECT MANAGEMENT		6	AL
Initial meeting			
Meetings with in-house staff			
Direct work of in-house staff		10	RTS
Consultant coordination		4	RTS
Correspondence/Reports/etc.		2	RTS
Travel time			
Government agency coordination		1	RTS
Monitor fee expenditures		2	RTS
Review time sheets and invoices		1	RTS
TOTAL 101		26	
102 BUDGET DEVELOPMENT			
Obtain owner's budget requirements		4	RTS
Research similar facility costs		4	RTS
Research furnishings costs		6	DKB
Research non-construction costs		6	WRI
Apply unit costs to requirements		1	RTS
Finalize and layout budget form		4	RTS
In-house budget meetings		3	AL
Revisions		2	RTS
TOTAL 102		30	

Figure 2.3-1
Work Task Estimating Form

52

```
Project:  ABC Corporation
Date: 4/15/86
Completed by: AEA
```

FEE CALCULATION WORKSHEET

Programming				Personnel		
Tasks	Type Rate	Principal 23.00	RTS 17.75	WRI/DKB 12.50	PDC 9.25	Total
Project management	Hours	6	20			26
	$	138	355	0	0	493
Budget development	Hours	3	15	12		30
	$	69	266	150	0	485
Meetings/Presentations	Hours	10	10	20		40
	$	230	178	250	0	658
Existing facilities survey	Hours			30	40	70
	$	0	0	375	370	745
Interviews	Hours			32		32
	$	0	0	400	0	400
Tabulate/synthesize	Hours			24	24	48
	$	0	0	300	222	522
Evaluate program data	Hours		10	32		42
	$	0	178	400	0	578
Develop written program	Hours		10	16		26
	$	0	178	200	0	378
	Hours					0
	$	0	0	0	0	0
	Hours					0
	$	0	0	0	0	0
Total this phase	Hours	19	65	166	64	314
	$	437	1,154	2,075	592	4,258

Figure 2.3-2
Fee Calculation Worksheet

each subphase will require. These are the totals that will be entered into your computer spreadsheet.

4. Following the directions of your software, set up your spreadsheet to accommodate the most likely number of subphase tasks you will have and the number of columns for personnel or unique billing rates you expect. Figure 2.3-2 shows a portion of a fee calculation worksheet for just the programming phase of a project. You can do all of the calculation with one spreadsheet file (including the fee calculation summary described later) or you can have several spreadsheets if your software is capable of reading data from one file into another. For example, you could have one file for each phase and then a summary sheet. Unless you

want an extra amount of detail this is not necessary; all the work can easily be put in one spreadsheet.

5. Once the template is set up, simply enter the total number of hours you calculated earlier and enter them in the appropriate cells of your matrix. At the top of each column, enter the hourly rate for the personnel or staff positions needed to accomplish the project. A spreadsheet can include only those people you expect will be working on the job or you can develop one "master" matrix with all staff listed. If someone is not scheduled to work on a job you are estimating, then simply enter a "0" for their hourly rate. Formulas entered in the matrix will automatically multiply hours times rates and produce subtotals and totals with the press of a key.

If staff members with different billing rates are doing work within the same subphase task group, divide the total number of hours into different billing rate groups. Make your best estimate at this time.

There are several hourly rates you can use to multiply by the estimated hours required to complete the job. One is direct payroll cost not including direct personnel expense. Another is direct personnel expense and the third is actual billing rate. Since the method illustrated here attempts to establish actual costs for you to do the job (break even), you should enter direct salary (payroll) costs. Factors for benefits, indirect expenses and profit should be added in with the summary.

6. Once the totals for each subphase and phase are calculated they can be added to get the final direct payroll budget for the entire job. This total will be placed on the first line of the fee calculation summary. Once again, this summary can physically be a part of the same spreadsheet or in a separate file. The only critical factor is that the computer be able to get the totals from one place to another so your data entry time is kept to a minimum.

Figure 2.3-3 illustrates one type of fee calculation summary matrix giving two options for calculating fees. In this example, the overhead allocation figure was used to account for direct personnel expense and office indirect expenses prorated to this job. You can also figure these separately, depending on how you do your office accounting and how accurate your financial records are. If you expect any nonreimbursable direct expenses include these as well.

The spreadsheet should be set up to add the direct payroll costs, overhead costs, and nonreimbursable direct expenses to give you a total office cost. This amount represents the absolute *minimum* fee you need just to break even on the job.

Additional line items include consultants, contingency and profit. All of these are added to the total office cost to give you the total project fee. Since total office cost is separate from the last three items, you can change your profit percentage, contingency and consultant's scope of services as you like to explore the "what if" possibilities that spreadsheet software is so good at. This way, minimum break even costs are not reduced in your analysis efforts.

54

Practical Steps to Help Streamline Your Business Management Needs

```
Project:  ABC Corporation
Date: 4/15/86
Completed by: AEA


FEE CALCULATION SUMMARY

Programming Phase
============================================================
Item                                           Estimate
============================================================
A   Direct payroll budget                        4,258
       (Summary of fee calculation
       worksheets)

B   [ Direct personnel expense @     % of A
C   [ Indirect expense @             % of A
              OR
D   [ Overhead allocation @      157 % of A      6,685

E   Nonreimbursable direct expense
                                               -----------
F   Total Office Cost               >>> $        10,943

G   Consultant's fees                             1,000

H   Consultant upcharge          10 % of G          100

J   Contingency                   5 % of F          547

K   Profit @                      8 % of F          875
============================================================
    TOTAL PROJECT FEE             >>> $         13,466
       (F+G+H+J+K)
```

Figure 2.3-3
Fee Calculation Summary

Sources for More Information on Financial Management

The American Institute of Architects. *Compensation Management Guidelines for Architectural Services.* Washington: The American Institute of Architects, 1975.

Kliment, Stephen. *Compensation Guidelines for Architectural and Engineering Services.* Washington: The American Institute of Architects, 1978.

———*Architect/Engineer Supplement to: Compensation Guidelines.* Washington: The American Institute of Architects, 1978.

Piven, Peter. *Compensation Management: A Guide for Small Firms.* Washington: The American Institute of Architects, 1982.

2.4

FINANCIAL MANAGEMENT SIMPLIFIED

One of the most valuable uses of a microcomputer is to keep track of the firm's money. With costs of hardware dropping and software prices within reason for the small firm, no office should be without this application. This section describes integrated financial management and accounting applications that are appropriate for firms of about 5 to 50 or more employees. The upper limit is variable depending on which software package you buy and how fast the system operates. If your firm has five or fewer people you may want to stick with manual methods or implement some simple time sheet tracking and job cost accounting with a spreadsheet program.

Basic Application Requirements

Integrated financial management software simply means that you only enter information once and the program takes care of posting it to all the appropriate accounts (files) in the system. For example, time sheet information entered once is then used to develop job costing information, accounts receivable, payroll, project management reports and productivity reports.

A good accounting and financial management program should include at a minimum accounts receivable, accounts payable, general ledger, payroll and project costing. Additional reports may include such things as income statements, trial balance, aged accounts receivable, invoice log, time analysis reports, detailed project reports and profit planning, among others. The program should follow the AIA accounting guidelines.

Additional Application Requirements

What may be considered additional application requirements depends on your office's needs. Some firms, for example, may feel that password protection is something they don't need while others would consider this a basic requirement. You may also want to look for programs that let you transfer your data to a spreadsheet program for further analysis or have that capability built in. One program on the market has 2-D and 3-D graphics that let you generate graphs and charts that can be manipulated in perspective, zoom and pan. In addition, you may want to have the ability to generate custom reports according to your specifications without complicated reprogramming.

Some accounting consultants recommend that the program allow for "batch" processing of data entry. With this method, the computer holds all of your entries in a separate file until you are ready to have it "post" entries to all the files. This way, you can check for errors and change entries before committing the data to the system. A report-generating facility should go along with this.

Requirements of Software

Some of the specific requirements of a good financial accounting program include the following:

1. It should accommodate the number of projects you have active in your office at any one time.

2. It should accommodate the number of employees you presently have as well as future employees. Even though some programs can technically handle a given number of employees they begin to slow down over a certain number.

3. The program should give you flexibility in numbering projects and phases. Look for at least an eight-digit project number capability that can be formatted according to your needs. You should also have the flexibility to have as many phases to a project as you need. A total of 99 possible phases is good as a top limit.

4. There should be a method to develop an audit trail so you or your accountant can trace an item back to its source.

5. There should be several billing types. At a minimum you want hourly, hourly to a maximum, fixed fee, cost plus fixed fee and percent of construction. Other possibilities include phased percent of construction cost, square footage, nonbillable and direct costs plus overhead.

6. It should maintain costs for each phase of a project as well as the total project cost in case you are contracting and billing on individual phases of the work.

7. The program should have the ability to handle job costing on both a billing-rate basis and an actual labor cost plus overhead allocation basis.

8. The software should provide the kinds of reports required by your office's accounting methods and your needs for management review such as the ones listed above. These reports should give you costs in both dollars and hours comparing the budgeted amount to the actual amount spent.

9. Your program should allow you to set minimum and maximum limits on numbers entered. This is one way to catch many of the gross errors inherent in accounting data entry.

Requirements of Hardware

RAM. Depending on the model of computer on which it was designed to run, most integrated financial accounting packages require at least 128K, some as much as 256K to 512K.

Disks. A ten-megabyte hard disk is either required or recommended for these larger programs although two floppy disks can be used on some of them.

Printer. A dot-matrix printer is sufficient for reports that are used in house, but you will probably want a letter-quality printer for invoices, billing backup and other forms that your clients will see.

Cost Variables

Hardware. A complete setup with a hard disk drive and a dot-matrix printer can be purchased for about $3,000 to $4,000.

Software. Integrated financial accounting software is either purchased as one entire system or in "modules" such as a project costing module, a general ledger module, and so forth. A complete package runs between $2,500 and $7,000 depending on whether it is for a floppy disk or hard disk system, how many employees and jobs it will handle, what "modules" it contains and how sophisticated these are.

Setup. Many of the A/E packages include one or several days of training; some require that you purchase training separately. The training is really the significant variable rather than the actual configuration of the program for your particular computer.

Update versions. Most programs provide periodic updates that range in cost from $50 to $500. This is a considerable range so ask specific questions about this when you are shopping for software.

Data entry. Data entry can be performed by a secretary or bookkeeper based on time sheets, invoices received and other forms.

Output. Printing reports can be time consuming, especially when you are preparing detailed progress reports for each job. You may want to consider a high-speed printer or a print buffer so you can use the computer while printing is taking place.

Implementation Procedures

1. Decide if you need financial accounting software at all. If your firm is under five employees and you intend to stay small you may be better off to have your bank or accountant do the work manually or on their computer.

2. If you decide to implement this application, analyze your needs. This in-

cludes how many employees you intend to have in one or two years, how many projects you intend to have in the office in the same time period and what kinds of financial reports you will need in addition to simple bookkeeping. Talk to your accountant to get his or her suggestions.

3. List your requirements in order of priority. You may find that there are some "must have" features and some "nice to have" features that you can live without initially. If the software is designed around "modules" you can purchase only those you need to get started and buy the others later.

4. Develop a list of vendors who provide financial management software specifically to the architectural market. Stay away from general accounting packages; these do not work for design offices. Your list can be developed from software directories listed elsewhere in this book, current magazine articles constantly appearing in the architectural press and advertisements. Some of the more popular software is listed at the end of this section to give you a place to start.

5. From your list narrow the choices to those vendors who provide software for your current computer, give the kinds of options you want or simply seem worth exploring.

6. Request detailed information from those vendors on your list so you can begin to further narrow the choices. Also request demonstrations of the packages you are considering. This may include getting demonstration disks you can review in your office without the pressure of a vendor's demonstration.

7. Ask the vendors to supply the names of architects who currently are using the system so you can talk to them directly. Demonstrations, while useful for preliminary evaluation, do not show all the idiosyncrasies of a piece of software.

8. Once you decide on a system, make sure you get vendor training. Although you can stumble through a manual on your own, the extra cost (if there is any) is well worth the time saved to get your financial management on the right track in the fastest way possible.

Case in Point

Carter/Cody Associates in Palo Alto, CA uses the *AEPEX* financial accounting system from Timberline Systems. They also use *Lotus 1-2-3* for setting up their time card information so it is compatible with the input requirements of the financial accounting system. This allows them to collect and keep track of time on a weekly basis and have the properly formatted information for data entry into the more complex financial management program.

Virgil Carter makes several suggestions when discussing this application:

1. Involve the people who will be closest to the system in all steps of its selection and implementation for their education and support of the system. This includes principals, technical staff and administrative staff.

59

2. Provide manual backup for your system for the first one to three months in case you have computer problems.

3. Anticipate annual maintenance and upgrade expenses.

4. Be prepared for implementation of your system to take longer than you think. Establish a schedule and then double it.

Additional Tips

- Make sure you know what kind of vendor support is available. If you have a problem in the middle of sending out bills or preparing a statement for the IRS you must be able to call someone for help.

- Make sure the manuals the vendor provides are clearly written and give easy-to-understand instructions.

- Carefully consider the number of employees you plan to have against what the program will accommodate. Firms with around 50 people may need a larger, mini-computer–based system.

Sources for More Information

Getz, Lowell and Frank Stasiowski. *Financial Management for the Design Professional.* New York: Whitney Library of Design, 1982.

Mattox, Robert F. *Standardized Accounting for Architects.* Washington: The American Institute of Architects, 1983.

——— *Financial Management for Architects.* Washington: The American Institute of Architects, 1980.

DAEDALUS—The Accounting and Management Information Software Directory Update. American Consulting Engineers Council, 1015 Fifteenth St. N.W., Washington, DC 20005, Order 94.

Partial List of Application Software Available

There are dozens of accounting and financial management software packages available for the architect. The following list includes some of the more popular and complete packages. Since the software development field changes constantly, use this list only as a starting point. Refer to any of the several directories listed elsewhere in this book for a current sampling of programs available and for current addresses and phone numbers.

BILLING & JOB COSTING
Binggeli Enterprises
P.O. Box 2568
Spring, TX 77383

FULLY INTEGRATED A/E ACCOUNTING PROGRAMS
ACCI Business Systems, Inc.
12707 N. Freeway, 140
Houston, TX 77060

PROFESSIONAL MANAGER
Automate Computer Software
7475 Callaghan Road Suite 201
San Antonio, TX 78229

PROFESSIONAL TIME ACCOUNTING
Briston Information Systems
84 N. Main Street
Fall River, MA 02720

INTEGRATED PROJECT MANAGEMENT/GENERAL ACCOUNTING
SYSTEM
BST Consultants, Inc.
P.O. Box 23425
Tampa, FL 33623

ARCHITECT'S BUSINESS MANAGER
Concept Group, Inc. Suite 301
4849 N. Mesa
El Paso, TX 79912

ARCHITECTURAL/ENGINEERING MASTER ACCOUNTING SYSTEM
Data-Basics, Inc.
11000 Cedar Road
Cleveland, OH 44106

MICROTECTURE
Data-Graphic Systems
218 W. Main Street
Charlottesville, VA 22901

PROJECT ACCOUNTING SYSTEM
Designers & Builders of Information Systems
1 Mayfair Road
Eastchester, NY 10707

AE/dB
Halford A/E Systems Corporation
5207 McKinney Avenue, Suite 24
Dallas, TX 75205

MICRO/CFMS
Harper and Shuman
68 Moulton Street
Cambridge, MA 02138

KEYSTONE PROJECT MANAGEMENT ACCOUNTING SYSTEM
Information Engineering Corporation
1155 Louisiana Avenue, Suite 200
Winter Park, FL 32789

INTEGRATED FINANCIAL MANAGEMENT/GENERAL ACCOUNTING
PACKAGE
Micro Mode
4006 Mount Laurel Dr.
San Antonio, TX 78240

OCC-JOB COSTING
Occupational Computing Company
22311 Ventura Boulevard, Suite 123
Woodland Hills, CA 91364

AEPEX
Timberline Systems
7180 S.W. Fir Loop
Portland, OR 97223

2.5

FINDING THE RIGHT CONSULTANT OR SERVICE

Over a period of years an architectural firm may employ dozens, often hundreds, of consultants, vendors and other suppliers of services. Keeping track of them all for future jobs can become a difficult task since some consultants are more appropriate for certain kinds of jobs than others and things like addresses and telephone numbers change frequently. A computer can help you maintain an orderly list of these kinds of people and provide you with a way of quickly finding the right one to meet a particular need. This is especially useful when you are preparing a proposal and you need to find consultants that have the appropriate type of job experience.

Basic Application Requirements

A file management type of data base management system is most appropriate for this application. If you are unfamiliar with this software type refer to Appendix A, Fundamentals of Data Base Management Systems.

This application is fairly straight-forward. You need to be able to set up a record for each consultant and service and then retrieve selected records based on search criteria such as name, project types worked on, and so on. If your potential list of consultants, vendors and services is large you may want to consider setting up a file for each, but for most applications you can combine all of them. This will result in some unused data space in each record, but the extra record length is negligible when compared with the ease of use in having everything in one file.

For setting up this application you need the following basic capabilities:

1. ability to define a data entry form on the screen
2. ability to search on any desired field in a record
3. ability to print out reports based on a sorted order and your selected search criteria
4. ability to easily add, edit and delete records

Additional Application Requirements

This application can be integrated with other marketing information in a relational data base management system. The link to other files would be through the project information file and the data field in that file listing who the consultants were. Refer to Sections 1.2 and 1.4 for more information on integrated systems.

Requirements of Software

The following are some of the specific software requirements you will need to successfully implement this application.

1. The system should be menu-driven for ease of use.
2. For a file management system the program should allow at least 20 fields per record.
3. You should be able to index and search on at least five data fields.
4. The software should allow you to sort on several key fields together instead of just one alone.
5. The program must have flexible methods of querying the data base, both on screen and in printed reports. This includes relational queries, Boolean searches and partial string searches.

Requirements of Hardware

RAM. Many simple file management systems will work with as little as 48K of RAM. Some relational data base management programs operate with as little as 64K of RAM with the more sophisticated ones requiring 128K or more.

Disks. You should have at a minimum two disk drives, one for the program and one for your data. Since many database management applications require a

63

great deal of storage you should estimate your needs prior to buying a system. Hard disks have the advantages of more storage space as well as faster access time, an important consideration when using a FMS or RDBMS.

Printer. A dot-matrix printer is the minimum requirement for this application.

Cost Variables

Hardware. A complete setup with two disk drives and a dot-matrix printer can be purchased for as little as $2,000 or less. A ten-megabyte hard disk drive will add about $800 to $1,300.

Software. Simple file management programs range from under $100 to $400 with a few costing more than $400. Relational data base management programs range from about $400 to over $1,000, but with many very good programs under $800.

Setup. Setup costs depend on the complexity of your application. You may need from one to two hours to set up a simple file management system while a more complex RDBMS may take from eight to twenty hours.

Implementation Procedures

1. Determine what information you need to maintain. Do you want to just keep a consultants file or do you want to add vendors and services such as architectural photographers and model builders?

2. Establish the data fields for each record. You should have enough to give you the information you need for accurate searching and evaluation of each consultant or service. Use the following list as a starting point for your decision making.

consultant (or service) name

address

city

state (You may want to keep "state" separate from "city" since you will often want to isolate consultants who work in a particular geographical region.)

zip code

phone

person to contact

title of contact

type of firm (Set up a code system so you don't use up storage space and so data entry is faster.)

firm size (Again, set up a code system for 1–5 employees, 6–10, 11–25, etc.)

years in business

specialties (Here, use the same project types you establish for your marketing information system.)

typical project size

date information entered

past projects worked on

evaluation (Use a 1–10 scale, a long verbal description, or break this down into several fields, each with one aspect of the evaluation.)

comments

Case in Point

Carter/Cody Associates in Palo Alto, California uses a data base management software called power-base (PowerBase Systems, Inc., Birmingham, MI) to maintain information on consultants, contractors, vendors and clients. They keep separate files on each since they all have different data field requirements.

This firm believes that a system must be easy to use so their setup is menu driven without the need for any programming skills. Virgil Carter suggests that someone contemplating purchasing a DBMS should first discuss the various types available with professional peers and computer stores. The search can be rounded out by examining magazine reviews of the software. You should then see demonstrations provided both by software and hardware vendors and by other architectural offices using the system.

Additional Tips

- Check to see how easy it is (if it is possible at all) to change or add data fields once you have set them up and entered information into the system. If it is not possible consider adding a few "extra" fields at the end of the record for later use.
- Consider your need to have the data interchangeable with other programs. For example, you may want to select certain information from your consultant data base and include it in a proposal being prepared with a word processing program.

65

CHAPTER 3

How to Use Your Computer for Higher Profits through Programming and Feasibility Services

The use of computers offers an untapped potential for design professionals. In the area of predesign services you can use them to improve existing programming services and to expand into other areas. With their ability to accurately and quickly manipulate numbers and vast quantities of data they make it possible for you to perform such services as real estate analyses, building pro formas, site utilization analyses, building component studies, rentable area leasing studies, as well as programming at a level of detail and accuracy that is impossible without them.

As a tool, computers make possible a level of productivity that lets you offer new services at reasonable fees while still making a profit. They also help you complete your work quickly and accurately. This chapter shows how to make the best use of automation in the areas of programming and "nondesign" applications. Once you have a grasp of the fundamentals you can easily expand your range of service offerings.

3.1
IMPROVING PREDESIGN EVALUATIONS

There are many instances in which an architectural firm is asked by a client to assist in analyzing the feasibility and constraints of developing a particular project. The issues that must usually be considered involve zoning restrictions, parking requirements, basic site layout, floor area, number of stories and preliminary cost estimates. Reaching a final recommendation requires a thorough study of the interrelationships among these issues and selection of the optimum approach for further design study.

There are dozens of ways a microcomputer can help you improve your professional services in this area. By employing simple, readily available software you can evaluate more alternatives in greater depth than you can with manual methods. You can expand services to existing clients and, with a little imagination, set up new service offerings to expand your market and create more work for your firm. This section briefly describes how a simple spreadsheet program can be used to assist with the various numerical problems found in many predesign evaluations.

Basic Application Requirements

There are innumerable ways you can use spreadsheets for preliminary feasibility and design studies. What specific application you decide to implement will depend on what kind of work your office does and the exact needs of your clients. For instance, one office may do work for speculative office developers where optimizing floor space is critical while still meeting parking, open space and other zoning restrictions. Another office may serve clients who need to achieve the best ratio of occupancy types in a mixed-use development balanced against varying construction costs for those occupancies.

A spreadsheet is an ideal piece of software to perform many of these studies because of its versatility and simplicity of use and its ability to perform iterative calculations to optimize the solution to a problem. Although there are special application programs available for certain kinds of feasibility studies, they are usually expensive and limited to only one problem type.

Additional Application Requirements

In addition to the standard features available with all spreadsheet programs, you can enhance your analyses with graphs and charts developed from the data. Some of the integrated programs are ideal for this although separate graphic programs can be purchased that can use data from some spreadsheet programs. It is also useful if the spreadsheet data can be exported to a word processing program for easy inclusion into reports.

Requirements of Software

Most of the ways you can use spreadsheets for predesign studies only require the basic features you will find in all programs. In addition, you may want your software to have the following capabilities:

1. The ability to perform different calculation based on relational functions such as "greater than," "less than" and "if-then-else."

2. The ability to retrieve data from other files. For example, one file could contain cost information generated in various ways based on certain variables. The final costs per square foot could then be retrieved by another file to plug into a formula as part of a summary analysis.

3. The ability to sort numerically and alphabetically.

Requirements of Hardware

RAM.   Many spreadsheet programs can operate on hardware with a minimum amount of RAM (64K or less), but if you want integrated software to allow you to draw graphs of your data you will need 128K, 256K or more depending on the program.

Disks.   For many programs, a single disk drive is sufficient, but you will most likely want at least two. A hard disk is desirable for faster operation of some of the integrated software packages.

Printer.   A dot-matrix printer is the minimum requirement, but for final printing to include in a programming report, you will want a daisywheel, laser or ink-jet printer.

Plotter.   If your program can produce charts from the data will need a plotter capable of supporting the output.

Cost Variables

Hardware.   A complete setup with two disk drives and a letter-quality printer can be purchased for as little as $3,000 or less.

Software.   Spreadsheet programs range from about $100 to $400.

Setup.   Depending on the complexity of the template you want for this application, setup time may range from two to eight hours.

Examples

The Denver office of Gensler and Associates, Architects uses spreadsheets for several kinds of applications. Figure 3.1-1 shows an analysis of costs based on the shape of a building. The analysis was for an office building on a given site to give some direction to the designer concerning the shape and proportions of the building on the site. In this case, the exterior wall costs were converted to a cost per *floor area* square foot parameter so it could be viewed in the context of other building component costs.

With this information, the designer can readily see the cost implications of various building shapes and can use the data in combination with other planning requirements. For example, although a circular building encloses the most floor area for the least wall surface, it is probably not appropriate for most office build-

M36 WALLCOM
AFFECT ON BUILDING COST PER SQ. FT. DUE TO EXTERIOR "SKIN" COST RELATIVE TO BUILDING SIZE AND SHAPE
ASSUMING: 10000 SQ. FT. PLATE SIZE
            12.50' FL./FL. HEIGHT
            27.50/SQ. FT. "SKIN" COST

GENSLER & ASSOCIATES
ARCHITECTS

BUILDING SHAPE	FLOOR PLATE AREA	PERIMETER	WALL AREA	RATIO WALL/FLOOR	WALL COST	COST/SQ.FT. FLOOR AREA
CIRCULAR BUILDING	10000 SQ. FT.	354.49 LIN. FT.	4431 SQ. FT.	.4431135	121856	12.19/SQ. FT.
OCTAGONAL BUILDING	10000 SQ. FT.	364.07 LIN. FT.	4551 SQ. FT.	.4550899	125150	12.51/SQ. FT.
HEXAGONAL BUILDING	10000 SQ. FT.	372.24 LIN. FT.	4653 SQ. FT.	.4653024	127958	12.80/SQ. FT.
SQUARE BUILDING	10000 SQ. FT.	400.00 LIN. FT.	5000 SQ. FT.	.5	137500	13.75/SQ. FT.
RECTANGULAR BUILDING (ASSUME L.= 2W.)	10000 SQ. FT.	424.26 LIN. FT.	5303 SQ. FT.	.5303301	145841	14.58/SQ. FT.
RECTANGULAR BUILDING (ASSUME L.= 3W.)	10000 SQ. FT.	461.88 LIN. FT.	5774 SQ. FT.	.5773503	158771	15.88/SQ. FT.
RECTANGULAR BUILDING (ASSUME L.= 4W.)	10000 SQ. FT.	500.00 LIN. FT.	6250 SQ. FT.	.625	171875	17.19/SQ. FT.
RECTANGULAR BUILDING (ASSUME L.= 5W.)	10000 SQ. FT.	536.66 LIN. FT.	6708 SQ. FT.	.6708204	184476	18.45/SQ. FT.
RECTANGULAR BUILDING (ASSUME L.= 6W.)	10000 SQ. FT.	571.55 LIN. FT.	7144 SQ. FT.	.7144345	196469	19.65/SQ. FT.
TRIANGULAR BUILDING	10000 SQ. FT.	455.90 LIN. FT.	5699 SQ. FT.	.5698768	156716	15.67/SQ. FT.

Figure 3.1-1
Wall Cost as a Function of Building Shape

70

```
SCHEMATIC FEASIBILITY ANALYSIS                GENSLER AND ASSOCIATES
                                                        ARCHITECTS
=====================================================================

LAND AREA      53175
OPN SPACE      20395
BLD FOOTP      32780

---------------------------------------------------------------------

ARCADE          9000    TYP FL    23780
RETAIL         23780    HEIGHT     1.00

---------------------------------------------------------------------

RESIDENT:
  NO UNITS        36
  SF./UNIT      1200    TYP FL     8640
  TOT AREA     43200    HEIGHT     5.00

---------------------------------------------------------------------

OFFICE
  ALLOWABL    145720    BON.FAR    2000
  ADD ALLO    720000    TYP FL    28872
  TOT ALLO    217720    HEIGHT     7.54

---------------------------------------------------------------------

PARKING
  OFFICE         435    AREA/OFF    500
  RESID.          36    #/RES      1.00
  TOT CARS       471    AREA/CAR    375
  TOT AREA    176790    TYP FL    50130
                        HEIGHT     3.53

---------------------------------------------------------------------

SUMMARY:     ARCADE    RETAIL    RESID.   OFFICE   PARKING      LAND
            -------   -------   -------  -------   -------   -------
    UNITS         -         -        36        -       471         -
     AREA      9000     23780     43200   217720    176790     53175
UNIT COST        0        60       100       60        30       200
     COST        0   1426800   4320000 13063200   5303700  10635000

  BLDG CST 24113700
  LAND CST 10635000
   DEV CST  3617055
   TOT CST 38365755
```

Figure 3.1-2
Schematic Feasibility Analysis

ings. However, the cost difference between buildings where the length to width ratio is two or three may be enough to affect the final design of the structure.

Figure 3.1-2 shows a portion of a feasibility analysis made for the design of a mixed-use facility to optimize the project cost and value under various zoning constraints and incentives. The zoning restrictions included height, floor area ratio, parking, open space and number of residential units. There were also incentives for arcade and retail space.

Since the optimum combination of elements was not self-evident simple modeling with a spreadsheet allowed the designers to better understand the interrelationships and start planning with concepts that were most likely to lead to the best solution.

Additional Tips

- When you develop a template to help you with a particular kind of problem, make it reusable for other projects or as part of a larger, multifile system. This may require that you simply leave more blank rows and columns for data or for calculation space.

- Set up your templates so the primary variables need only be entered in one place at the beginning of the form. The formulas in the various parts of the spreadsheet can then pull this data as required. This makes it easier for you to enter data, make "what if" calculations, allows the template to be reused for other jobs and lessens the chances for mistakes.

3.2

FAST AND ACCURATE PROGRAMMING WITH SPREADSHEETS

One of the primary purposes of programming is to determine the amount of space required both at move-in and at future dates. Whether you are doing programming as a separate service or as part of the basic design services you and your client need an accurate, up-to-date tabulation of the space needs of the project.

In addition, a good program should document the required adjacencies among spaces and departments and well as record specific requirements of each space, such as the type of furniture and equipment needed, special electrical and mechanical services, and so forth.

This section will describe how to implement a simple programming tabulation using spreadsheet software. Section 3.3 describes how to use a data base management system to record and analyze more comprehensive program information.

72

Basic Application Requirements

There are three major variables in programming tabulations: personnel projections, the identification of spaces for the personnel and the amount of square footage required for each. Any application should have the ability to record these, perform the mathematics to get department and grand totals, and print out reports for review. In addition, you should have the ability to make changes as the programming proceeds and print updated reports reflecting those changes.

A spreadsheet program is the most useful type for this application because it is easy to set up, performs all the mathematics required, and can be easily changed. It also allows the option of setting up very simple summary matrices or more complex reports that can include, for example, detailed information on each individual space, various formulas for growth projections and space analyses.

Additional Application Requirements

You may want to include more data in your tabulations than just numbers of people, space standards and square footage totals. Other application requirements you may want to consider include:

1. The ability to translate the data into graphs or charts. Integrated programs including both spreadsheet and graphics are useful for this.

2. The ability to retrieve data from other files. For example, separate files can contain very detailed information on each department of a large organization while one smaller, summary file can extract just the area requirements from each and total them for an executive synopsis.

3. The ability of the program to perform different calculations based on relational functions such as "greater than," "less than," and "if-then-else." With this ability, the program can look at a subtotal for a department's assignable square footage requirement and decide what circulation factor to apply—circulation generally being more efficient as the assignable square footage increases.

Requirements of Software

The spreadsheet program you select for this application should have the following minimum characteristics:

1. the standard mathematical functions
2. the ability to vary column widths

73

3. the ability to add rows and columns at the end and in the middle of the matrix

4. a column formatting capability to allow right justification, decimal point location, comma location and percentages

5. the ability to print only selected portions of the matrix

6. the additional mathematical functions of percentage, average, count, minimum and maximum

Refer to the Additional Application Requirements listed above for other software features you will find useful.

Requirements of Hardware

RAM. Many stand-alone spreadsheet programs can operate on hardware with a minimum amount of RAM (64K or less), but if you want integrated software to allow you to draw graphs of your data you will need 128K, 256K or more depending on the program.

Disks. For many programs, a single disk drive is sufficient, but you will most likely want at least two. A hard disk is desirable for faster operation of some of the integrated software packages.

Printer. A dot-matrix printer is the minimum requirement. For speed of operation a dot-matrix, laser or ink-jet printer is the best choice. For final printing to include in a programming report, you will want a daisywheel, laser or ink-jet printer.

Plotter. If your program can produce charts from the data you will need a plotter capable of supporting the output.

Cost Variables

Hardware. A complete setup with two disk drives and a letter-quality printer can be purchased for as little as $3,000 or less. A ten-megabyte hard disk drive will add about $800 to $1,300.

Software. Spreadsheet programs may range from about $100 to $400.

Setup. Depending on the complexity of the template you want for this application, setup time may range from two to eight hours.

Data entry. Time required for data entry depends on the size of the job you are programming and its complexity. Most of the information will come from interview forms or questionnaire forms so the actual data entry can be done by a secretary or other clerical staff.

Implementation Procedures

1. Decide whether you can use a simple program tabulation as described in this section or need to use a data base management system outlined in Section 3.3. In many cases you will want to do both.

Advertising Agency
Space Allocation Summary

Person/Area	0	1	3	5	Area sq ft	Closed or Open	Move-in	1 yr.	3 yr.	5 yr.	Comments
ADMINISTRATION											
President	1	1	1	1	250	C	250	250	250	250	
Secretary	1	1	1	1	120	C	120	120	120	120	
Reception	1	1	1	1	400	O	400	400	400	400	Seating 8 with display
Main conference					750	C	750	750	750	750	20 w/ rear proj. & pantry
VP Finance	1	1	1	1	170	C	170	170	170	170	
Accounting asst.	1	1	1	1	120	C	120	120	120	120	
Accounting clerk	1	2	2	2	50	O	50	100	100	100	
Computer station					50		50	50	50	50	
Records storage					15	C	15	15	15	15	
Office services	1	2	3	3	50	O	50	100	150	150	
Mail room	1	1	1	1	100		100	100	100	100	
Main copy room	1	1	1	1	250		250	250	250	250	With key operator
Lunch room					200		200	200	200	200	Seat 8, w/ full kitchen
Library	1	1	1	1	300		300	300	300	300	With librarian near media & acct. services
Dept Net Sub-total							2,825	2,925	2,975	2,975	
Circulation @ 25%							706	731	744	744	
ADMIN. GROSS TOTAL	10	12	13	13			3,531	3,656	3,719	3,719	
MEDIA											
Media director	1	1	1	1	150	C	150	150	150	150	
Media buyer	2	3	3	4	100	O	200	300	300	400	
Media asst.	1	1	1	1	50	O	50	50	50	50	
Computer station					50	O	50	50	50	50	
Conference room					100	C	100	100	100	100	Could share, seats 4
Waiting area					75	O	75	75	75	75	If separate, seat 2-3
Dept Net Sub-total							625	725	725	825	
Circulation @ 25%							156	181	181	206	
MEDIA GROSS TOTAL	4	5	5	6			781	906	906	1,031	
PUBLIC RELATIONS											
Public relations	0	2	3	4	150	C	0	300	450	600	
Secretary	0	0	1	1	50	O	0	0	50	50	
Dept Net Sub-total							0	300	500	650	
Circulation @ 25%							0	75	125	163	
P. R. GROSS TOTAL	0	2	4	5			0	375	625	813	
ACCOUNT SERVICES											
Sr. VP Acct. Serv.	1	1	1	1	225	C	225	225	225	225	
Account supervisor	2	2	4	4	150	C	300	300	600	600	
Account executive	4	8	12	16	115	C	460	920	1,380	1,840	
Account coordin.	2	4	6	6	75	O	150	300	450	450	
Secretary	0	2	3	3	50	O	0	100	150	150	
Conference room					275	C	275	275	275	550	Seating 8-10
Word process. sta.					50		50	50	50	50	
Storage room					15	C	15	15	15	15	
Copy machine					10	O	10	10	10	10	
Dept Net Sub-total							1,485	2,195	3,155	3,890	
Circulation @ 25%							371	549	789	973	
ACCT. SERV. TOTAL	9	17	26	30			1,856	2,744	3,944	4,863	
CREATIVE											
VP Creative Dir.	1	1	1	1	225	C	225	225	225	225	
Assoc. C. Director	2	3	3	3	150	C	300	450	450	450	
Art director	3	3	4	5	115	C	345	345	460	575	
Copywriter	2	3	4	5	115	C	230	345	460	575	
Designer	1	1	1	1	75	C	75	75	75	75	
Secretary	0	1	1	1	50	O	0	50	50	50	
Conference room					275	C	275	275	275	275	Seating 8 w/ A-V
Production manager	1	1	2	2	150	C	150	150	300	300	
Traffic manager	1	1	2	2	75	O	75	75	150	150	
Clerical asst.	1	1	1	2	50	O	50	50	50	100	
Mechanical artists	4	5	6	6	50	O	200	250	300	300	
Typesetting					120	C	120	120	120	120	With word processing
Work room					625	C	625	625	625	625	With art storage
Stat room					50	C	50	50	50	50	
Light room					50	C	50	50	50	50	
Dept Net Sub-total							2,770	3,135	3,640	3,920	
Circulation @ 25%							693	784	910	980	
CREATIVE TOTAL	16	20	25	28			3,463	3,919	4,550	4,900	
GRAND TOTAL	39	56	73	82			9,631	11,600	13,744	15,325	
	0	1	3	5			Move-in	1 yr.	3 yr.	5 yr.	

Figure 3.2-1
Space Allocation Summary

2. Review your current method of obtaining programming information. The reports from this application will only be as good as the information going into it so check your questionnaires, programming forms, interviewing techniques and general programming processes to make sure you are getting the best information possible from your clients. Revise any of your printed forms as required so the information can be transferred easily onto the computer by clerical staff.

You might want to consider using a portable computer to take with you to interviews or to the client's site to avoid the intermediate step of paper forms.

3. Decide on the format of the reports you will want and set up the template following the directions of the program you have. Try to make it as generic as possible so you can use it on other jobs with little or no modification.

```
WorldWide Savings
Space Requirements
October 1, 1986
-------------------------------------------------------------------------------
Department:  Construction Loans

Circulation factor:     .28
===============================================================================
                  Personnel     Space Std.      Area
                  ---------------             -----  -----  ----- Date last
Space                                                               update
                  1986 1988 1990 Type Area    1986   1988   1990
===============================================================================


VP Const. Lending   1    1    1   A   225     225    225    225    4/12/86
Residential Admin.  1    1    2   B   150     150    150    300    4/12/86
Commercial Admin.   0    1    2   B   150       0    150    300    4/12/86
Loan Secretary      1    2    3   D   100     100    200    300    4/12/86
Loan Const. Super.  1    1    1   B   150     150    150    150    5/22/86
Loan Servicer Income 1   1    2   B   150     150    150    300    5/22/86
Loan Poster         1    2    3   C   100     100    200    300    5/22/86
Loan Specialist     1    1    2   C   100     100    100    200    4/12/86
Residential Disb Ser 1   2    3   C   100     100    200    300    4/12/86
Commercial Disb Ser 2    2    3   B   150     300    300    450    5/18/86
Asst Supervisor     0    0    1   C   100       0      0    100    4/12/86
Reception           1    1    1       400     400    400    400    5/18/86
Work Area/Storage   0    1    1       175       0    175    175    5/22/86
Conference room     1    1    1       300     300    300    300    5/18/86
Lateral Files       8   11   14        18     144    198    252    5/18/86


                  ----- ---- ----
Department subtotal 11   15   24             2,219  2,898  4,052
Circulation                                   621    811  1,135
                  ==== ==== ====            ====== ====== ======
DEPARTMENT TOTAL    11   15   24             2,840  3,709  5,187
```

Figure 3.2-2
Department Space Summary

4. Enter the data you collect and print reports as required. Make sure each report is titled with the date included so you have a record of the progress of the job as changes are made. In addition to the printed reports you can save each variation of the program on disk.

Examples

Figures 3.2-1 and 3.2-2 illustrate two layouts for programming tabulations. Figure 3.2-1 contains all the space requirements for an entire office with each department subtotaled and a grand total. Figure 3.2-2 shows just one department in a larger facility. Another spreadsheet template takes the department totals from several files and creates a summary sheet.

3.3
PROGRAMMING WITH A DATA BASE MANAGEMENT SYSTEM

Section 3.2 describes how to use spreadsheet software to tabulate programming requirements for a client. Spreadsheets are good for small jobs or as space requirement summaries for any size of job, but they have some inherent limitations that can be overcome by using a data base management (DBMS) system.

Although a DBMS is slightly more difficult for the first-time user to learn, it offers several advantages. First, a greater quantity of more detailed information can be accommodated much easier. Trying to include dozens of data fields in a spreadsheet for each space in a building would soon create an unwieldy size of matrix. Additionally, spreadsheets are not well suited to text fields that require many character spaces to contain the necessary information.

Second, it is easier to change and update information. With a DBMS you can go directly to the record you need and change just the fields you are interested in without having to search through a large matrix.

Third, report formats are more flexible. You can sort the information any way you desire and print out just the data you need.

There are specific application programs that are designed for programming and space management, some of which include the ability to draw adjacency diagrams. You may want to consider reviewing some of these that are listed at the end of Section 8.3. This section, however, will focus on using a DBMS to develop your own application program to do space requirement tabulations.

Basic Application Requirements

For this application you want to identify each space (whether occupied full-time with a person or not) or type of space, and record the requirements of that space. For example, a person's office would require a certain amount of square footage, the occupant would need particular kinds of furniture and equipment, there would be electrical and communications needs and so forth. You also need the ability to summarize requirements by departments or other types of groups and tally the results to include such things as square footage, number of desks of a certain type and numbers of people.

There are two ways to set up a data base management for program information. See Figure 3.3-1. The first method treats each identifiable space (whether occupied or not) as a record with its own particular attributes. There may be only one space of a particular type or several; if there are several each is listed, even if it is identical to others. Examples of space "types" are a typical classroom or a 200 square foot manager's office.

The second method considers each *type* of space as a record with one of the data fields being the *quantity* of that type of space. For example, one record

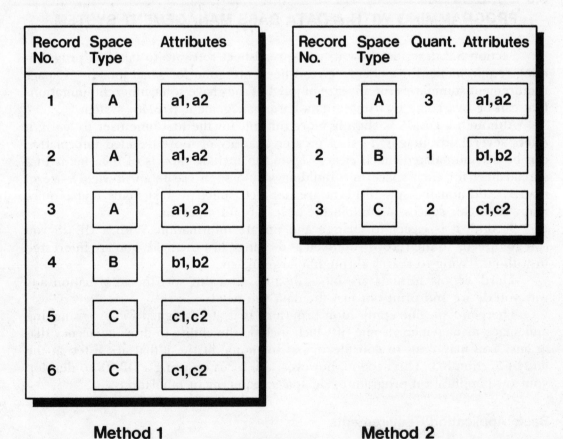

Record No.	Space Type	Attributes
1	A	a1, a2
2	A	a1, a2
3	A	a1, a2
4	B	b1, b2
5	C	c1, c2
6	C	c1, c2

Method 1

Record No.	Space Type	Quant.	Attributes
1	A	3	a1, a2
2	B	1	b1, b2
3	C	2	c1, c2

Method 2

Figure 3.3-1
Approaches to Programming with a DBMS

may be a "private hospital room" and there may be 65 of them in a hospital. The advantage of setting up a DBMS like this is that you only have to enter information concerning a private hospital room once instead of 65 times. The disadvantage is that there is less flexibility. For a final program report you may want only a space summary. Later, during design development and construction documents, you may want a detailed listing of all those 65 hospital rooms to serve as an invaluable quality control checklist.

You will have to make the final decision concerning which approach you want to take based on the needs of the project. In most cases you will want to treat each space as a separate record so you have the flexibility of recording data and getting the kinds of reports your client will need. The problem of having to enter identical information on similar or identical spaces can be taken care of by using a two-file relational data base system with the space "type" linking the two files. See Figure 3.3-2. This approach is described in more detail in the implementa-

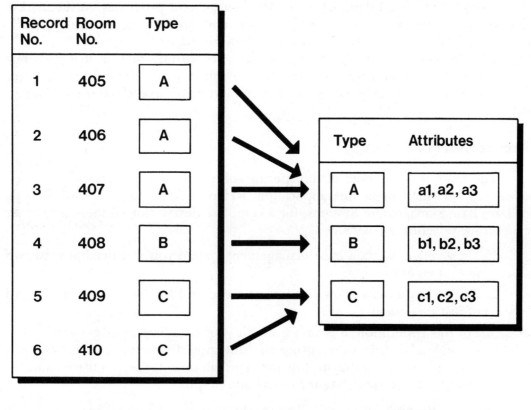

File 1   File 2

Figure 3.3-2
Relational DBMS Schema

tion procedures later in this section. Maintaining a design requirement data base is also discussed in Section 4.1.

Additional Application Requirements

In its simplest form, recording program information with a data base management system can be accomplished with a file management system (FMS). All the information concerning one space or one *type* of space is contained in the record for that space. As mentioned above, this can become a problem if you want one record for each space, but have a lot of identical spaces. To overcome this problem a relational data base management system (RDBMS) is helpful. Refer to Appendix A, Fundamentals of Data Base Management Systems, for a more complete explanation of this type of software.

Your decision concerning which type to use will depend on the size of the project you are programming and how much flexibility you want to have. Because there are several good relational data base management programs on the market that are fairly simple to use, I would recommend considering this approach. If you use a RDBMS you may want to include a file that can contain "free text"; that is, a file of variable length where you can record information that does not fit neatly into a fixed-length data field. Some software has this feature built in, others force you to set up fixed-length alphanumeric fields in each record to contain the data.

Requirements of Software

The following are some of the specific software requirements you will need to successfully implement this application. Refer to Appendix A, Fundamentals of Data Base Management Systems, for a complete description of these and other criteria for selecting a DBMS.

1. For a relational data base management system you will need at least two files open at one time.

2. The software must allow you to sort on several key fields together instead of just one alone.

3. For this application, it is very useful if your data base management system is compatible with other programs. Integrated programs, of course, will have this feature built in, but for stand-alone software, you will want to be able to use your data for charts and graphs.

4. Since this application can become complex and each record lengthy, the program should allow more than one "screenfull" of information per record.

5. The program should have the ability to make "mass changes" to a particular

80

data field to save you time. For example, you may want to change the square footage requirements for all type "B" spaces in a program from 150 square feet to 175 square feet with one command rather than having to change the data field in each record.

6. The program must have a flexible report generator since you will want to print out results in various ways. For a RDBMS this includes being able to access more than one file at a time for report generation.

7. The program must have at least basic four-function arithmetic calculation capability. The program must also be able to "count" the number of records of a particular type so program data can be summarized.

Requirements of Hardware

RAM. Some relational data base management programs operate with as little as 64K of RAM with the more sophisticated ones requiring 128K or more.

Disks. You should have at a minimum two disk drives, one for the program and one for your data. Since many data base management applications require a great deal of storage you should estimate your needs prior to buying a system. Hard disks have the advantages of more storage space as well as faster access time, an important consideration when using a FMS or RDBMS.

Printer. Since you will want reports produced quickly in house, but will also want letter-quality output for reports and client use, you should consider having both a dot-matrix printer and daisy wheel printer, or a laser or ink-jet printer.

Cost Variables

Hardware. A complete setup with two disk drives and a letter-quality printer can be purchased for as little as $3,000 or less. A ten-megabyte hard disk drive will add about $800 to $1,300.

Software. Simple file management programs range from under $100 to $400 with a few costing more than $400. Relational data base management programs range from about $400 to over $1,000, but with many very good programs under $800.

Setup. Setup costs depend on the complexity of your application. You may need from two to six hours to set up a simple file management system while a more complex RDBMS may take from eight to twenty hours. Keep in mind that much of this setup time will include thinking through your method of collecting program information and how this is transferred to electronic form.

Data entry. Data entry may be performed by a secretary or other clerical assistant if data collection forms are set up properly. You may want to consider bypassing this step by using a portable computer for interviews and on-site data collection.

Implementation Procedures

1. Decide which of the methods illustrated in Figure 3.3-1 you want to use. The following steps describe using a relational data base management system (Method 1 in Figure 3.3-1 and Figure 3.3-2), but if you want to use Method 2, simply combine the data fields described below into one file instead of two.

If you conduct a complete survey of *every* person and space you will want to use a single-file system because the data for each space will probably be slightly different and it would be cumbersome to attempt to group this information into space types. In this case, each record of your data base will represent a single space and contain the complete information on that space.

2. Decide on the kinds of programming information you will be collecting. This should be specific to the project you are working on, but general enough so you can reuse the application program for other jobs.

3. Set up interview forms and questionnaires as appropriate to collect the data. These should be similar to the data entry "screen forms" you use on the computer to make data entry as easy as possible, either for the programmer or for clerical help. If you have a portable computer, do the data entry on site.

4. Following the directions of your particular software, set up data entry screens, indexes, report formats and other files as required. How you set up data fields will depend on the kinds of information you are collecting and on the capabilities (or limitations) of your software's report-generating program. See Figure 3.4-3 for examples of records from a two-file RDBMS.

5. Make changes as they occur. One of the advantages of using a RDBMS for this application is that changes are easy to make. For example, if one space among several designated as "Type A" changes to become a new type you only have to modify the designation on that one record and create a new record in the second file to reflect a new type of space. If the space changes to another type you already have in the data base it is even easier since you will only need to change the contents of one data field in one record.

6. To include circulation area (corridors, space around workstations, etc.) you can either include a circulation factor with each space or have your program multiply department subtotals by some factor you select.

Additional Tips

- If you need tabulations for move-in requirements and expansion at given future intervals, set up one data field in the first file for each expansion time. Make it a numeric field type of one character length. If the space is needed during the expansion interval, enter a "1," otherwise enter a "0." This way you can list the space whether it is needed at first or not. Later,

```
            ID#:  307-4
     Space name:  Bookkeeping
     Department:  Accounting
     Space type:  D
  Personal name:  John Smith
  Existing size:  138
   Move-in (1=Y): 1
3-yr expan. (1=Y): 1
Special comments:  Needs 2 terminals
```

Individual Space Record

```
     Space type:  D
     Space name:  Office
   Open/Closed?:  C
   Sq. Footage:   150
     No. people:  1
           Desk:  30" x 60", single pedestal
  Typing return:  N
   Terminal sta.: Y
  Visitor chairs: 1
          Files:  4-dwr. lateral; configuration C
     Electrical:  2-duplexes
      Telephone:  Yes, with auto dial
            CRT:  Y
```

Space Type Record

Figure 3.3-3
Relational DBMS Records

when you are calculating square footages, the program can take the number and multiply it by the square footage assigned to the space type.

- Send intermediate reports to the client for review. Don't wait until the final report is due before verifying that you are on the right track.

- Set up a coding system so each space has a unique identifying number, but in such a way that departments are grouped. In Figure 3.3-3, for example, the 300 series is the accounting department, the "7" indicates bookkeeping and the "—4" represents the fourth bookkeeping office.

3.4

EXTRA PROFITS WITH RENTABLE AREA STUDIES

In the competitive office and retail leasing market, having an accurate accounting of a building's rentable square footage is vital to the economic success of that project. In many instances, rentable square footage calculations are made by the architect during the design development or working drawing phase of a project. These are passed on to the building owner or leasing agent to use in writing leases and figuring income based on the current lease rates.

Many times the area calculations are done haphazardly or incorrectly, resulting in a loss of rental income for the building owner. Even a miscalculation of 100 square feet per floor of a 30-story office building would result in a 3,000 square foot mistake. At a lease rate of $25.00 per square foot that would represent a total yearly loss to the owner of $75,000!

In addition to simply verifying area calculations, rentable area leasing studies serve other purposes. They can document for the tenants how rentable area was calculated, they can be used to develop financial pro formas showing the effect of measurement alternatives, and they can provide area controls during leasing to assure that the building will be leased according to original pro forma calculations.

This kind of study can be a valuable addition to an architect's marketable services and a microcomputer is a natural tool to make it a profitable service.

Basic Application Requirements

A spreadsheet is the most appropriate program to use for this application since mathematical calculations and the ability to examine various alternatives are the primary requirements. You can use spreadsheet templates two different ways: as a "worksheet" for actually calculating areas to determine the total usable and rentable square footages on each floor and as a summary, listing floor by floor the usable and rentable areas for both single-tenant and multiple-tenant occupancies, usable/rentable ratios, and any other data your client needs.

Additional Application Requirements

If you have a CAD system it may have the capability to do area calculations by simply outlining the various usable, rentable and nonrentable areas. This simplifies the process, but you will still want to set up a matrix sheet showing the various figures floor by floor.

Requirements of Software

The spreadsheet program you select for this application should have the following minimum characteristics:

1. the standard mathematical functions
2. the ability to add rows and columns to the matrix after initial setup
3. the ability to print only selected rows or columns of the matrix

4. the ability to retrieve data from other matrices (With this, your summary sheet can get the area totals from various "worksheets" and then use these totals to calculate rentable/usable ratios.)

Requirements of Hardware

RAM. Many stand-alone spreadsheet programs can operate on hardware with minimal RAM of 64K or less, but if you want integrated software to allow you to draw graphs of your data you will most likely need 128K or 256K, depending on the software.

Disks. Two floppy disks are recommended as a minimum configuration. A hard disk allows faster access to large spreadsheets, but is not absolutely necessary.

Printer. A dot-matrix printer is sufficient for this application as a minimum configuration.

Cost Variables

Hardware. A complete setup with two disk drives and a dot-matrix printer can be purchased for as little as $2,000 or less. A ten-megabyte hard disk drive will add about $800 to $1,300.

Software. Spreadsheet programs may range from about $100 to $400.

Setup. Setting up your first spreadsheet for this application may take from three to six hours, depending on its complexity. Once you have a worksheet and summary sheet set up, however, using them for new jobs is simply a matter of entering new dimensions for the building under review.

Data entry. The time required for data entry depends on the complexity of the building under study and how each floor varies. For example, with a high-rise building that tapers toward the top, each floor would have to be calculated separately.

Implementation Procedures

1. If you are not familiar with the standard method of measuring floor area get a copy of *Standard Method for Measuring Floor Area in Office Buildings* published by the Building Owners and Managers Association International, (BOMA) 1221 Massachusetts Avenue, N.W., Washington, DC 20005. This is also American National Standard number ANSI Z65.1. It gives definitions, the procedure for measuring usable and rentable areas in offices and stores and how to figure the rentable/ usable ratios. Figure 3.4-1 shows the difference between usable area and rentable area. However, keep in mind that the usable area on a multitenant floor is different from the usable area on a single-tenant floor because a single tenant will be able to use the corridor area normally required to access several office suites.

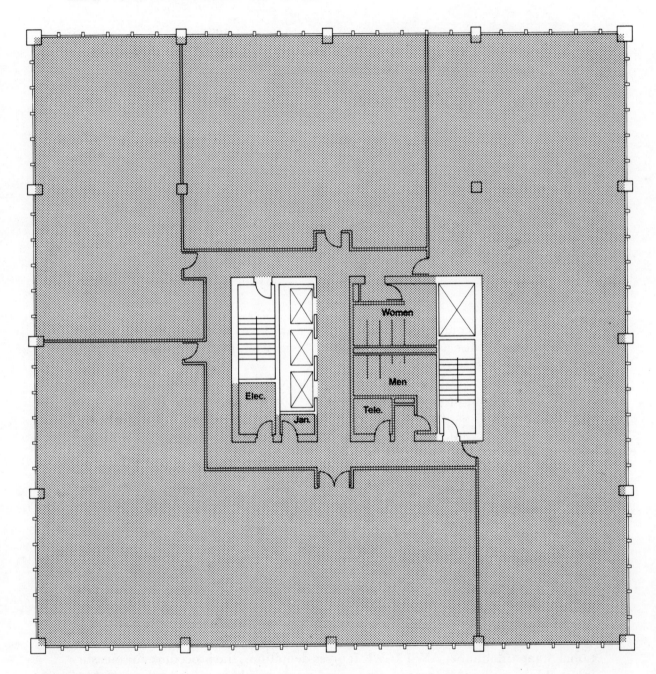

Rentable Area

Figure 3.4-1
Usable and Rentable Floor Areas

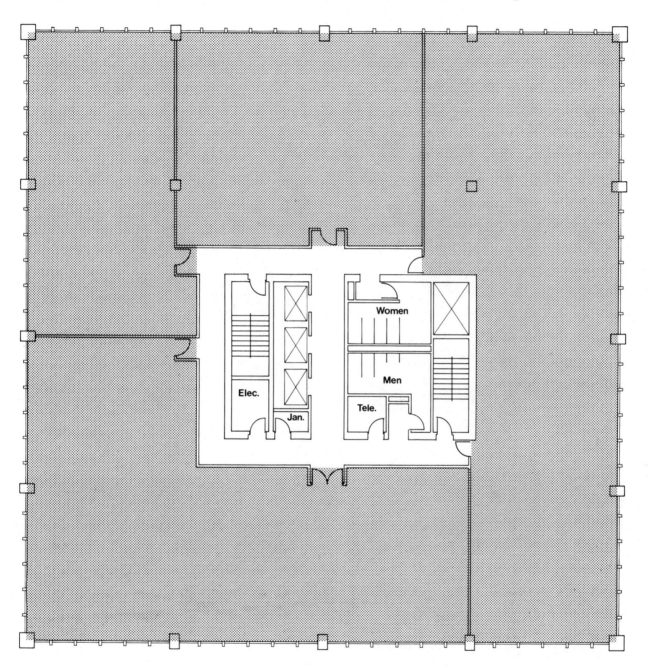

Usable Area

Figure 3.4-1 (*cont'd*)
Usable and Rentable Floor Areas

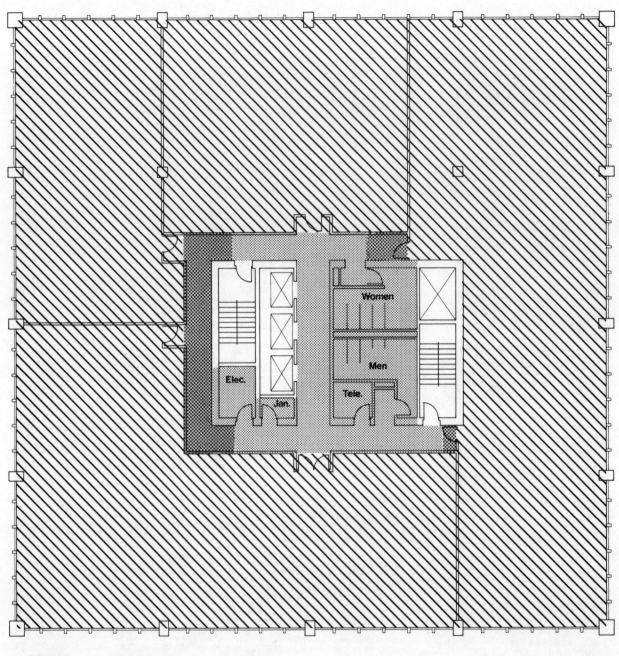

Mult·tenant usable

Mult·tenant corridor

Rentable

Non·rentable

**Figure 3.4-2
Calculation Areas for Leasing Study**

2. Obtain a copy of the working drawings for the building or buildings you will be studying or, if none exist for an old building, take accurate field measurements for a good set of measured drawings. Divide up the areas on a floor plan into multitenant usable, multitenant corridor, nonusable but rentable area on the floor (such as toilet rooms, electrical closets, etc.) and nonrentable area (elevator shafts, stairways, etc.). See Figure 3.4-2. Further subdivide the areas into simple geometric shapes so you can enter lengths and widths into your "worksheet" template. If you have curves or unusual geometric shapes, divide the areas into shapes for which you can enter a mathematical formula to calculate area—triangles, trapezoids, quarter circles and so forth.

3. Following the instructions of your software, set up a "worksheet" template to calculate areas. The columns should include the space identification number, its length, its width, the area and a column for subtotals. You may also want to include a column for comments. Each row should be one "subdivided area" that you identified in Step 2 so you can enter the length and width of each area.

At the top of the spreadsheet include a place for the title of the project, what floor (or floors) are being calculated, the date, and any other project identification you need. Either at the top or bottom of the spreadsheet, include a summary where you list the total rentable area for the floor, the single-tenant and multitenant usable area, and the single- and multitenant rentable/usable ratios.

If you are doing several different floors of a multistory building, these are the numbers that will be retrieved by your summary spreadsheet when it lists the total building rentable and usable areas. Figure 3.4-3 shows an example of this kind of worksheet. You may also want to include at the end of the spread sheet a "check" calculation to see if the usable, corridor, proratable area and nonrentable area adds up to the building gross area. Note that this is not "architectural gross area" but gross area as measured to the inside finish of the exterior walls as defined by the BOMA standard.

4. Set up a summary sheet to list the required information floor by floor. See Figure 3.4-4. The columns should include the floor number, the gross area, the nonrentable area, the total rentable area, single-tenant usable, minimum corridor required for multitenant occupancy, multitenant usable, single-tenant rentable/usable ratio and the multitenant rentable/usable ratio. Each row should be one floor of the building with the final row totaling the numbers.

You may also want to include various common areas of the building such as entrance lobbies that some building owners prorate to each individual tenant. If the building owner wants to study the effects of various measurement alternatives on the overall financial picture of the structure this is one of the valuable features of a spreadsheet application.

5. Based on the areas you defined on the floor plans, enter the length and width of each on your worksheet, using one worksheet for each floor that is unique in area. When the calculations are complete transfer the numbers to the summary

```
8990 AIRDALE STREET
Detailed Area Calculations
Floors - thru -                              GENSLER AND ASSOCIATES
September 31, 1985                                      ARCHITECTS
===============================================================================
SPACE    LENGTH     WIDTH      AREA SUBTOTAL  SUMMARY
===============================================================================
Multi-tenant usable area:
U1       31.54      24.87      784.40              Rentable area: 24140.52
U2       30.00      24.87      746.10
U3       30.00      24.87      746.10    Single Tenant Usable area: 23391.39
U4       30.00      24.87      746.10            Single Tenant R/U:     1.032
U5       30.00      24.87      746.10
U6       31.54      24.87      784.40    Multi-tenant Usable area: 22327.22
                                                Multi-tenant R/U:     1.0812
U7        7.50      23.21      174.08
U8       31.54      21.67      683.47
U9       22.92      21.67      496.68
U10       7.08       9.59       67.90
U11      30.00       9.59      287.70
U12      30.00       9.59      287.70
U13       7.08       9.59       67.90
U14      22.92      21.67      496.68
U15      31.54      21.67      683.47
U16       7.50      23.21      174.08

U17       7.50      24.88      186.60
U18       9.04      25.00      226.00
U19      30.00      25.00      750.00
U20      22.92      25.00      573.00
U21      22.92      25.00      573.00
U22      30.00      25.00      750.00
U23       9.04      25.00      226.00
U24       7.50      24.88      186.60

U25       7.50      24.87      186.53
U26      16.54      23.33      385.88
U27      30.00      23.33      699.90
U28      22.92      23.33      534.72
U29       7.08      16.25      115.05
U30      30.00      16.25      487.50
U31      30.00      16.25      487.50
U32       7.08      16.25      115.05
U33      22.92      23.33      534.72
U34      30.00      23.33      699.90
U35      16.54      23.33      385.88
U36       7.50      24.87      186.53

U37       7.50      24.75      185.63
U38      24.04      23.21      557.97
U39      30.00      23.21      696.30
U40      30.00      23.21      696.30
U41      30.00      23.21      696.30
U42      30.00      23.21      696.30
U43      30.00      23.21      696.30
```

page 1

Figure 3.4-3
Area Calculation Worksheet

```
8990 AIRDALE STREET
Detailed Area Calculations
Floors - thru -                           GENSLER AND ASSOCIATES
September 31, 1985                                    ARCHITECTS
======================================================================
SPACE    LENGTH    WIDTH    AREA SUBTOTAL  SUMMARY
======================================================================
U44       30.00    23.21   696.30
U45       24.04    23.21   557.97
U46        7.50    24.75   185.63

C1         5.41    44.16   238.91
C2        14.80     5.41    80.07
C7        14.80     5.41    80.07 22327.22
----------------------------------------------
Multi-tenant Corridor:
C3        20.69     5.41   111.93
C4        27.85     5.41   150.67
C5         5.41    44.16   238.91
C6         9.00    33.34   300.06
C8        20.69     5.41   111.93
C9        27.85     5.41   150.67  1064.17
----------------------------------------------
Single Tenant Usable Area:         23391.39 s.f.
----------------------------------------------
Pro-ratable Areas on floor:
P1         9.08    11.38   103.33
P2         7.59     5.33    40.45
P3         8.59     7.27    62.45
P4         8.59     7.27    62.45
P5        12.25    33.34   408.42
P6         6.33    11.38    72.04   749.13
----------------------------------------------
Rentable Area on Floor:            24140.52 s.f.
----------------------------------------------
Non-rentable areas:
N1         9.08    21.96   199.40
N2        10.50    33.34   350.07
N3         7.59    28.01   212.60
N4         8.59    18.80   161.49
N5         6.33    21.96   139.01  1062.56
----------------------------------------------
Net-Gross Area of Floor:           25203.09

Note:These areas were derived from working drawings by xxxxxxx dated
     xx/xx/xx and are accurate only to the extent that they conform
     to the dimensions explicitly shown thereon.

Check   243.08   118.08    1.00 28702.89
         30.00    23.33   -2.00 -1399.80
         22.50    23.33   -2.00 -1049.85
         15.00    23.34   -2.00  -700.20
          7.50    23.33   -2.00  -349.95
                                 ---------
                                 25203.09

                       page 2
```

Figure 3.4-3 (*cont'd*)
Area Calculation Worksheet

91

Extra Profits with Rentable Area Studies

8990 AIRDALE STREET
Summary Area Calculations
Alternative 1, Kitchen Sink Approach
September 31, 1985

GENSLER AND ASSOCIATES
ARCHITECTS

FLOOR	NET-GROSS AREA	NON-RENTABLE	FLOOR COMMON DEDUCT	FLOOR COMMON ADD	BUILDING COMMON DEDUCT	BUILDING COMMON ADD	TOTAL RENTABLE AREA	SINGLE TENANT USABLE	MIN. COR-RIDOR	MULTI-TENANT USABLE	SINGLE TENANT R/U	MULTI-TENANT R/U
SEE NOTES->	(1)	- (2)	- (3)	+ (4)	- (5)	+ (6)	= (7)	: (8)	- (9)	= (10)	(7)/(8)	(7)/(10)
BSMT	15951.87	1040.90	0.00	0.00	8857.38	391.30	6444.89	5319.16	0.00	5319.16	1.2116	1.2116
RESTR	14817.27	1792.50	0.00	0.00	0.00	841.90	13866.67	11331.07	0.00	11331.07	1.2238	1.2238
1	20053.03	1662.56	0.00	0.00	7420.11	709.11	11679.47	10794.99	0.00	10794.99	1.0819	1.0819
2	14530.27	1103.02	0.00	0.00	0.00	867.92	14295.17	12718.58	829.81	11888.77	1.124	1.2024
3	19889.34	1062.56	0.00	0.00	0.00	1216.94	20043.72	18077.65	1064.17	17013.48	1.1088	1.1781
4	25203.09	1062.56	0.00	0.00	0.00	1560.41	25700.94	23391.39	1064.17	22327.22	1.0987	1.1511
5	25203.09	1062.56	0.00	0.00	0.00	1560.41	25700.94	23391.39	1064.17	22327.22	1.0987	1.1511
6	25203.09	1062.56	0.00	0.00	0.00	1560.41	25700.94	23391.39	1064.17	22327.22	1.0987	1.1511
7	25203.09	1062.56	0.00	0.00	0.00	1560.41	25700.94	23391.39	1064.17	22327.22	1.0987	1.1511
8	25203.09	1062.56	0.00	0.00	0.00	1560.41	25700.94	23391.39	1064.17	22327.22	1.0987	1.1511
9	25203.09	1062.56	0.00	0.00	0.00	1560.41	25700.94	23391.39	1064.17	22327.22	1.0987	1.1511
10	25203.09	1145.86	0.00	0.00	0.00	1555.03	25612.26	23308.09	1076.67	22231.42	1.0989	1.1521
11	25203.09	1145.86	365.69	182.68	0.00	1543.20	25417.42	22942.40	710.98	22231.42	1.1079	1.1433
12	25203.09	1102.90	0.00	183.01	1671.92	1461.56	24072.84	21730.44	974.42	20756.02	1.1078	1.1598
TOTAL	312069.59	16431.52	365.69	365.69	17949.41	17949.41	295638.07	266570.72	11041.07	255529.65	1.109	1.157

Figure 3.4-4
Area Calculation Summary

92

sheet. If your software has the ability to get data from one file and enter it in another, this is a simple procedure. An alternate approach is to set up different "areas" on one very large spreadsheet.

Even if you have to manually transfer the numbers most of the data will be calculated by the computer. For example, the total rentable area is simply the subtraction of nonrentable area from gross area.

Examples

Gensler and Associates in Denver offers rentable area management studies as one of their special services. They measure, calculate and document rentable area of office buildings to provide the building owner with an accurate accounting of lease area. In most cases, the additional "found" rentable area they find more than justifies their fee. When a building is being sold, an accurate measure of its "rentable potential" is vital to the real estate transaction.

Additional Tips

- When you are using working drawings to take measurements for area calculations, verify that the building was built according to the dimensions shown. Remember, even a variation of a few inches in a large building with multiple floors can result in a significant variation.

- When setting up a worksheet, leave plenty of extra rows for calculating areas of other projects so you can reuse the template. You will need only a few rows for a simple, rectangular structure, but you will use dozens of subdivided areas for a complex building with an unusual shape.

- When you enter lengths and widths of areas the numbers must be in decimal format, not feet and inches. Although you can use a standard conversion table of decimals of a foot such as found in *Architectural Graphic Standards* you may want to consider spending a little extra time on your spreadsheet setup and devise formulas that allow you to enter dimensions in a feet/inches/fractions format and let the computer do the conversions.

Sources for More Information

Building Owners and Managers Association International (BOMA)
1221 Massachusetts Avenue, N.W.
Washington, DC 20005

CHAPTER 4

How to Improve Design with Computer Tools

Most architects and interior designers think of computer-aided design when they think of improving their services with computers. This is understandable because the most dazzling advances in technology have come in the area of graphics. Multicolor CAD, solids modeling, perspective generation, animation and other impressive techniques make every designer long to have the latest development in a CAD workstation.

While computer-aided design and drafting can vastly improve your practice, there are many other nongraphic ways you can use microcomputers to enhance your design work. The key is realizing that much of design is the management of information and the organization of that information into forms that make it possible for other people to build what is conceived in the imagination. Some of the information is managed and organized into lines, symbols and other graphic elements, but much of it consists of words and numbers that represent ideas.

This chapter focuses on some of the methods of managing design information. If you have not yet taken the plunge into computer-aided design, you can still enhance this phase of your practice without expensive equipment. If you are thinking of expanding into CAD, Section 4.5 provides the basic information you need to evaluate the powerful low-cost CAD systems now available. There is also an entire class of "design" software written for specific applications. Solar heating programs, structural design and lighting calculations are some examples of this type of software. Refer to the various directories listed in Appendix C or be aware of magazine advertisements for these kinds of programs.

4.1
MAINTAINING A DESIGN REQUIREMENT DATA BASE

Most architects and interior designers consider the programming phase of a project to be the time when most of the client's needs are established. While this is generally true, the setting down of design requirements is an on-going process with some decisions not being made until late in the working drawing stage and with many decisions being changed frequently. It is usually these late and changed decisions that cause most of the problems for architects. These are the ones that result in one window in a room where the client wanted two, or an electrical outlet being placed three feet too low.

Recording design requirements and tracking them during the course of a project is vital to the success of a job and can eliminate many of those embarrassing and costly "oversights." A microcomputer can make this job easier for you by improving communication between you and your client and by "remembering" the thousands of details involved in a design project.

This section discusses how you can use a microcomputer with a data base management system (DBMS) to help you with this task. It is an extension of some of the basic programming functions described in Sections 3.2 and 3.3, but includes more detailed information. It is also complimentary to the application described in Section 6.4, Project Transactions, in that it records who makes what decisions about design questions. If you have a great deal of programming information to maintain you may want to consider this application as one of the files in the relational data base management system described in Section 3.3.

Basic Application Requirements

This application requires that you identify each space in the design project and record the various requirements of that space, whether they are dictated by specific client needs, suggested by the designer or are generated as a byproduct of other decisions. For example, a request by the client to have extra heavy-duty shelving built into a room may require heavier studs—something the client isn't concerned with directly, but something that becomes a technical design requirement in addition to the shelving itself.

Even though there may be several identical spaces, such as hotel rooms, offices and the like, you should list each of them separately. There are several reasons for this. First, you want to have the ability to print out a complete report on the entire building at any time for your client's review as well as yours. This can improve communication by forcing both of you to see the entire scope of the work and check off each space.

Second, when you work at the level of detail of this application, even seemingly identical spaces can have slight, but important, differences. One office may be exactly like another except that its occupant needs an extra electrical outlet.

Finally, listing each space makes it easier to print reports showing individual components of the whole job. For example, you can have the computer count and list the number of file cabinets required or the number of fire-rated doors and their locations.

96

You also need the ability to sort and print out your information in various ways. At one time you may want design requirements listed by department while another time you may need them arranged alphabetically by room name. In some instances only a simple listing of required areas may be necessary.

Additional Application Requirements

As mentioned above, you may want to organize this application as part of a relational data base management system linked with area requirements. That way, you could maintain a simple file of information for space planning, but still have all the detail you needed during design development and working drawing production. Refer to Section 3.3 for more information.

Another, more sophisticated, way to implement this application is to use a computer-aided design program that has a data base management component. AutoCAD by Autodesk, Inc. is one example of a low-cost CAD system that has this capability. With this kind of system, you "sketch" each space and show furniture, equipment, electrical outlets, doors and other components graphically. You then assign each of these items certain "attributes" that correspond to data fields in a standard DBMS. For example, a sketch of an electrical outlet in a room can be assigned a voltage, whether it is switched or not, if it needs to be on a dedicated circuit and so forth. You also record who made the decision concerning the component, and the date.

This not only gives you a detailed listing of design requirements but can be the start of schematic design drawings!

Requirements of Software

The following are some of the specific software requirements you will need to successfully implement this application. Refer to Appendix A, Fundamentals of Data Base Management Systems, for a complete description of these and other criteria for selecting a DBMS.

1. For a file management system the program should allow at least 30 fields per record. However, you may need many more if you want to keep a very detailed record of all the possible requirements of a complex building type.

2. You should be able to index on all the data fields.

3. The software should allow you to sort on several key fields together instead of just one alone.

4. Since this application can become complex and each record lengthy, the program should allow more than one "screenfull" of information per record.

5. The program should have the ability to make "mass changes" to a particular data field to save you time. For example, if a type of ceiling finish was eliminated from several types of rooms it would be faster to make one change rather than calling up each record and changing one field.

6. The program must have flexible methods of querying the data base, both on screen and in printed reports. This includes relational queries, Boolean searches and partial string searches.

7. The program must have at least basic four-function arithmetic calculation capability. In addition, it is helpful if the program can perform simple counts of the number of records in the data base where the contents of a given field are of a certain value.

Requirements of Hardware

RAM.   Many file management systems will work with as little as 48K of RAM. The ones that are part of an integrated package require more, usually 128K or greater.

Some relational data base management programs operate with as little as 64K of RAM with the more sophisticated ones requiring 128K or more.

Disks.   You should have at a minimum two disk drives, one for the program and one for your data. Since many data base management applications require a great deal of storage you should estimate your needs prior to buying a system. Since this application is specific to a particular job you will probably be able to contain all the programming data on one disk.

Printer.   A dot-matrix printer is the minimum requirement for this application.

Cost Variables

Hardware.   A complete setup with two disk drives and a dot-matrix printer can be purchased for as little as $2,000 or less.

Software.   Simple file management programs range from under $100 to $400 with a few costing more than $400. Relational data base management programs range from about $400 to over $1,000, but with many very good programs under $800.

Setup.   Setup costs depend on the complexity of your application. You may need from one to two hours to set up a simple file management system while a more complex RDBMS may take from eight to twenty hours.

Implementation Procedures

1. Decide on the typical kinds of design requirements you need to keep track of. These will depend on the project types your office designs and your judgement

of how much detail is important to record. Review your experience with past jobs. What kinds of problems did you have? What information "fell through the cracks"? What communication problems did you have with the client and consultants regarding programming data? Answers to these types of questions will give you some guidance in making your decision.

2. Based on your decisions in step one list the data fields for each data base record and decide on which fields will be "key" fields; that is, which field or fields uniquely identify the room or space. Room number is the most likely candidate, but during the early stages of setting up design requirements you will not have room numbers. Instead, you might consider a combination of the room name field and an arbitrary sequential series number. Thus, you might have Office-1, Office-2 and so forth. Later, when a plan is finalized, you can assign them room numbers that will be carried through working drawings.

Another possibility if you are dealing with known occupants is to use the last name of the person occupying the space. In this case you might have Office-Smith, Office-Jones, and so on.

In either case, keep the room name in a separate field from the second identifying key field so you can index and sort on the room name alone. Figure 4.1-1 lists some of the possible data fields for this application. Use this as a starting point for making your list.

3. Based on the data fields established in the previous step and the particular requirements of the building type you are working on, design a data entry form to use when you interview the client or tour the client's existing facility. The forms can be completed over a period of several days or weeks, then compiled for initial data entry at one time. This makes input easier and allows the people collecting the information to concentrate on that task.

To completely avoid this step you can use a portable computer and enter the data as you interview.

4. Following the directions of your software set up data entry screens, indexes, report formats and other files as required.

5. Be diligent in making changes as they occur. This can yield one of the greatest benefits from this application, since it is "lost" changes that often cause the most problems. Include a single-character data field in your record such as a Y or N to allow you to mark the records that have changed. Using the select feature of your DBMS you can then print out a list at any time of all current changes to give to the designers or drafters on the job. The information concerning changes should also include a description of the change, who made it, why it was made and the date of the change.

6. Establish an office policy concerning one person who should maintain this data base, what kinds of reports should be produced and when. For most offices the project manager is in the best position to keep track of design requirement and changes since he or she maintains communication with all members of the

```
Room name
Series number (or occupant's last name)
Department
Room number
Area
Optimum dimensions
Ceiling height
Floor finish
Wall finish
Ceiling finish
Illumination level
Power requirements
Telephone
Data communication
Ventilation
Acoustic requirements
Equipment
Furniture
Other special requirements
This record changed? (Y/N)
Change description
Change made by
Reason
Date of change
```

Figure 4.1-1
Data Fields for a Design Requirement Data Base

project team—client, consultants, code authorities, designers, firm principals and manufacturer's representatives.

Additional Tips

- If you need to keep track of a great deal of information on each room in the building you are designing (such as a hospital) consider keeping several records for each room. They would all have the same number or other identifying key, but be separated into such areas as "electrical/mechanical" requirements, "furniture" requirements, "interior finish" requirements and so forth.

- Print complete reports on the current status of your information at various times for review by the client. You give the client the opportunity to catch any misunderstandings early in the design process and set up a "paper trail" of reasons for your design decisions in case there are disputes later.

4.2
STAYING COMPETITIVE WITH COMPUTERIZED SPACE PLANNING

Computers can be a valuable tool to assist architects with the detailed planning of building interiors, either as an adjunct to an architectural commission or as a separate service. Space planning is similar in process to laying out an architectural floor plan, but involves much more data including layout alternatives, furniture and equipment requirements, lighting, exact locations of telephone and electrical outlets and innumerable other details.

In this application it is necessary to link graphics with a data base so that you can keep track of the lists of items associated with a particular space, but still design, view and manipulate two-dimensional images. This usually requires a more sophisticated and expensive mini-computer along with more elaborate software. However, there are several low-cost CAD programs that can provide you with the capability to improve your space planning services. While they may not have *all* the refinements of some of the larger systems they are extremely powerful for their cost. As continuing improvements are made in the CAD market for designers, the ability of these programs to emulate some of the more powerful programs will likely increase. Refer to Sections 4.5 and 8.3 for a listing of some of the low-cost programs available.

This section outlines some of the requirements for implementing computer space planning to help you make an intelligent choice when shopping for software and hardware. It gives guidelines for how to proceed with starting up the system in your office to keep you ahead of your competition.

Basic Application Requirements

Good space planning involves several interrelated activities: determination of move-in and future space needs, the location and adjacency of those spaces, deciding on the detailed furniture and equipment of each space and designing for movement of people and goods between the spaces. Some aspects of these activities can be handled simply with other types of computer programs such as data base management systems and spreadsheets. Refer to Chapters 3 and 8 for ways to implement these applications. Others, however, are only possible with computer graphics tied to data based in the system.

The specific kinds of graphic functions you want a system of this type to perform include the following:

- Allocation of space including size, shape and adjacencies. Types of drawings include bubble diagrams, block plans and stacking diagrams.

- The ability to show detailed information of each space including furniture, equipment, storage requirements, lighting requirements, power and communication requirements and space standards, if any. The data base part of the system needs to be linked to these items.

- Layout of circulation for people, goods and paper.

Additional Application Requirements

More sophisticated software can handle the requirements listed above in addition to allowing you to make space projections (something you *could* do with a separate spreadsheet or data base management program) and creating detailed inventories of spaces, furniture and equipment. At the top end of the spectrum, some CAD programs can turn the data into three-dimensional images.

Requirements of Software

The primary requirement of the software is that it link the graphic functions with the data base. This includes being able to assign "attributes" to the graphic elements. For example, a desk shown in an office has attributes such as type, manufacturer's name, size, finish, types of drawers, a code number and so forth. When you want a listing of all the desks in the project sorted in a particular order the computer can do it very easily.

Taking this one step further, the software should be able to automatically add a record to the data base when you "draw" it on the plan. Thus, as you fill in a series of offices with a desk that has a particular code number, the computer adds each to the data base without you having to type in every attribute. Another advanced feature of some software is the ability to automatically assign furniture and equipment to various departments based on where you draw the boundaries for the department. If you move a desk from one department (area on the drawing) to another, the data base is modified to reflect this desk being in another department.

The software should also be able to calculate floor areas based on your graphic layout by individual space, department, floor and entire building. Refer to Section 4.5 for more detailed requirements of CAD software.

Requirements of Hardware

Because of the extreme range of capabilities of software that can perform some or all of the functions listed above, it is impossible to give exact hardware requirements. The primary differences over other applications described in this book include greatly increased random access memory (RAM) and disk storage, and a plotter to produce the graphic output. High-resolution, color screens are desirable, but not always necessary. Another choice you must make is whether to have stand-alone workstations or a multiuser system.

Cost Variables

Hardware.   As mentioned above, hardware requirements are quite variable. A low-cost CAD setup may cost about $10,000 to $15,000 depending on the screen type and plotter while a top-of-the-line system may cost $75,000 to $100,000.

Software.   Like hardware, software is quite variable depending on the capabilities of the system. Your needs will dictate how much you spend.

Setup and training.   CAD systems are complex and time-consuming to learn. Setup and training account for a good portion of the total cost of the system, even if you decide to use simple, low-cost CAD software.

Maintenance.   For any kind of CAD system you should have a maintenance contract. This is a monthly charge paid to the vendor who sold the system or to a third-party maintenance company. On larger, more sophisticated systems this monthly cost can be substantial so find out early what it will be.

Implementation Procedures

1. Determine the kind of space planning work you will be doing; this determines how sophisticated the program needs to be. For instance, will you be doing simple graphics for small jobs or handling projects with several hundred thousand square feet in multiple buildings? Do you want (or need) matrix analysis of adjacencies? Do you need a multiuser system or is a stand-alone workstation sufficient?

2. Define the kinds of reports the system must generate. Will you need simple space summaries and lists of equipment, or will you want more detailed analysis of the data?

3. Determine the amount of data you will be manipulating. This includes the number of individual drawing components (spaces, desks, chairs, etc.) and the number of attributes (data fields) each will have as well as the complexity of the drawings the system must handle.

4. Shop for software and hardware with these requirements in mind. Make sure the hardware has enough computing power and disk storage to handle your present needs as well as future requirements.

5. Plan the number of data fields in your data bases carefully. Some software (especially the less expensive programs) do not allow you to add fields to the data structure once it is set up. Leave extra, blank fields if you are not sure what additional attributes of each graphic element you need to track.

6. Once the system is up and operating, establish procedures for how the data base is to be updated.

Case in Point

The Stewart Design Group, Boston, uses a sophisticated computer-aided drafting system for all phases of architectural design. The firm does a great deal of health care facility design and uses the space planning capabilities of the computer extensively to analyze programming information, evaluate space planning alternatives, and draw the final solution.

On a typical project a designer first develops adjacency requirements by selecting one of six types of relationships between spaces for each pair of spaces in the proposed building. This is done with the involvement of the client. From this data the computer develops a bubble diagram indicating the best mathematical fit for the required adjacencies.

After the bubble diagram is edited, it is translated into a block diagram where simple rectangular blocks shown to scale are laid out, along with the required circulation. As many alternative block diagrams can be developed as required. This diagram can also be edited and the computer can compare the original adjacency relationships with those actually represented in the block diagram.

As a further refinement, standard room layouts with furniture and equipment (developed by the firm and stored in the computer) can be superimposed on the block diagram and edited to fit. The final drawing is a refined space plan meeting the original requirements of the client and containing all the detailed equipment and finish needs of each space. This information is stored in the data base portion of the program but linked to the graphic symbols on the drawing.

The system also allows the 2-D drawing to be transformed into a 3-D drawing to give an indication of what the spaces will look like.

Additional Tips

- Make sure the vendor from whom you buy your system provides continuing support so that when you have a problem or a question you know who to call.

- When you see a vendor's demonstration make sure it includes handling a large amount of data, not just a few offices or workstations. Practically all systems look good when they only have small amounts of information to process; the true test is operating under normal data loads.

- Plan on plenty of time for initial setup of the system and debugging. This step always takes longer than expected. It is important that the system users do not get discouraged because the application does not work perfectly immediately.

4.3
DESIGN CHECKLISTS FOR SUCCESSFUL QUALITY CONTROL

Most firms design similar types of projects time after time whether they are schools, office buildings, stores or factories. And many firms make the same mistakes time after time. One of the primary reasons why this occurs is that the lessons learned from one project remain only in the minds of the people who worked on that project. If these people leave the firm, don't work on the next, similar, job or simply forget, the knowledge is not applied to a new situation.

This kind of "corporate forgetfulness" occurs in large and small firms alike. With the pressure of the next project and no organized way to save information, the project managers, designers and others simply don't record what they have learned and how to avoid similar mistakes in the future.

Developing design checklists can be an important ingredient of your firm's overall quality control program. It can organize a standard way of reviewing projects, help catch mistakes before the job is carried too far, and serve as a learning tool for new employees or for younger, less experienced staff members. Such a checklist developed in house can also be tailored to *your* firm's project types, unique design and detailing methods and geographical area.

This section describes how to apply a computerized checklist to the design process. Refer to Section 5.2 for a discussion on maintaining a working drawing checklist and Section 6.3 for information on project management checklists.

Basic Application Requirements

For this application you need to manipulate words, lists and blocks of text. A word processing program with a "merge" capability works perfectly well for this kind of checklist production. Refer to Section 4.4 and "Additional Application Requirements" in Section 6.3 for guidelines on using a spreadsheet or data base management program for checklists.

Automating the production of a design checklist has several advantages over manual typing. Of course, there is the obvious feature of being able to easily change, add and delete portions of the checklist. The real power comes in being able to quickly customize lists for a specific job based on the project type, site location, applicable codes and any special program requirements.

A word processing program selected for this application should be able to read files or portions of a file into the file on which you are working. It should also be able to merge predefined files into a "calling" file the same way you would send similar letters to names on a mailing list.

Requirements of Software

The software requirements for this application are minimal. Almost any but the least expensive programs will work as long as they have the "merge" capability described earlier. The software must also allow you to "read" another file into the file you are working on at any time or "write" a block of text into another file. Underlining and boldface printing is also advantageous if you need to highlight some portion of the text.

Requirements of Hardware

RAM. For word processing, minimum RAM is required for developing this kind of checklist. It will depend more on your software requirements than on the application.

Disks. A single disk drive is sufficient for most word processing programs, but it is preferable to have two, one for the program and one for the disk containing your project data.

Printer. The minimum requirement is a dot-matrix printer.

Cost Variables

Hardware. The required hardware for basic word processing is minimal. If you are starting from scratch you could get an entire setup with a dot-matrix printer for $2,000 or less.

Software. Word processing programs with merge capabilities may range from about $200 to $500. Spelling checkers, indexing programs and other add-ons to word processing are in addition to this price.

Setup. Initial development of your checklist is the most time-consuming part of this application unless your office already has some rudimentary form of list.

Data entry. Typing the checklists into the various files can be time consuming. If most of your list is already developed, this task can be handled by a secretary. If you are starting new, the responsible project manager or designer can enter the items directly into the computer. A copy can be printed for review by others in the office and revised as many times as required.

Implementation Procedures

1. Develop a framework for organizing your checklist data base. This will be the collection of individual, standard components you put together to make a

custom checklist for a particular project. These components can be broken down into two broad areas: those based on building types your office does most frequently and those based on groups of design decisions. During the design phase of a project, architects make decisions related to several recurring issues. For example, there are always design decisions related to sitework, floor plan layout, lighting, dimensioning, exterior materials and so on. These are common to any job regardless of the building type and can be grouped with building types to form a matrix. See Figure 4.3-1.

The *groups* of design decisions are common to any type of project, but the individual checklist items in each group will change to reflect the particular needs

		Bldg. type	1	2	3	4	5	6	7			99
	Decision group		Residential	Apartments	Condominiums	Offices	Retail Stores	Warehouse	Office interior			
A	Site development		A1	A2	A3	A4	A5	A6				A99
B	Layout			B2	B3	B4	B5	B6	B7			B99
C	Exterior Materials		C1	C2	C3	C4	C5	C6				C99
D	Interior Materials		D1	D2	D3	D4	D5	D6	D7			D99
E	HVAC		E1	E2	E3	E4	E5	E6	E7			E99
F	Lighting			F2	F3	F4	F5		F7			F99
G	Power		G1	G2	G3	G4	G5	G6	G7			G99
H	Communication			H2		H4	H5		H7			H99

Figure 4.3-1
Checklist Module Organization

of each building type. For example, lighting design decisions will be different in apartments than in office buildings. Figure 4.3-1 shows a matrix organization that one type of office may use. Some cells are blank since not all decision groups are applicable to all building types. However, you should develop the individual headings based on *your* firm's design procedures and project types.

Some of the groups of design decisions you might want to consider include:

sitework

layout

exterior materials

interior materials

lighting

HVAC

power distribution and switching

communications

In the cell of each matrix is a designation that you will use to title the individual word processing files. By looking at the matrix you can quickly tell which modules you want to copy into your working checklist file.

2. Write the individual checklist items for each module. These will be based on your experience, checklists you may already have, and ideas gleaned from reference books. For each of the groups of design decisions, you may want to have two files, one for checklist points unique to a particular building type and one for points common to any kind of project. This way, if you are doing a project type new to your office you still have something to start with.

Each module should be developed with the idea of flexibility in mind so you can easily print customized lists to fit any particular job. However, don't fall into the trap of making an excessive number of modules. The system will become so unwieldy that no one will use it.

3. Develop master files on your word processor for each of your offices most common building types. These are the files that will "call" each of the specified modules into your working file and build the final checklist. If your software does not have this "merge" capability, you can open a file and manually read in each module in the desired order.

4. Print a reference copy and place it in a notebook. The project manager or senior designer can use this along with the matrix to select the appropriate modules when a project begins.

5. When you are ready to develop an individual project checklist use the master file you developed in Step 3 or set one up to call your selected files. When this is done, review it on screen and add any special requirements dictated

by the project and delete any that may not be appropriate. Print out the file and you are ready to begin.

6. Test the adequacy of your list by using it on one or two jobs. Revise it as necessary based on feedback from project managers and designers.

7. As your office uses the checklist, update it as required to reflect data gathered from completed jobs. This is *the most important* step in implementing this application. Without continuous updating, the checklist cannot become the valuable data base of information it should be.

Example

Figure 4.3-2 shows a portion of a checklist developed for an office building and design decisions relating to interior materials (module D4 in Figure 4.3-1). This example simply shows a brief description of each item and one place to check it off as it is reviewed or verified. You can make the list more elaborate if you like by including places for the date, check-off by a second person, and additional notes by the designer.

```
MODULE D4--INTERIOR MATERIALS/OFFICE BUILDINGS


Floor finishes

[ ]   Review material selected for traffic expected

[ ]   Flooring acceptable for heavy fixed loads--files, etc.

[ ]   Durability of transitions at change in flooring materials

[ ]   Flamespread meets building code

[ ]   Maintenance requirements consistent with available personnel

[ ]   Repair and replacement possible within life cycle guidelines

[ ]   Material can accommodate floor outlets

[ ]   Furniture casters usable without chair pads

[ ]   Color doesn't adversly affect light reflectance

[ ]   Material, color approved by client
```

Figure 4.3-2
Design Checklist Module

Additional Tips

- Since this is a *design* checklist stick with issues that are typically encountered during the schematic and design development phases of a project. You should develop a separate working drawing checklist (See Section 5.2) for more specific questions dealing with detailing, cross-referencing, materials construction and coordination with the specifications.

- Involve all appropriate people in the office when you begin to develop the individual checklist items. Tap into the collected experience and knowledge of the entire professional office staff.

Sources for More Information

The Guidelines Pre-design and Planning Manual Guidelines, P.O. Box 456, Orinda, CA 94563

Rosen, Harold J., and Bennett, Philip M. *Construction Materials Evaluation and Selection.* New York: John Wiley & Sons, 1979.

Architectural and Engineering Performance Information Center
University of Maryland
3907 Metzerott Road
College Park, MD 20742 (301.935.5544)

This center collects, analyzes and disseminates data on the performance of buildings and civil structures. The information deals with the structural, electrical, mechanical, functional, aesthetic and environmental performance of materials, elements, systems and processes. They maintain a computer data base that can be searched on a fee basis as well as a dossier library and visual materials library.

4.4

GETTING THE MOST FROM CODE CHECKLISTS

Repetitious problems with building code requirements arise almost as often as recurring design mistakes. There are several causes, but one of them is the complexity of codes. Most architects and designers would rather design than wade through the lengthy, often contradictory dictates of a building code. Because of this, many offices have developed their own checklists to help minimize the problems caused by oversights in complying with regulatory requirements. Other firms, however, still plod through as best they can, usually relying on the person in the office who is most knowledgeable in this area.

For the firms who do not use code checklists, a computer can be a simple way to get started in this area of quality control. For those firms who already rely on them, automating the application can improve compliance with the multitude of regulations in the building industry.

Basic Application Requirements

The requirements of any building code depend on a great number of interrelated variables. This is one of the difficult aspects of compliance, but it is a fact of life. A code checklist should do more than simply repeat the provisions of the written document; it should help organize the information in a way that follows (as much as possible) the architect's design process so that the necessary data is at hand when a design decision is being made. For example, portions of a code influencing setbacks and exterior wall openings are scattered in several chapters. A good list will pull all of these requirements together so the architect can lay out a building quickly and do it right the first time.

A good checklist should also include provisions of other regulations that affect the same design component as provisions in the local code. For example, a local housing code may be more stringent in a particular area than one of the national model codes. A checklist is an ideal way to pull together the various regulations that impinge on one project.

Finally, you should be able to access and arrange the checklist in various ways. In one case you may want the items organized according to specific subject areas such as "wall finishes." In another, you may want all the provisions related to a particular occupancy sorted by major topic areas such as "exiting," "exterior openings," and "fire-resistive standards." In this way, the checklist can help you isolate only those provisions that relate to the particular project at hand and not inapplicable sections related to other occupancies and construction types.

A data base management program is an ideal type of software to implement this application. With a DBMS you only have to enter the information once and can then print checklists for certain building types (occupancy classifications), design specialties or broad subject areas. For example, you can print a complete checklist for the project manager or project designer and then an abbreviated list of "finish" requirements for the interior designer. A DBMS also makes it easy to change individual provisions and to add new sections as you improve and refine your checklist.

Requirements of Software

A file management type of data base management program is all you need to computerize this application. The following are some of the specific software requirements you will need. Refer to Appendix A, Fundamentals of Data Base Management Systems, for a complete description of these and other criteria for selecting a DBMS.

1. The program should allow at least 15 fields per record.
2. You should be able to index on at least five data fields.
3. The software should allow you to sort on several key fields together instead of just one alone.
4. The program must have a flexible report generator since you will want to print out results in various ways.

Requirements of Hardware

RAM. Many file management systems will work with as little as 48K of RAM, most with 64K. The ones that are part of an integrated package require more, usually 128K or greater.

Disks. You should have at a minimum two disk drives, one for the program and one for your data. This application is not memory intensive so a hard disk is not required.

Printer. A dot-matrix printer is the minimum requirement for this application.

Cost Variables

Hardware. A complete setup with two disk drives and a dot-matrix printer can be purchased for as little as $2,000 or less.

Software. Simple file management programs range from under $100 to $400 with a few costing more than $400.

Setup. You will need from one to two hours to set up this application using a file management system.

Data entry. Data entry is the most labor-intensive part of organizing a code checklist. In addition, much of the work will have to be done by someone knowledgeable in the various codes your office uses. If you already have some type of list the work will be reduced somewhat, but to organize a data base management system will take a great deal of thought and data entry time.

Implementation Procedures

1. Determine the level of detail you want in your checklist system. Should each listing be in very brief outline form or provide prompting and a description of the code provision to which it relates? Consider the difference in each of the following checklist items that both refer to the same topic.

_____Wall finish flame-spread ok?

or

_____Maximum flame-spread of 75 (class II) required for interior walls and ceilings of exitways in occupancies A, E, I, H, B and R-1. Maximum of 200 (class III) in R-3 and no restrictions in M.

```
 1. Section number      1726(e)
 2. Section title       Atriums, smoke detectors
 3. Seminar keyword     Fire and life safety, smoke detectors
 4. Design keyword      Smoke detectors
 5. Cross reference     Chapter 38, 1726(c)X1
 6. Related standard    NFPA 72E
 7. Standard title      Automatic fire detectors
 8. Summary 1           Smoke detectors shall be placed on the occupied
 9. Summary 2           side of any door opening into the atrium. When
10. Summary 3           level is open to atrium, that level shall be
11. Summary 4           fully detectored.
12. Summary 5
13. Blank 1
14. Blank 2
```

Figure 4.4-1
Building Code Data Entry Screen

The first one calls the user's attention to the topic and makes for a much shorter checklist, but requires that whoever is using it knows about flame-spread ratings and that minimum requirements differ by occupancy type and location.

The second one is very specific and gives guidance in what is required. Even if an inexperienced staff member were using the checklist and did not completely understand flame-spread requirements, this kind of notation is sufficiently involved that he or she would ask someone else for clarification. The disadvantage is the lengthy document produced and the time required to enter the information in the data base.

2. Decide on the other information you want to include in each data record. This will be determined by how much of a problem code compliance is for your office, the experience level of your staff and how much time and effort you want to devote to automating this application. Figure 4.4-1 shows one example of a data entry screen prompting for a checklist entry.

As a minimum, you should have the following data fields:

the checklist description

the code provisions to which it refers

the chapter of the code involved

a broad topic heading such as "exiting"

a specific keyword subject heading such as "handrails"

In addition you may want to consider the following additional data fields:

cross-reference to other articles in the code

references to industry standards not printed in the code

occupancy types to which the item applies

3. Following the instructions of your software, set up the various file definitions, indexes and report formats you will need.

4. Print out the checklists sorted by whatever method is most useful to you. You may want to have one for each occupancy type your firm works with the most. As an alternate, you can print one "master" checklist and then just print various indexes that refer to the master. Indexes provide the added benefit of giving you double duty from your efforts because you can use the checklist as a reference tool as well as a project-specific guide.

Figure 4.4-2 shows a partial listing of a checklist outlining stairway requirements for schools.

5. Be diligent about updating and adding to your checklist. Like the design checklist described in Section 4.3, this tool is only useful if it reflects current code requirements and the accumulation of your firm's ongoing experience in this area.

Additional Tips

- Although a well-developed code checklist can be a valuable aid to design and quality control, it is not a *substitute* for the code. Do not rely on it exclusively because no checklist can contain all the subtle relationships and exceptions of most codes.

- Consider keeping items from *all* applicable codes in one data base—building codes, zoning ordinances, housing codes, food service regulations, and so forth. This way your checklist reminds you of all the requirements that impinge on your design. By adding an additional data field to mark what kind of code the listing is from, you can have the DBMS select only those records related to one document if you need it.

Sources for More Information

Goldberg, Alfred. *Design Guide to the 1985 Uniform Building Code.* Mill Valley, CA: GRDA Publications, 1985.

4.5

LOW-COST COMPUTER-AIDED DESIGN AND DRAFTING

Computer-aided design and drafting (CADD) is the one computer application that has captured the interest and imagination of practically every architect and

```
Check  Item                                           Code ref.
================================================================
```

Exiting, stairways
_____

____	Min. two stairways provided above 1st story?	3319 (g)
____	Exit stairs from basement open directly to exterior?	3319 (i)
____	Min. width determined by occupant load divided equally?	3319 (g)
____	Stairs with occupant load over 100 min. width of 5'-0"	3319 (g)
____	Stairway enclosure minimum 1-hour except for type I and type II non-combustible which is 2-hour.	Table 17-A
____	Wall and ceiling finish flame-spread maximum of 25 (class I)	Table 42-B
____	Dimension of landing in direction of travel equal to width of stairway?	3306 (g)
____	Landing at doors not less than stair width?	3304 (i)
____	Stairway doors do not reduce landing size more than 7"?	3304 (i)
____	With occupant load >50 doors do not reduce landing dimn. more than 1/2 required?	3304 (i)
____	Maximum 12' vertically between landings?	3306 (i)
____	Stair riser min. 4", max. 7"?	3306 (c)
____	Minimum stair tread 11"?	3306 (c)
____	Handrails each side of stair?	3306 (j)
____	Max. handrail projection 3 1/2".	3306 (b)
____	Handrails 30" to 34" above nosing.	3306 (j)
____	Intermediate handrail if width over 88"	3306 (j)
____	Does one handrail extend 6" beyond top and bottom risers with a return or safety terminal?	3306 (j)
____	Handgrip 1 1/4" to 2"?	3306 (j)
____	Not less than 1 1/2" between rail & wall?	3306 (j)

Figure 4.4-2
Building Code Checklist

interior designer. It is the most "visible" to the profession because it most closely resembles what they produce: graphic images and drawings. As a result, there have been hundreds of magazine articles written, books published, roundtables held, newsletters created and an intense marketing effort set in motion by scores of software and hardware vendors. Although CADD has been around for decades, the interest has intensified because of the recent development of low-cost CADD that brings the application within reach of practically every architect and interior designer.

Computer-aided design and drafting offers the design professional the benefits of increased productivity, improved accuracy and generally allows him or her to offer better service to clients. More alternatives can be tested faster and at a lower cost. Changes can be made easily and quickly. Finally, repetitive graphic elements can be reused, thus helping to keep fees steady as service increases.

Although this book focuses on the non-CADD applications of microcomputers, a brief discussion of CADD is necessary for those who are new to the profession, new to computers or are contemplating purchasing a CADD system along with implementing some of the other applications described in this book.

This section is by no means intended to be a complete guide to evaluating, selecting and implementing a computer-aided design and drafting application; that would require a separate book in itself. Instead, it is intended to give the nonuser a general idea of what is available in micro-based CADD, what to expect in the way of software and hardware needs, a general idea of cost and some basic tips in getting started with selecting a system. For more detailed information, refer to the sources of information listed at the end of this section and in Appendix C.

Basic Application Requirements

All CADD systems, whether they are based on a microcomputer or a large mainframe do essentially the same thing; they allow you to create a drawing, edit it and print it out. The differences come in ease of use, speed, amount of data processed (perspectives and color, for example), number of workstations accommodated, integration with other programs and miscellaneous "bells and whistles."

Since most of the time a person spends at a CADD workstation is spent in entering information to create a drawing, the system should make this as easy and fast as possible. Early systems allowed you to do little more than what is possible today, but the procedures were laborious and time consuming. Even now, some software forces you to go through many separate steps to perform a relatively simple process like breaking a wall to insert a window opening.

You should have a system that allows simple selection of commands and graphic symbols from a menu so drawing generation is as fast as possible. Time is money and greatly increased productivity will not occur unless you can minimize the time the operator spends entering commands. Other "user-friendly" features include help screens, error recovery and a good manual.

Additional Application Requirements

Every firm will have requirements that they consider "must have" features and others that may be considered "nice to have." For example, many people may consider data base extraction to be beyond the basic application requirements of drawing. However, this is such a powerful use of CADD that it should be considered a basic requirement.

The following are my choices of features that most offices will not need if they are just starting with CADD, but that are available if you want to find the systems and spend the extra money.

1. *3-D drawing.* This includes isometrics, perspectives in wire-frame mode or with hidden lines removed and solids modeling. Software and hardware for 3-D is more sophisticated and often takes the application out of the low-cost category. However, there are some economical software packages available that perform 3-D drawing.

2. *Sketch mode.* This allows you to enter free-hand drawings apart from the orthographic rigidity of most programs.

3. *Associative dimensioning.* This feature automatically changes dimensions as the object is changed. Again, some economical software has this feature.

Requirements of Software

The following are some of the features you should consider when shopping for CADD software. Some, like creating lines, are found in all programs while others are implemented in varying degrees of sophistication in different packages. Consider the following as minimum features that will allow you to use CADD efficiently.

Setup

Limits. When you set the limits of the coordinate system, can they be changed later if you need more room. For example, if the size of a building is 75 by 100 feet and your limits are 100 by 120 feet, and the building is later lengthened to 125 feet, can you enlarge them to accommodate this change?

Size of units. These are the smallest dimensions that the program will deal with and represent the accuracy of the drawing. They are defined each time you start a drawing and may be, for instance, one-quarter inch for an architectural floor plan. Can they be changed any time during the creation of the drawing?

Layers. Like overlay drafting, CADD allows you to keep different entities

117

like structural grid, notes, walls and room names on different "layers." Can entities be switched between layers once created?

Line style. Does the program offer a variety of styles such as center lines, dashed lines, etc?

Color. Although not absolutely necessary, color makes it much easier to see the components of different layers on the screen.

Creating the Drawing

Line. How easy is it to create lines, the basic component of CADD?

Circles and arcs. How easily are they created?

Fillets. Fillets are curves tangent to any two intersecting lines with a user-defined radius.

Mistakes. Does the program offer an easy way to undo your mistakes?

Grid. Can you set up a grid (much like using graph paper under a drawing sheet) that helps you lay out the drawing?

Snap to grid. The program automatically aligns any entered line to the nearest grid point so you don't have to be exact with your input device.

Snap to end points. If there is an existing line and you want to connect it with a new line the program automatically connects the two as long as your input device is close to the existing line.

Rotate grid. Can the grid be oriented at any angle?

Orthogonal snap. This feature forces a line to be either horizontal or vertical regardless of exactly how it was entered.

Isometric snap. Same as orthogonal snap but oriented to the isometric grid you establish.

Dimensions. How easy is it to make dimension lines, extension lines and label the dimension. Does the program automatically calculate the dimension from the length of the objects already entered?

Text. You should have a choice of determining the location, height, font, justification and angle of text.

Hatching. This fills in shapes with cross hatching and other patterns.

Editing the Drawing

Erase. This deletes a line, group of lines or object from the data base.

Move. This moves a line or entire group of elements from one part of the drawing to another. Part of this command should allow you to rotate or mirror image the element you are moving.

Cut. Can you easily break into an existing drawing element to make an opening for something else?

Copy. Similar to "move" but it leaves the copied element intact. You should also be able to copy several times for an array, rotate, mirror image or change scale.

Group elements. This command allows you to define a group of lines and elements and save it as a file for later reuse. This is one of the most powerful features of CADD since it lets you create something only once, like an elevation of a window, and use it over and over. Also called object definition, this feature is used to create symbol libraries for very fast drawing production.

Search and replace. Can the program find a particular element in the file and automatically replace it with another?

Screen Display

Zoom. Since you can never see an entire drawing at a scale large enough to read on a small screen, the zoom command lets you "step back" or "look close" at a portion of the drawing. With programs that use a floating-point number format the zoom ratios are very high, allowing you to include an incredible amount of detail in one drawing.

Pan. This allows you to "move around" and view different parts of the drawing on the screen.

Status line. There should be someplace on the screen (or a separate screen) that constantly tells you the commands you have entered, what layer you are currently using, how much memory is left, cursor coordinates, current system settings and similar information.

Resolution. What kind of screen resolution does the program support? With a good zoom capability high resolution is not critical, but it often makes creating a drawing a little easier.

Drawing regeneration. Can you toggle off layers, text and solid fill-in to speed up drawing regeneration? If not, you will find yourself waiting for complex images to regenerate on the screen after you have edited them.

Input

The software should support a variety of input devices such as digitizers, mice and stylus pens.

Output

Scaling. As with manual drawing, this determines what small distances will represent full-size dimensions.

Selective plot. Are you able to plot layers selectively with different colors or line widths and types? Can you also plot just a portion of a drawing?

Other

Macros. Macros are sequences of commands that perform a particular function. If you use a particular sequence over and over it speeds things considerably if you can substitute one keystroke or menu selection for many. With parametric programming a macro will pause to allow you to enter a variable that controls how the macro performs. This feature allows you to create your own menus. Some people consider macros and user-defined menus as an advanced feature but they are critical to fast use of the system.

Help command. This gives on-screen assistance and may refer you to the appropriate section of the users' manual.

Data base extraction. Sometimes called a bill of materials feature, this very powerful capacity allows you to assign attributes to graphics elements. For instance, a door on a floor plan can have all the typical door schedule information "attached" to it—size, thickness, fire-rating and so forth. These attributes are usually not displayed on screen, but held internally for later examination or print out. If you delete a door, one door in the data base is automatically deleted.

This is one of the most important features you should look for in a CADD system. While it is a standard feature on mini- or mainframe systems, not all microcomputer-based programs have it. It makes applications such as facility management, quantity takeoffs and schedules almost automatic.

Area. The program should be able to calculate the area within a defined space.

Number format. There are two types, floating point and integer. Always look for floating point format as this allows greater accuracy and higher resolution. The main disadvantage is that it requires more storage and processing power.

File interchange. Can your drawing files be interchanged with other programs or computers? Does the program meet the IGES standard (Initial Graphic Exchange Specification) by the National Bureau of Standards?

Requirements of Hardware

Computer-aided design and drafting requires a wider range of hardware components than other applications and these components must all be compatible with each other. This is one of the reasons why setting up a functional workstation is often difficult. Practically all micro-based software will operate on IBM computers and compatible equipment. Other brands can be used as well, but your choices of software are diminished.

The real variable is the kind of central processing unit the computer uses. Most programs will run much faster if a math co-processor is also installed. Unless you plan to assemble all the pieces of your system, it probably isn't necessary to worry too much about the technical details of the CPU, but you should be aware that some modifications to standard hardware may have to be made at an additional cost.

RAM. 512K RAM is usually the minimum necessary.

Disks. Many systems can operate with two floppy disks, but you should consider one floppy and one ten-megabyte hard disk as a minimum. Operation is simply too slow without a hard disk.

Backup for hard disk. Backing up a ten-megabyte hard disk or anything larger

120

is too slow and tedious for floppys. Plan on buying a tape cartridge or disk cartridge backup system.

Ports. These are another little technical concern depending on the kinds of input and output devices you will be using. Both serial and parallel ports are required. Once again, you will probably depend on your dealer's knowledge to make the right match.

Input devices. This is a very personal (and important) part of the system. Some people are more comfortable with some kinds of devices than others. Some devices can actually slow up the input process. Try several kinds before buying. The common devices include the keyboard, digitizer (in either a stylus or puck configuration), mouse, light pen and touch pen. The light and touch pens used to contact the screen are very awkward and shouldn't be considered.

A variation of the stylus is one that works on a digitizing tablet. It recognizes your freehand marks so that a "Z" scribbled on the pad would be recognized as the command for "zoom."

There are also scanning cameras that can be used to convert existing drawings to an electronic format without the need to manually trace over each line on a digitizing tablet.

Screen. There are many types of screens with varying resolutions and color capabilities. Generally speaking, the higher-resolution monitors are easier to look at over a long period of time and color monitors allow you to make full use of layering while creating or editing a drawing. However, be aware that low-cost color monitors have a lower resolution than comparably priced monochrome monitors.

When you buy a color monitor you usually need to get a compatible color graphics board that costs extra and is critical to the proper functioning of the monitor. The kind of monitor you select will be a compromise between resolution, color and cost.

Output devices. The output device is one of the most important parts of your system. Not only is it the limiting factor in hard copy resolution (the software is always more precise) but it also greatly affects the total cost of your system. You can easily spend as much or more on a plotter than your entire hardware and software setup.

The common output devices include dot-matrix printers, ink-jet printers, electrostatic plotters, drum plotters and flat bed plotters. For most low-cost CADD applications, a drum plotter offers the best compromise between performance and cost.

Cost Variables

Because there are so many variables and combinations of hardware and software components, it is nearly impossible to give general cost figures. Generally, low-cost CADD can be considered to be any system less than about $15,000 and a modest configuration can be purchased for less than $10,000.

The following prices will give you an approximate idea of the costs of some of the components. However, as with any prices in the industry, they change frequently so use them only as rough guidelines.

Software. Most of the popular and *usable* micro-CADD software costs between $1,000 and $2,000. The variables are which version is available at the time of purchase and various optional add-ons. Third-party software vendors also sell programs to run with some of the base programs. These add to the cost. For example, AE/CADD is available as an add-on to AutoCAD. It is a master template with a symbol library and many of the most needed macro commands to speed the creation of drawings.

Computer. A computer such as the IBM/XT with a monochrome monitor, one floppy disk drive and a ten-megabyte hard disk may range from $5,000 to $6,000. A math co-processor will add about $250.

Plotter. This is one of the major cost variables. Generally, the cost increases as the size of the plotter increases. Other variables include drawing speed and the number of pens supported. The following are some general ranges of plotter prices based on drawing sheet accommodated.

A size (8 ½″ × 11″): less than $1,000

B size (11″ × 17″): $1,000 to $3,000

C size (17″ × 22″): $3,000 to $14,000

D size (22″ × 34″): $3,000 to $14,000 (D size is really about the minimum for professional applications unless you are working strictly with small detail sheets.)

E size (34″ × 44″): $7,000 to $17,000

Color monitor. Adding color graphics increases the cost about ten percent over monochrome, but a high quality color monitor may run from $1,500 to $10,000.

Digitizers. Small digitizers may range in price from $900 to $1,500. Large ones may cost about $6,500.

Implementation Procedures—Selecting a micro-CADD System

This is a very abbreviated list of steps to take in selecting a system. Beyond the initial steps of analyzing your needs, deciding what you are willing to spend and some initial research, you will save a lot of time (and ultimately money) if you select a dealer you trust who specializes in putting together systems for designers.

1. As with all computer applications, first determine your needs, now and

in the future. With a CADD system more than with any other application in this book, this step of the process will determine the success of the application and the final cost. One firm may need a system that can produce three-dimensional drawings while another only needs 2-D drawings on "B" size paper. Also, decide on whether you need single-user workstations, multiuser systems or a network configuration.

2. Research current software and make up a "short list" for consideration. This research can be based on your preview of magazine articles, conversations, trade show attendance, advertisements and comparison reviews in directories and other sources. There is no shortage of independent information on CADD for architects and interior designers today. Start with some of the sources of information listed at the end of this section to help you make detailed evaluations.

3. Talk with other designers who are using the systems. This is one of the best ways to get honest, in-the-field evaluations. However, don't take all negative responses at face value. Often, a user dislikes some aspect of a program because it doesn't match his or her method of working or particular needs. Yours may be different and the same feature that your friend dislikes may be perfectly suited for you.

4. Research the hardware that can run the software you decide on. This should include not only the CPU and RAM required, but also the type of input device you like, the quality of the screen and the output device.

5. Arrange for demonstrations from both users and value-added dealers who know architectural needs. Beware of "canned" demos, however, as they are designed to show the system at its best. Try using the system yourself with drawings you are likely to draw.

6. Once you select a system, buy training from the dealer if it is not included in the purchase price. The extra money will more than pay for itself in getting you to one-to-one productivity (and beyond!) faster.

7. Allow sufficient time for you and your staff to learn the system. For many people, computer-aided design and drafting is a totally new way to view design and drawing creation. Just the eye-hand coordination required often takes considerable time to learn.

Additional Tips

- Buy from a value-added dealer that can assemble an entire package of software, hardware and peripherals to meet *your* exact needs and that can follow up with training, maintenance and support. It just isn't worth your time and trouble (and money!) to mix and match components to get a system up and running. It is also nearly impossible for a practicing professional to stay current with all the latest software updates, peripherals and other add-ons that can make a system run better. Although value-added

123

dealers tend to promote only a few of the dozens of available hardware and software components available, they do so because the ones they sell have been found to be the best for most design firms.

• Remember that once you get a CADD system, your ability to think up new tasks for it to do and the amount you depend on it may outstrip its capacity. Plan for this when you buy, either by buying more capacity than you think you need initially, or by getting a system that can grow with the demands you place on it.

• Before you buy software, check to see how stable the company is. How many installations are there? Does the company offer telephone "hotline" assistance? Is there a local users' group? Is there a newsletter to keep you advised of new developments, tips and other useful news?

2-D Low-cost CADD software

The following list includes some of the more popular low-cost CADD software packages current at the time of this writing. Since companies come and go in the fast-changing computer business and addresses change, check with the directories listed later in this section for the latest in micro-CADD.

AUTOCAD
Autodesk, Inc.
2658 Bridgeway
Sausalito, CA 94965

BENCHMARK
Metasoft Corporation
6509 West Frye Road, Suite 12
Chandler, AZ 85224

Robo CAD-PC
Robo Systems Corp.
111 Pheasant Run
Newtown, PA 18940

CADKEY
Micro Control Systems, Inc.
27 Hartford Turnpike
Vernon, CT 06066

CADPLAN
Personal CAD Systems, Inc.
981 University Avenue
Los Gatos, CA 95030

CADVANCE
CalComp, Personal Systems
200 Hacienda Boulevard
Campbell, CA 95008

CASCADE I
Cascade Graphics Development
16842 Von Karman
Irvine, CA 92714

DESIGN BOARD 3-D
MegaCadd, Inc.
401 Second Avenue South
Seattle, WA 98104

DRAWING PROCESSOR
BG Graphics Systems, Inc.
6632 S. 191st Street Place, Building E 103
Kent, WA 98032

MICROCAD
Imagimedia Technologies, Inc.
P.O. Box 210308
San Francisco, CA 94121–0308

MICROGRAFX
Micrografx, Inc.
1820 North Greenville Ave.
Richardson, TX 75081

MICROTECTURE
Data Graphic Systems of Virginia
218 West Main Street
Charlottesville, VA 22901

PERSONAL ARCHITECT
Computervision Corporation
100 Crosby Drive
Bedford, MA 01730

PC CAD
Houseman & Associates
Box 474
Allied Cypress Bank
Cypress, TX 77429

VERSACAD ADVANCED
T & W Systems, Inc.
7372 Prince Drive, Suite 106
Huntington Beach, CA 92647

Sources for More Information

Books

American Consulting Engineers Council. *Computer-Aided Design and Drafting for Design Professionals.* Washington: ACEC, 1983.

GSB Associates. *Implementing and Managing CADD in the Design Office.* GSB Associates, Inc., 3400 Edge Lane, Thorndale, PA 19372.

Guidelines. *How to Set Up a Microcomputer CADD System.* Guidelines, Box 456, Orinda, CA 94563.

Kemper, Alfred M. ed. *Pioneers of CAD in Architecture.* Pacifica, CA: Hurland/Swenson Publishers, 1985.

Orr, J. *The Architect's CADD Primer.* New York: McGraw-Hill, 1984.

Orr, J. *Computer Aided Design & Drafting.* New York: Van Nostrand Reinhold.

Teicholz, Eric. *CAD/CAM Handbook.* New York: McGraw-Hill, 1984.

Directories

CAD/CAM Computer Graphics: A Survey and Buyers' Guide. Daratech, Inc., 16 Myrtle Avenue, Cambridge, MA 02238.

PC CADD: A Buyer's Guide. Graphic Systems, Inc. 180 Franklin Street, Cambridge, MA 02139.

The S. Klein Directory of Computer Graphics Suppliers: Hardware, Software, Systems and Services. Technology & Business Communications, Inc. 730 Boston Post Road, Suite 25, Sudbury, MA 01776.

Newsletters

The A/E Computerization Bulletin. Guidelines, P.O. Box 456, Orinda, CA 94563.

A/E Systems Report. P.O. Box 11316, Newington, CT 06111.

Today's SCIP. EMA Management Associates, Inc., 1145 Gaskins Road, Richmond, VA 23233.

Magazines

Computers for Design and Construction. MetaData Publishing Corp., 310 E. 44th Street, New York, NY 10017.

Computer Graphics World. Computer Graphics World Publishing Co., 1714 Stockton, San Francisco, CA 94133.

Design Graphics World. St. Regis Publications, Inc., 390 Fifth Avenue, New York, NY 10018.

CHAPTER 5

Cost-Saving Methods of Producing Construction Documents

As with design, most architects first consider computer-aided drafting when they think of ways to speed production of construction documents. As with computer-aided design, however, graphics is only part of the story. There are many ways to trim the expense of producing all the documents required for a construction project while improving their quality without using computer drafting. Of course, these should not be used *in place* of CADD, but in conjunction with it. Together they can give you an edge on the competition.

The following sections outline some ways to use word processing, spreadsheet, and data base management software to improve the quality of your documents and speed up their production. Section 5.3 will be of particular interest to those who prefer to write their own specifications rather than using a purchased master. It shows how to use some of the advanced features of word processing programs to go beyond the simple "cut and paste" approach to automated specification production.

5.1 SPEED PRODUCTION WITH COMPUTER KEYNOTING AND SCHEDULES

Some of the greatest efficiency gains in producing working drawings can be made with the simplest of applications. Three areas that lend themselves to easy computerization are general notes, keynoting and schedules. General notes are those verbal descriptions that are placed on a drawing, usually a plan sheet, that provide the contractor with basic information concerning the drawing and how it should be interpreted. For example, a note on a floor plan might read, "All dimensions shown are to finish face of wall unless otherwise noted."

127

Speed Production with Computer Keynoting and Schedules

Keynotes are groups of numbered notes placed at the side or bottom of a drawing. The corresponding number is placed in the field of the drawing with an arrow to the item being described. Instead of hand lettering the same note several times (such as "porcelain enamel panels" on a series of elevations) it is done once and the same reference number shown where required. Keynoting is also useful in cases where the description of the item should be placed on the drawing sheet but is too long to sensibly fit next to the drawing image itself. Food service equipment plans are an example of this.

Schedules are grids of rows and columns of data that give variable information about a number of similar items such as door schedules. They are extremely valuable in the construction document production process; you can pack more organized, condensed information in a schedule than in any other kind of graphic communication.

All three of these communication devices have one thing in common—the data or form of the data is reusable from job to job. The majority of general notes reflect the experience and concerns of a particular office and the project types they do, and so are reused on nearly every project. The same is true for keynoting. Schedules, while they contain unique information on every job, are usually in the same format of rows and columns with the same headings.

Because of these similarities the architect and interior designer has a choice of using word processing, spreadsheet or data base management systems to assist in streamlining production and turning out more accurate and understandable drawings. All three types of software allow you to organize, save, change, reuse and print out information for a project.

Basic Application Requirements

General notes and keynoting only require a simple word processing program. Schedules can be produced with a word processor, spreadsheet or a data base management program. No matter what software you choose, it must be able to format text and numeric data in the way you desire. You must also be able to copy a "master" file for reuse and change its contents easily. The advantages and disadvantages of using a particular type of program will be discussed in "implementation procedures."

Additional Application Requirements

This section describes how to use nongraphic software to improve document production. You can do many of the same things with some of the low-cost CADD systems now available. There are also programs that allow you to convert your existing text files for notes into "drawing" files that can be read by some CADD

128

software. You can then place the note anywhere on the CAD drawing much as you would with a graphic image.

Requirements of Software

The most basic versions of word processing, spreadsheet and data base management software will work for the applications described in this section. If you already have one or more of these programs they will probably work just fine. If you are thinking of purchasing one, the requirements of other applications described in this book will be more stringent. For a data base management system (DBMS), you only need a "file management" type of DBMS software. Refer to Appendix A, Fundamentals of Data Base Management Systems, for a complete description of the criteria for selecting a DBMS.

Requirements of Hardware

RAM. Some word processing programs, spreadsheets and simple file management systems will work with as little as 48K of RAM if you must use an older system. However, try to have at least 64K. The ones that are part of an integrated package require more, usually 128K or greater.

Disks. You should have at a minimum two disk drives, one for the program (or programs) and one for your data. The "master" notes and schedules should be kept on one disk and then copied to a "project disk" for modifications. The project disk then becomes part of the archival records when the job is completed.

Printer. A dot-matrix printer is the minimum requirement for this application, but you may want a letter-quality printer to produce better images for reproduction. If you use a dot-matrix printer it should have a "double strike" mode, "correspondence quality" or some way to make dark image suitable for running through a diazo machine. For very wide schedules, you will need a 132-column-wide printer.

Cost Variables

Hardware. A complete setup with two disk drives and a dot-matrix printer can be purchased for as little as $2,000 or less.

Software. Basic word processing programs can be purchased for less than $300. Spreadsheet programs may range from about $100 to $400. Simple file management programs range from under $100 to $400 with a few costing more than $400. An integrated program with all three may be the ideal solution to your needs.

Setup. Setup costs depend on the complexity of your application. General notes and keynotes set up with word processing take only as long as required for typing.

You may need from one to two hours to set up a simple file management system. However, keep in mind that much of the setup time includes thinking through your methods of keynoting and scheduling and how they coordinate with other aspects of your documentation such as specification numbering, drawing indexing and filing systems.

Output. Output can be handled two ways. You can print out the notes and schedules on paper and then tape them to a carrier sheet with other drawing images as part of a paste-up drafting system. The other method is to print them on drafting appliqué film and place them directly on the drawing sheet. Appliqué film is available in continuous form with holes punched for tractor feed printers so this method may be the easiest and fastest.

Implementation Procedures

1. Begin your implementation of these applications with general notes and keynoting. These are the simplest and fastest ways to make use of your computer, and for the firm that is new to computers they are the least threatening. To start, you may want to emulate the standard method of typing notes on translucent appliqué film. Later, you should begin to organize the notes into functional groups including those that remain the same from one project to the next and those that need to be slightly modified for each job.

2. As you gain experience with keynoting, identify each note with a number that corresponds to the *Masterformat* section numbers you use for specifications. This way, the notes also tell the contractor what parts of the specifications relate to the drawing he or she is looking at. If there is more than one note for one specification section use a decimal point and sequential numbers after it. For example, for marble veneer you might have notes numbered 04455.1, 04455.2 and 04455.3.

3. Limit yourself to keynoting only on those drawings where notes are repeated several times such as elevations, sections and details.

4. For schedules, decide on which ones your office uses the most. Some schedules you should consider computerizing include those for doors, windows, finishes, millwork, electrical fixtures, plumbing fixtures, equipment and signage. There will be some you use so infrequently that it will not make sense to automate them.

5. Decide on whether to use spreadsheet or data base management software. Because of their inherent grid nature, spreadsheets may seem to be the most appropriate for schedules. You can set up enough rows and columns to contain the number of elements you have, make the columns wide enough to accommodate the data and then simply fill in the blanks.

While a spreadsheet format may work for quick, small schedules, you may find a simple file management type of data base management program much more flexible. Once you set it up there is no limitation on the number of elements you can have so the same format can work for a job with 15 doors or a job with 200 doors. In addition, you can generate several types of reports from the same data. With a door data base, the doors can be listed in numerical order as with any standard door schedule. However, if you like, you can arrange them by hardware group number to check for correct hardware. At another time you can sort them by door material so separate lists can be given to wood door suppliers and hollow-metal suppliers for preliminary cost budgeting. A DBMS is also easier to change and update as the job progresses. "Check" schedules can be printed for review at any time with final printing held until the schedules are either bound into the project manual or pasted onto the drawing sheets.

Figure 5.1-1 shows what a typical data entry screen might look like for developing a door schedule. The operator is prompted for the necessary information and given instructions concerning the data entry format. The person filling in the door schedule is only faced with one door (DBMS record) at a time, making what often seems an insurmountable task with a drawn grid into a simple, step-by-step procedure. The process can begin at any time during the design develop-

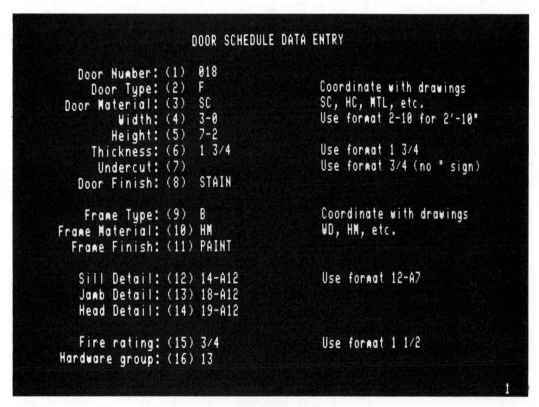

Figure 5.1-1
Data Entry Screen for Door Schedule

DOOR SCHEDULE

	TYPE	MTL	WD	HT	THK	UCUT	FINISH	FRAME		FINISH	SILL	JAMB	HEAD	FIRE	HWD
018	F	SC	3-0	7-2	1 3/4		STAIN	B	HM	PAINT	14-A12	18-A12	19-A12	3/4	13
019	F	SC	2-6	7-2	1 3/4	3/4	STAIN	B	HM	PAINT	14-A12	20-A12	19-A12		9
020	B	SC	2-6	7-2	1 3/4		STAIN	D	WD	STAIN		21-A12	25-A12		9
021	D	HM	3-0	7-0	1 3/4		PAINT	F	HM	PAINT		4-A11	5-A11		8
022	D	HM	3-0	7-0	1 3/4	3/4	PAINT	F	HM	PAINT	7-A11	4-A11	5-A11		15

Figure 5.1-2
Door Schedule Generated from Data Base

132

ment or construction document phase. Whatever information is known is entered. As more decisions are made, the data base is easily updated.

Figure 5.1-2 shows a portion of the final schedule developed from the individual data base records. A similar process can be used for any schedule.

Additional Tips

- Be aware of contractors' likes and dislikes of keynoting. Many of them do not like to go back and forth from the drawing to the legend just to read a simple section or elevation. Use some judgement in deciding how much keynoting to do.
- Make sure your abbreviations and nomenclature are consistent throughout. This includes general notes, keynotes and schedules.
- Keep a master list of printed general notes, keynotes and schedule formats in a notebook for reference by the project manager, job captain and production people.

Sources for More Information

The Guidelines Master Notation and Keynote Manual. Guidelines, P.O. Box 456, Orinda, CA 94563

5.2

IMPROVED QUALITY CONTROL
WITH WORKING DRAWING CHECKLISTS

The production of working drawings is one of the most complex technical aspects of design practice. Even with computer-aided drafting making things a little easier there are thousands of chances for errors during this phase of design. Checklists are a time-tested method of finding mistakes and omissions in construction documents. Now, with the use of a microcomputer you can vastly improve your performance in this area. If your firm does not employ some kind of working drawing checklist, developing a system on your personal computer is an ideal way to begin. If you already have some type of list you can improve its usefulness by computerizing.

As with any kind of checklist, one for construction documents can be developed using the traditional typewriter and cut and paste method. However, using a computer yields several advantages:

1. Changing and adding to the list is much easier.
2. Several versions of the same checklist can be developed that relate to

133

specific building types. This way, versions customized for particular building types can be quickly produced and targeted to the project you are checking.

3. The list can be coordinated with other automated functions such as specifications, design checklists (See Section 4.3) and standard detail indexing.

Refer to Sections 4.3 and 6.3 for ways of automating design and project management checklists.

Basic Application Requirements

This application requires simple word processing capabilities: editing words and manipulating lists and blocks of text. In addition, to make the most productive use of it, you should have the ability to read one file into another so you can build a custom working drawing checklist from groups of standard lists. This procedure will be described in more detail in the implementation portion of this section.

Additional Application Requirements

Although it is possible to develop checklists from a data base management system it is usually not warranted unless you want to integrate the checklist items with other components of your office's production method. Refer to "Additional Application Requirement" in Section 6.3 for a description of how you can do this.

Requirements of Software

The software requirements for this application are minimal and can be satisfied with practically any word processing program as long as it is possible to read one file into another. Underlining and boldface printing are useful for highlighting important parts of the text. A search and replace function is also helpful if you need to quickly change repetitive words or phrases to tailor one master list to a particular job.

Requirements of Hardware

RAM.　For word processing, minimum RAM is required. It will depend more on your software needs than on the application.

Disks.　A single disk drive is sufficient for most word processing programs, but it is preferable to have two, one for the program and one for the checklist.

Printer.　The minimum requirement is a dot-matrix printer.

134

Cost Variables

Hardware.   The required hardware for this application is minimal. If you do not already have a word processor you can buy a simple system with a dot-matrix printer for $2,000 or less.

Software.   Word processing programs may range from under $100 to $500 depending on their complexity.

Setup.   Initial development of the checklist is the most time-consuming part of its implementation. If your office is already using one, what you have can be a good starting point. If not, several sources contain checklists that you can use to begin one for your office. Refer to the Sources for More Information at the end of this section.

Data entry.   Typing a lengthy checklist takes time. However, if you follow the procedures described below the task will seem a little more manageable. Most of the work can be done by a secretary with project architects, job captains and other technical staff making recommendations and corrections.

A logical approach to developing a working drawing checklist begins with understanding what happens during a drawing check. When working drawings are reviewed there are seven major checking parameters that the architect or interior designer is concerned with. These exist whether the documents are prepared manually or with a CADD system. For every drawing type in the set some of these parameters are relevant and some are not. See Figure 5.2-1 for a summary of these parameters and the types of drawings to which they generally apply. The seven items that a checker normally looks for include the following:

1. *Conformance to design.*   Do the working drawings actually reflect the original design intent of the project? During the time it takes to complete construction documents many changes take place. Since the emphasis during this period is on technical accuracy, design goals are sometimes unknowingly compromised. This parameter is one that will vary among building types. You should consider developing a separate checklist section for each major building type you do. There is no sense in going through a lengthy list of items appropriate to a school when you are checking drawings for a speculative office building. This parameter can be coordinated with the design checklist discussed in Section 4.3.

2. *Technical accuracy.*   This is the heart of working drawings and one of the most important parts of the check. Does the drawing represent a complete, buildable and workable portion of the building? Will the roof detail keep the water out? Does the reflected ceiling plan show all the fixtures in the correct locations? Are all the required components shown on the exterior elevations? These kinds of questions are answered during a technical check.

This parameter will also vary slightly among building types. For example,

135

some technical requirements for a window detail of a manufacturing plant will be different from those of a church.

3. *Dimensional accuracy.* Are the dimensions correct and all required dimensions included? Do strings of dimensions add up? CADD programs help with the arithmetic in this area, but a program doesn't know if a particular item *should* be dimensioned.

4. *Coordination with other architectural drawings.* Are all the components of one drawing consistent with the other drawings? For example, is a wall on the reflected ceiling plan in the same place as it is on the floor plan? Do detail references on one sheet contain the correct detail numbers they refer to?

5. *Coordination with specifications.* Since specifications and drawings are usually developed separately by different people this is one area especially prone to error. Is there any overlap of information between the two documents? Are all items included in one or the other? Is the same terminology used?

6. *Coordination with consultant's drawings.* This is another recurring source of problems. Consultants usually don't check their drawings against the architect's; it is the architect who must 'do the checking.

7. *Graphic completeness.* This parameter includes all the nontechnical aspects of the drawings. Are north arrows on the plans? For every note is there a leader line and arrowhead pointing to the correct part of the drawing image? Are the line weights correct for best reproduction? Do all rooms have a name and number?

As shown in Figure 5.2-1, where a checking parameter intersects with an appropriate drawing type, a checking "module" is created—a related group of checklist items that can be manipulated as desired with other modules without losing the essentials of that component.

Implementation Procedures

1. Set up an overall framework for organizing the individual components of your checklist system. Use the matrix in Figure 5.2-1 as a starting point. List the drawing types your office generates and any consultant drawing types you need. Beginning this way not only helps to organize your efforts but also makes it easier to solicit ideas from various people in the office. You will get more input by asking someone to write down their checklist ideas for coordinating the building sections with the specifications than you will by asking them to generally comment on "a working drawing checklist."

In addition, developing modules like this gives you more flexibility when it comes time to assemble the checklist. Specifically, you can assemble all the matrix columns of one row for a complete list of those items to check on a particular drawing type. Or, you can assemble all the rows of *one column* to give to someone who has an expertise in that parameter. The specification writer, for instance, can review all specification coordination items for all drawing sheets.

136

Checking parameter → Drawing type	A Conformance to design	B Technical accuracy	C Dimensional accuracy	D Coordination w/ arch. dwgs.	E Coordination w/ specs.	F Coordination w/ consult's	G Graphic completeness
1 Cover & Index sheet				●		●	●
2 Demolition plan				●	●		●
3 Site plan		●	●	●	●	●	●
4 Floor plans	●	●	●	●	●	●	●
5 Reflected clg. plans	●	●		●	●	●	●
6 Roof plan		●		●	●	●	●
7 Exterior elevations	●		●	●	●	●	●
8 Interior elevations	●		●	●	●		●
9 Building sections	●	●	●	●	●	●	●
10 Details	●	●	●	●	●		●
11 Schedules	●	●		●	●		●
12 Finish plans	●	●		●	●		●
13 Civil dwgs.		●	●	●			●
14 Structural		●	●	●			●
15 Electrical		●	●	●			●
16 HVAC		●	●	●			●
17 Plumbing		●	●	●			●
18 Fire protection		●	●	●			●
19 Landscape dwgs.	●	●	●	●			●

Figure 5.2-1
Working Drawing Checklist Module Organization

2. Assign one senior person to be the coordinator for the development of the checklist. All suggestions and comments should be funneled through this one person who should assemble the final checklist.

3. Have all architects, job captains, project managers and other technical staff submit their suggestions for the checklist. The final document should represent a collective "office experience" data base—especially from those people who have been employed for some time. They are in the best position to know the firm's method of operating and the expected quality of work. The coordinator can request that people only involve themselves in the modules they may know most about.

4. Decide what form the individual checklist items will take. As with code checklist items mentioned in Section 4.4 you must determine how much guidance to give the user. For example, the following two items can refer to the same thing:

_____Caulking and sealants

_____Verify caulking is called out in details at all minor joints and changes of materials such as exterior door and window frames, penetrations through exterior wall, etc. Verify high-performance sealants with backer rod at major vertical and horizontal joints subject to movement. Verify proper depth/width ratio.

Which one you choose will depend on the experience of the people using the checklist and the amount of time you want to devote to developing it.

5. Enter the checklists using your word processing program. Give each module a letter/number combination name corresponding to the intersection of the rows and columns in the matrix you developed in Step 1. If you have several modules written for different building types, add a suffix such as 5B-SCH for the module for technical accuracy of reflected ceiling plans for SCHools. You can then easily refer to the matrix when you want to "read" the various files into one master file developed for a particular job.

6. When you are ready to check the construction documents for a specific job assemble the required modules. As always, the person doing the check should be someone who has not worked on the job so he or she can view it with a fresh eye. If you want to do a double check, assemble the list by rows so someone reviews the set drawing by drawing. Assemble the list by columns for review by someone who is a specialist in that area. A specification writer to check coordination with specs, an experienced field person to review for technical accuracy, a designer to verify conformance with original design intent and so on.

Examples

Figure 5.2-2 illustrates one "module" of an abbreviated checklist.

Module 6/B

ROOF PLAN/TECHNICAL

[ ] Show overall building dimensions, overhangs, and canopies.

[ ] Show column grid lines.

[ ] Call out materials: roofing, coping, etc.

[ ] Does roof construction meets fire-resistive requirements?

[ ] Show expansions joints, reference to details.

[ ] Fire walls extending above roof, if applicable.

[ ] Positive drainage at every point? Show drainage, location of roof drains, scuppers, gutters and leaders, crickets, saddles.

[ ] All penetrations shown? Skylights, chimneys, scuttles, hatches, vents, etc.

[ ] Show all roof-top equipment: HVAC, solar panels, antennas, window washing scaffolding, protection pads, lighting rods, snowguards, flagpoles, etc.

Figure 5.2-2
Working Drawing Checklist Module

Sources for More Information

The Guidelines Working Drawing Planning and Management Manual Guidelines, P.O. Box 456, Orinda, CA 94563

Stitt, Fred A. *Systems Graphics.* New York: McGraw-Hill Book Company, 1984.

Duggar, John Frederick III. *Checking and Coordinating Architectural and Engineering Working Drawings.* New York: McGraw-Hill Book Company, 1984.

5.3

ADVANCED WORD PROCESSING APPLICATIONS
FOR CREATING YOUR OWN MASTER SPECIFICATIONS

Writing specifications has traditionally been one of the most time-consuming and error-prone phases of architectural practice. For offices that produce their own specifications (as contrasted with those who contract with independent specification consultants) the situation has been helped with the wider availability and use of word processing, along with nationally recognized guide specifications such as *Masterspec* and *Spectext*. Still, many offices do not take maximum advantage of the microcomputer's power to streamline this task while producing better quality documents.

Most small and medium-size offices stay away from developing their own master specifications because of the amount of time required and the potential liability. They either contract with an outside consultant or use a nationally recognized set of guide specifications. However, there are advantages in developing your own set of "master" specs and the time required can be less than you imagine.

Custom specifications can be tailored to your office's type of practice, special needs and preferences for materials and construction methods. They can contain information that your office has learned over the years and include those materials that are particularly suited to your geographical area of practice and unique project requirements. In addition, if each master specification section is written so it is edited by deleting items not needed, it also serves as a valuable checklist to remind you of the many variables involved with the project.

This section will describe how to set up your own master specifications using advanced features of word processing software to enable you to streamline the production of better contract documents. Since most offices limit themselves (either consciously or unconsciously) to a relatively few building types the number of technical sections is actually quite small. You can first concentrate on only those sections that you use the most, adding less used sections as time permits. By using past specifications as starting points, you can quickly identify those provisions of each section that you must include in your "master."

Basic Application Requirements

There are currently some very sophisticated computer programs being developed to assist with specification writing. At some future time these may be widely available at a cost low enough to justify their purchase by a large number of architectural firms. In the meantime, however, there are ways to use word processing software to speed the production of specifications. This section will describe two methods—one using basic word processing capabilities and the other using the "merge" function many of the more advanced programs include.

For the first method, you need the standard editing and printing functions found in even the low-cost word processing programs. These include such things as deleting and inserting text, moving blocks of text, underlining, boldface printing and the like. In addition, you need to be able to include notes to the specifier in the "master file" that can be printed for review, but that do not print when the final project specification is produced. A "find and replace" function is also required to make it easy to search your specification for one word or string of words and replace it with another. For example, you may want to change the word "Architect" to "Architect/Engineer."

Additional Application Requirements

For the second method you need to assign variable names to certain portions of the master sections and assign values to these variable names to fit the unique requirements of a project. For example, where there might be a choice of flame-spread rating for a finish you could assign the variable name "FLAMESPREAD" within the body of some standard "boilerplate" text and at the beginning of the specification section be able to type in Class I, Class II or Class III as required. The program would then "read" what you typed and automatically insert it in place of the variable "FLAMESPREAD," reformat the paragraph where it occurred so the right and left margins were correct, and print it out.

You should also have the ability to "read in" separate files into a command file so you only need to type boilerplate text once. Then, when you want to use the standard sentence, paragraph or section, you simply type in a command where you want it placed in your specification and the file name you have given it. When the program is printing it reads the entire "boilerplate" file from the disk and inserts it where you want. After the file is inserted, the program returns to the calling file and proceeds.

Another advanced application involves the automatic renumbering of paragraphs so if you delete section 2.04 from the master, section 2.05 is renumbered so it follows 2.03. There are separate software packages that are designed for specification writing that add some of these features that even most of the advanced word processing programs do not have.

You can also use one of the many spelling checkers available to help you catch typographical errors as well as spelling mistakes. You can add to the standard dictionary with technical words unique to specifications.

Requirements of Software

In addition to the basic editing functions the abilities of the software for this application should include:

pagination
centering
automatic hyphenation
right margin justification
headers and footers

underline and boldface type

user-defined line and character spacing

nonprint lines

screen-oriented formatting

search and replace functions

superscript and subscript

For the more advanced application you will need the following softward capabilities:

a "Merge" function so values can be assigned to variables and one file can read data from another file

automatic renumbering of paragraphs

automatic table of contents generation

Requirements of Hardware

RAM.   Most word processing programs (even the more sophisticated ones) will operate with as little as 64K of RAM.

Disks.   At least two disks are needed, one for the program and one for your data files. For this application it is better to use floppy disks because each disk can contain certain *Masterformat* divisions or sections that can be filed away without cluttering up a hard disk. Further, individual project specifications can be put on one or more disks to make archiving easier.

Printer.   Either a dot-matrix, impact printer or laser printer is acceptable for this application. The choice depends on your budget, what speed you need, and how refined you want the final copy to look.

Cost Variables

Hardware.   A complete system can be purchased for as little as $2,000 or less with a dot-matrix printer. If your office does a lot of specifications it may be worthwhile to devote one stand-alone system to just this one application.

Software.   Word processing programs may range from under $100 to $500 depending on their complexity. Spelling checkers, indexing programs and other add-ons to word processing are in addition to this price. One of the more sophisticated programs used to enhance specification writing with automatic paragraph renumbering runs about $750.

Setup and data entry.   Setup costs are significant for this application. If you are starting from scratch without any office guide or master specifications at all, not only do you have to do the research and writing of the technical sections, but you also have to type them into a particular format. However, you can spread out the work by doing a little at a time—developing a few master sections each time you write a project specification. Keep in mind that the extra time you put in at the beginning will more than pay off later on in-time savings and more accurate technical documents.

If you have a good set of office masters you may be able to have them digitized by an optical character reader if they are printed in a "readable" type face. Services to do this on a fee basis are available in most cities.

Output. The time required for output of a long specification depends on the speed of the printer. Unless you have a laser printer or are satisfied with the appearance of a dot-matrix document, you may want to invest in a separate printer for specifications so you don't tie up other office production.

Implementation Procedures

Method 1: Using Basic Word Processing Capabilities

There are several preliminary decisions you must make about your method of writing and editing specifications before you begin. If you write your own specifications you probably have already decided on many of them. However, setting up a good set of master specification may require that you rethink your method of operation.

1. The first decision is whether you will establish a "guide" or a "master" specification. This section assumes you will write masters and not guide specifications. Guide specifications are essentially outlines of each technical section that must be extensively modified, added to and deleted to fit the requirements of a particular job. Master specifications are more complete and contain prewritten text that can be used "as is" without extensive modification. They are usually edited by deleting whole blocks of text or by making one choice out of several within a section of text.

Because a master is supposed to cover most any situation an office may encounter they are often difficult to write. The process can be streamlined, however, by writing paragraphs and articles to cover the most common situations and custom writing for special situations as they occur.

For this application you should write a variation of a master specification. Not only does it make producing a project document faster but it also serves the "checklist" function mentioned earlier by recording what your office has learned.

2. Decide on whether to use several narrowscope sections of a specification or a larger broadscope section. For example, do you want to write a section for "Resilient Wood Flooring Systems" or break it down into "Cushioned Wood Flooring," "Mastic-Set Wood Flooring," and so on? The decision should be based on what kind of work you do, how often you use various narrowscope sections and

how much editing you want to do each time a section is used. You will probably want a combination of both. You may also want to write two or more "masters" for the same section to cover different type of clients. For instance, there may be one master for government work and one for private work.

3. Decide on the format for your specifications. You should follow The Construction Specifications Institute's three-part section format and page format, but occasionally you will need to use a government guideline or one dictated by a special client.

4. Set up a list of section titles you will require. This should follow CSI's *Masterformat* list of section titles and numbers. Establishing this list will help you coordinate the various sections and gives direction to your efforts. You can set priorities from this list on what sections should be written first.

5. Begin writing the various master technical sections you require. This, of course, is the most difficult part of the process. You can begin with previous specifications your office has produced or use one of the commercially available guide specification. Consider reviewing information from other sources such as industry associations, government master specifications, manufacturer's suggested specifications and the like.

Part of this process should include adding "notes to the specifier" that assist the person editing the master in making decisions and reminding him or her what to consider. This is really one of the most powerful uses of a good master specification because it is a good place to record what you have learned from past successes and failures. These notes are marked in such a way that they do not print in the final job specification. How they are marked depends on the particular software package you are using.

Figure 5.3-1 shows one page from a master specification written primarily for an interior design office. The notes to the specifier are all capitalized and heavily indented so they are easily distinguished from the other text and each line is preceded by a ">>" in the first two columns of the page. In order to print out the comments these symbols are changed from a double period (..) by using the "search and replace" function of the word processing program, in this case WordStar. Once the master specification is printed out as a reference copy for inclusion into a notebook, the >>'s are easily changed back to double periods (..) which is WordStar's nonprint comment command.

When the master specification is copied for editing as a project specification these "notes to the specifier" appear on the screen but are not printed.

Note how editing is provided for in this example. In some cases the specifier has a simple choice such as between [square] or [trimmed with cove] for internal corners in Figure 5.3-1. In other cases the choices that are *not* wanted are simply deleted line by line. In the case of thresholds in Figure 5.3-1, the most common choice is indicated as "marble," but a blank line is included for unusual circumstances.

144

B. Trim units: Provide trim units as shown on the drawings and as
    required for a complete installation. Trim units shall match
    wall tile in quality, color, pattern and finish unless otherwise
    noted on the drawings.

>>   DELETE OR ADD TO THE FOLLOWING AS REQUIRED AND
>>   NOTE ANY SPECIAL CONDITONS ON THE DRAWINGS.

    1. Provide bullnose units for wainscots and vertical
        termination of tile, except where wainscot is flush with
        abutting wall surface.
    2. Provide bead trim units on external corners.
    3. Internal corners shall be [squared] [trimed with cove].
>>   SELECT ONE
    4. Provide cove base units between tile wall and floor.

>>   SELECT ONE OF THE FOLLOWING SETTING MATERIALS.
>>   REFER TO THE TCA HANDBOOK FOR HELP IN SELECTING
>>   THE APPROPRIATE SETTING AND GROUTING MATERIALS.
C. Latex-portland cement mortar: ANSI A 118.4
>>   OR
C. Dry-set mortar: ANSI A 118.1
>>   OR
C. Organic adhesive [Type I] [Type II]: ANSI A 136.1
>>   SELECT TYPE I FOR PROLONGED WATER RESISTANCE AND
>>   TYPE II FOR INTERMITTENT WATER RESISTANCE.
>>   OR
C. Conductive dry-set mortar: ANSI A 118.2

D. Grout: Premixed commercial portland cement grout as recommended
    by tile manufacturer. Color to be selected by Architect from
    standard product line.
>>   *** OR ***
>>   SELECT ONE OF THE FOLLOWING GROUTING MATERIALS.
>>   REFER TO THE TCA HANDBOOK FOR HELP IN SELECTING
>>   THE APPROPRIATE METHOD.
>>
D. Dry-set grout
>>   OR
D. Latex-portland cement grout
>>   MUST BE USED OVER WOOD FLOORS

E. Thresholds: Provide [marble] [_____] thresholds as
    shown and dimensioned on the drawings.

>>   USE THE FOLLOWING ONLY IF THEY ARE NOT SPECIFIED
>>   IN OTHER SECTIONS. FOR SMALL JOBS THESE ITEMS
>>   MAY BE SPECIFIED HERE. COORDINATE WITH
>>   PARAGRAPH 1.1 (B) OF THIS SECTION.
F. Joint sealers:
    1. Single-component shall be non-sag type complying
        with Fed. Spec. TT-S-001543 or TT-S-00230c for non-
        trafficked area.
    2. Two-component sealant shall comply with
        Fed. Spec. TT-S-00227e; Type I (self-leveling) for
        horizontal surfaces and Type II (non-sag) for vertical
        surfaces.

09310-6

Figure 5.3-1
Page from a Master Specification

Also note the number of editing steps that would be required to modify this master to make it a project specification. Deleting the unwanted lines for mortar type would be easy—a single keystroke for each line. For selecting one of the choices within a sentence, however, you would have to first move the cursor to the beginning of the unwanted choice and then delete the choice word for word. Of course, you could write two similar sentences on separate lines, and then delete the unwanted sentence. This would make editing faster, but would increase the length of the file. Problems such as these can be solved with the procedures described in Method 2.

6. When you are ready to prepare a project specification, simply copy the section you are editing and give the file an appropriate name based on the requirements of your software. Since *Masterformat* numbers are five digits and most computers allow an eight-digit file name (with extension) you can begin the file name with a three-letter abbreviation of the job name followed by the *Masterformat* number.

Editing can be done on screen by the specifier. This is usually faster if the specifier is adept with the program and basic typing skills. Otherwise, a hard copy can be marked up and the changes made by a word processing operator.

Method 2: Using a "Merge" Program and Variable Name Assignment*

1. Proceed with steps 1–5 as listed above except instead of writing in various choices the specifier can make within the body of the text, these choices are given variable names in the text and the choices are listed at the *beginning* of the document for insertion by the "merge" program when the final specification is printed.

Where you have choices between entire paragraphs that are unique, you will still want to list these under the proper article number and delete the unwanted choices line by line (or with a "block" deletion), but the majority of editing can be taken care of with the use of variables.

It takes some thinking to anticipate the largest and smallest inserted variable possible so indentation and sentence continuity is not affected, but once this is done editing is easy. In many cases, a variable selection made once at the beginning of the document can be used several times throughout the section.

Figure 5.3-2 shows the same sample page as in Figure 5.3-1 except that it has been set up for use with variables. These are shown in **boldface** type. The variables are enclosed between ampersands (&) as a way of marking them for this particular word processing software. Other programs may use other symbols.

Figure 5.3-3 shows the method used at the beginning of the file for the specifier to make the various choices that are then substituted for these variable names.

---

* The following procedures are based on using *WordStar* and *MailMerge*, both programs of MicroPro International. Other word processing programs may require slightly different commands, but the basic method is the same.

B. Trim units: Provide trim units as shown on the drawings and as required for a complete installation. Trim units shall match wall tile in quality, color, pattern and finish unless otherwise noted on the drawings.

>>   DELETE OR ADD TO THE FOLLOWING AS REQUIRED AND
>>   NOTE ANY SPECIAL CONDITONS ON THE DRAWINGS.
1. Provide bullnose units for wainscots and vertical termination of tile, except where wainscot is flush with abutting wall surface.
2. Provide bead trim units on external corners.
3. Internal corners shall be **&CORNERS&**.
4. Provide cove base units between tile wall and floor.

C   Mortar: **&MORTAR&**.

D. Grout: **&GROUT&**.

E. Thresholds: Provide **&THRESHOLD&** thresholds as shown and dimensioned on the drawings.

>>   USE THE FOLLOWING ONLY IF THEY ARE NOT SPECIFIED
>>   IN OTHER SECTIONS. FOR SMALL JOBS THESE ITEMS
>>   MAY BE SPECIFIED HERE. COORDINATE WITH
>>   PARAGRAPH 1.1 (B) OF THIS SECTION.
F. Joint sealers:
1. Single-component shall be non-sag type complying with Fed. Spec. TT-S-001543 or TT-S-00230c for non-trafficked area.
2. Two-component sealant shall comply with Fed. Spec. TT-S-00227e; Type I (self-leveling) for horizontal surfaces and Type II (non-sag) for vertical surfaces.

PART 3 -- EXECUTION

3.1 INSPECTION

A. General: Prior to installation of the work of this Section, inspect the installed work of other trades and verify that thin-set applied ceramic tile can be properly installed. Do not install tile until all unsatisfactory conditions have been corrected.

B. Conditions of floor surfaces: Concrete slabs shall have steel trowel and fine broom finish. Maximum variation shall be 1/8" in 10 feet and not more than 1/16" in 12 inches. Concrete slabs shall be cured, dimensionally stable and free of waxy or oily films and curing compounds.
>>   VERIFY THAT CONTROL JOINTS ARE DETAILED ON THE
>>   DRAWINGS IF CRACKING IS ANTICIPATED

09310-6

Figure 5.3-2   147
Master Specification Page Using Variables

```
.he ABC Corporation                                              Ceramic Tile
.fo                                                                 09310-#
.dm
.dm Note: leave one space after the comma following the variable
.dm      name before entering the value for that variable.
.dm
.dm Enter which code is applicable, Denver Building Code, UBC, etc.
.sv CODE,
.dm
.dm Enter A108.5 for standard tile set with dry-set or latex mortar
.dm   or enter A108.7 for conductive dry-set mortar
.sv ANSI,
.dm
.dm Enter what grade you want (Standard grade, Seconds grade, Decorative
.dm   thin wall tile grade
.sv GRADE,
.dm
.dm Enter whether you want internal corners to be "square" or "trimmed
.dm   with cove"
.sv CORNERS,
.dm
.dm Enter what kind of mortar you want:
.dm      Latex-portland cement mortar: ANSI A 118.4
.dm      Dry-set mortar: ANSI 118.1
.dm      Organic adhesive: [Type I] or [Type II]: ANSI A 136.1
.dm        (Type I for prolonged water resistance and type II for
.dm        intermittent water resistance)
.dm      Conductive dry-set mortar: ANSI A 118.2
.sv MORTAR,
.dm
.dm Enter what kind of grout you want:
.sv GROUT, Premixed commercial portland cement grout as ^Nrecommended by tile m
.dm
.dm Substitute for above grout if desired:
.dm   Dry-set grout
.dm   Latex-portland cement grout
.dm
.dm Select type of threshold (if any). If none, delete from text.
.dm   marble
.dm   wood
.sv THRESHOLD,
.dm
.dm Select type of installation:
.dm   "latex-"
.dm   "dry-set"
.dm   "conductive dry-set"
.sv INSTALLTYPE,
.dm
```

Figure 5.3-3
Format for Setting Variables

B. Trim units: Provide trim units as shown on the drawings and as required for a complete installation. Trim units shall match wall tile in quality, color, pattern and finish unless otherwise noted on the drawings.

    1. Provide bullnose units for wainscots and vertical termination of tile, except where wainscot is flush with abutting wall surface.
    2. Provide bead trim units on external corners.
    3. Internal corners shall be square.
    4. Provide cove base units between tile wall and floor.

C. Mortar: Latex-portland cement mortar: ANSI A 118.4.

D. Grout: Premixed commercial portland cement grout as recommended by tile manufacturer. Color to be selected by Architect from standard product line..

E. Thresholds: Provide marble thresholds as shown and dimensioned on the drawings.

F. Joint sealers:

    1. Single-component shall be non-sag type complying with Fed. Spec. TT-S-001543 or TT-S-00230c for non-trafficked area.
    2. Two-component sealant shall comply with Fed. Spec. TT-S-00227e; Type I (self-leveling) for horizontal surfaces and Type II (non-sag) for vertical surfaces.

PART 3 -- EXECUTION

3.1 INSPECTION

A. General: Prior to installation of the work of this Section, inspect the installed work of other trades and verify that thin-set applied ceramic tile can be properly installed. Do not install tile until all unsatisfactory conditions have been corrected.

B. Conditions of floor surfaces: Concrete slabs shall have steel trowel and fine broom finish. Maximum variation shall be 1/8" in 10 feet and not more than 1/16" in 12 inches. Concrete slabs shall be cured, dimensionally stable and free of waxy or oily films and curing compounds.

C. Conditions of wall surfaces: Wall surfaces to receive tile installation shall have square corners, be plumb and true with variations in plane not exceeding 1/8" in 8 feet. Concrete or masonry wall surfaces to receive tile shall be free of sealers, cleaning compounds, curing compounds, waxy or oily films, dirt and dust.

09310-5

Figure 5.3-4
Final Project Specification

The two-letter "dot commands" are *WordStar*'s method for entering these kinds of instructions. The ".dm" simply allows you to enter a nonprinting comment without it affecting the running of the program. The ".sv" is the "set variable" command in which you actually assign a value (your choice) to the variable name (in this case CODE, ANSI, GRADE, CORNERS, etc.). The program then substitutes what you type in on the right side of the comma in the proper place in the specification. The ".he" and ".fo" are commands to insert header and footer lines on each page of the specification.

Notice that the choice for ".sv GROUT" has already been inserted. For this master, it is the most common selection so instead of retyping it every time it is the default choice. If another one is desired it is substituted for the default. Also notice how this entry runs off the page. In the computer it is entered on one line after the ".sv" command with embedded carriage return commands so that it will print out on three lines as shown in Figure 5.3-4.

2. When you are ready to produce a project specification, copy the appropriate "master" section and give it a file name as described previously.

3. Go through the checklist at the beginning of the file entering the appropriate variables after the variable names.

4. Edit other portions of the master as required and add any new articles, paragraphs or other provisions you might need.

5. Save the file to disk and run the "merge" program. The output will be the final specification section ready for reproduction. Figure 5.3-4 illustrates one page of the project specification produced from Figures 5.3-2 and 5.3-3.

Additional Tips

- Notice that Figure 5.3-3 shows comments preceding each ".sv" (set variable) choice telling the specification writer or operator what to enter. This is where you should put the appropriate "notes to specifier" to help make the proper entry. These comments can be as extensive as you like so they serve as a checklist of points to remember.

Sources for More Information

The Construction Specifications Institute

Preparation and Use of an Office Master Specification. Alexandria, VA: The Construction Specifications Institute, 1980.

———*Page Format.* Alexandria, VA: The Construction Specifications Institute, 1981.

———*Three-Part Section Format for Construction Specifications.* Alexandria, VA: The Construction Specifications Institute, 1985.

150

Gero, J.S. "Specifications." In *Computer Applications in Architecture,* edited by John S. Gero. London: Applied Science Publishers, Ltd., 1977.

Simmons, H. Leslie. *The Specifications Writer's Handbook.* New York: John Wiley & Sons, Inc., 1985.

Software

Specification-writing software includes two broad categories: Software that actually includes the technical sections in some "guide" or "master" form (such as Masterspec) and software that supplements word processing programs to allow you to do such things as paragraph renumbering. The following are two programs of the second type that can help you implement the suggestions contained in this section. They are not absolutely necessary if you have a good word processing program, but may speed up the process. Write to the companies for more information.

SPEC-WRITER
ACCI Business Systems, Inc.
12707 N. Freeway, Suite 140
Houston, TX 77060

DISCO-SPECS
MTI Software
600 B Street
P.O. Box 1659
Santa Rosa, CA 95402

5.4

SYSTEMATIC CONTROL OF DRAWINGS AND PROJECT RECORDS

All architectural and interior design offices produce a large quantity of drawings, specifications and other job-related documents. Every firm must have a way of maintaining control over these kinds of records, not only for legal purposes but also to aid in retrieving selected information to accelerate the production of documents for a new project. For many offices, drawings are rolled up and forgotten once the job is complete. The only filing that is done usually includes labeling a box with the project name and throwing everything related to it in that box.

Managing your drawings and other project records involves two separate, but related, areas: standard details that can be used on any project, and documents that are produced for a specific job. The former is an "active" kind of file while

151

the latter is "archival." Both are important, but involve slightly different application requirements. A computer is an ideal tool to help with each.

Basic Application Requirements

Standard Details

For offices that use standard details or are thinking of establishing a standard detail system, the method of numbering the drawings and keeping an index of them is critical. Some of the requirements of an indexing system include:

1. the ability for anyone in the office to find the appropriate detail for their immediate needs

2. the ability to pull together several associated details that may be filed in another order. For example, details may be stored according to the 16-division Masterformat system, but you need all those that apply to interior finishing—a group that crosses several division lines

3. the ability to handle both standard details (those that are adaptable to any job) and master details (those that were developed for a particular job, but are useful for reference)

4. the ability to allow for growth—new categories as well as an increase in numbers.

Archival Storage of Project Documents

An indexing system for project records should allow you to meet two basic requirements: the ability to retrieve specific documents relative to a project (such as when you do an addition to an existing building you designed) and the ability to retrieve all drawings and other data related to a particular building type that you want to reference for a new, but similar, job. An added bonus to this is the ability to easily produce lists of drawings and other documents for insurance purposes.

The software best suited for both of these applications is a data base management system. Either a file management system or a relational system can be used, but a relational data base management system (RDBMS) gives you more options when setting up a method of indexing archival records. Refer to Appendix A, Fundamentals of Data Base Management Systems, for a complete description of these two types of software.

Advanced Application Requirements

Since the archival record storage is based on project name and number, this application can be integrated with a project history data base (see Section 1.2) or a project transaction data base (see Section 6.4). You can then call up almost any information on a given project. Keep in mind, however, that setting up this type of data base structure is complicated and involves considerable storage requirements.

Requirements of Software

The following are some of the specific software requirements you will need to successfully implement this application. Refer to Appendix A for more information.

1. For a file management system the program should allow at least ten fields per record. This would be adequate for most record keeping of a standard detail data base.

2. If you decide to maintain a relational data base for archival records you will need at least four files open at one time.

3. You should be able to index on at least five data fields.

4. The software should allow you to sort on several key fields together instead of just one alone. This will be necessary when using a RDBMS for maintaining archival records.

5. If you decide *not* to use a relational data base management system for archival records and use a file management system instead each record will be lengthy. You will then need a program that allows more than one "screenfull" of information per record.

6. The program should have the ability to make "mass changes" to a particular data field to save you time. For example, if your office moves and you need to change the "location" data field of your records this feature is very welcome.

7. The program must have flexible methods of querying the data base, both on screen and in printed reports. This includes relational queries, Boolean searches and partial string searches. For example, you may want to find all the floor plan drawings of every condominium project your office did after a certain date.

8. The program must have a flexible report generator since you will want to print out results in various ways. For a relational data base management system this includes being able to access more than one file at a time for report generation.

9. Any relational data base management system that you use should be a stand-alone program. The integrated programs for microcomputers simply cannot handle the requirements that will be described later in this section.

153

Requirements of Hardware

RAM. Many file management systems will work with as little as 48K of RAM. Some relational data base management programs operate with as little as 64K of RAM with the more sophisticated ones requiring 128K or more.

Disks. You should have at a minimum two disk drives, one for the program and one for your data. Since a relational data base management application for archives may require a great deal of storage you should estimate your needs prior to buying a system. Hard disks have the advantages of more storage space as well as faster access time, an important consideration when using a FMS or RDBMS.

Printer. A dot-matrix printer is the minimum requirement for this application.

Cost Variables

Hardware. A complete setup with two disk drives and a dot-matrix printer can be purchased for as little as $2,000 or less. A ten-megabyte hard disk drive will add about $800 to $1,300.

Software. Simple file management programs range from under $100 to $400 with a few costing more than $400. Relational data base management programs range from about $400 to over $1,000, but with many very good programs under $800.

Setup. Setup costs depend on the complexity of your application. You may need from two to four hours to set up a simple file management system while a more complex RDBMS described below may take from ten to twenty hours.

Data entry. Data entry for on-going jobs will not be too much of a problem if you enter the information as you archive a project's records. If you want to computerize all your past projects, the time and cost will depend, of course, on the size of your collection.

Keyboarding information for a standard detail system will be a simpler job. Most of the data can be taken right off the detail sheet by a secretary.

Implementation Procedures

1. Decide what portions of the indexing methods described in this section you absolutely need to implement and at what level of detail. If your office and projects are small you may be able to use a simple file management system for your archives instead of the relational system described below. Or, you may simply need information on where to find your drawings and project records. If so, you will not need to use all the data fields suggested in the examples.

2. For indexing standard details, decide on a numbering and classification system if you don't already have one. There are many possible ways to do this. Refer to the sources of information listed at the end of this section for some good guidelines on how to do this.

```
Detail number:    09261-08

  Detail name:    Gypsum board partition at ceiling (1-hr)

 Date created:    86/04/15

Building element:  Interior partitions

     Keywords:    Partition, Gypsum board, Walls, Ceiling

        Scale:    1 1/2"

  Description:    Shows 1-hr. rated partition on 2 1/2"
                  mtl. studs passing through suspended
                  ceiling with reveal trim.

 Developed by:    MKA

   Evaluation:    Good.  "V" trim easy to install.
```

Figure 5.4-1
Standard Detail Data Base Record

3. For standard details, set up the data entry screens, indexes and report formats required by the particular software you have. Figure 5.4-1 shows one type of standard detail data entry screen. This gives the basic information required to find and evaluate the drawing the record refers to. Notice that there is an "evaluation" field to allow the recording of feedback concerning how the detail has performed. You can expand this to include such data fields as "structural integrity," "ease of cleaning," and other specific evaluation criteria.

4. For archival records the procedures are a little more complicated if you set up a relational data base management system. This requires that you have four separate files. See Figure 5.4-2. The project identification file holds data unique to all your projects; their names, numbers, clients, building types and so forth. The drawing set file lists all the individual drawing sheets you have and the data unique to them such as date, scale, revisions dates and the locations where they are stored. The project manual file contains information on those and the project records file itemizes all the various types of document "sets" that are part of any job. These include such things as the complete drawing sets, shop drawings, specifications, project notebooks and so on.

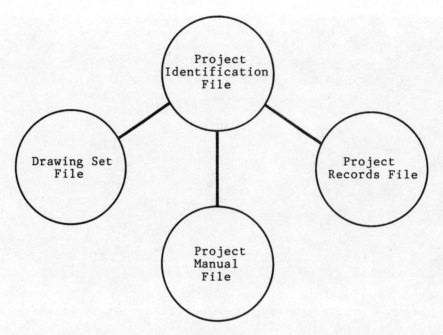

Figure 5.4-2
Project Archives Data Base Management File Structure

5. Review the diagram in Figure 5.4-2 and decide what portions of the system you require. You may only need the project identification file and the project records file, choosing to consolidate the project manual information and drawing set data into one file.

6. Set up a data base schema to plan the file structure you want. If you are not familiar with how to do this, refer to Appendix A, Fundamentals of Data Base Management Systems, for a discussion of the theory behind a RDBMS. Figure 5.4-3 shows one possible schema using four files. The illustration shows the files set up as tables, with each row representing a *record* and each column representing a *data field* in each record.

Each record in the project identification file represents one job only while in the drawing set file and the project records file there is more than one record to each project. However, the records are uniquely identified in those files by a *combination* of project number and drawing number or project number and document type code. The project manual file is simple, with just one set of data per record.

The four files are thus related by project number. If you want a complete printout of only one job, the computer finds the requested record in the project identification file and prints out the information. Then it searches the drawing set file and finds the records where the project number is the same as what you

Project Identification File

Proj. #	Name	Client	Building Type	Location	Completion Date
8714	Wallace	John Smith	Factory	Salt Lake	05/23/86
8715	Evans Bldg.	Pete Evans	Office	Phoenix	06/15/86
8716	ABC Corp.	Nick Peters	Office	Phoenix	09/01/86
8717	Linden sch.	Edna Winsome	School	Los Angeles	01/27/87

Drawing Set File

Proj.#	Dwg. #	Dwg. name.	Date	Revision
8716	A-12	Bldg. sections	11/02/86	11/23/86
8716	A-13	Door details	11/02/86	11/18/86
8716	A-14	Window details	11/02/86	none
8716	A-15	Misc. details	11/05/86	12/12/86

Project Manual File

Proj.#	Date	Addenda	Mech/Elec?
8714	05/23/86	none	Yes
8715	06/12/86	1, 2	Yes
8716	11/02/86	1, 2, 3	No

Project Records File

Proj.#	Doc. Code	Doc. Type	Location	Description	Disposal Date
8716	A	Design sketches	Warehouse, Box 149	Misc. diagrams	01/01/96
8716	B	Originals	Warehouse, Box 157	Arch, Struc, Mech	none
8716	D	Project manual	Office, Bookshelves	Specs, bidding info	none
8716	F	Shop drawings	Warehouse, Box 158	Complete set	01/01/94

Figure 5.4-3
Relational Data Base Management Schema
for Project Archives

requested and prints out the information on each drawing. It then does the same for the project manual file and the project records file. Of course, you can specify what data fields are printed out and their format.

7. Following the instructions of your software and using the graphic schema you developed as a guide, set up the files, data entry screens, indexes and report formats you need. Some software allows you to set up custom menus so the application can be a complete "turn-key" use. Others require you to use a command language or software-defined, menu-driven format.

Additional Tips

- Regardless of what numbering system you select, maintain the same number of characters for each record. For example, the detail number 07540–3–10 would be indexed *before* the number 07540–3–5 because the computer would sort the digit "1" before the digit "5." Instead, the second number should be 07540–3–05.

- Be careful not to make this application more complex than it needs to be for *your* needs. The illustration in this section for setting up an archival records system is probably the most complete you would ever need. Modify it according to your office's requirements.

Sources for More Information

Bennett, Philip M. *Construction Detail Banking: Systematic Storage and Retrieval.* New York: John Wiley & Sons, 1984.

This work includes a discussion of several types of classification and indexing systems for standard details as well as a recommended descriptor term system that uses a controlled vocabulary (thesaurus). Detailed guidelines are given for developing an in-house list of controlled terms to use for storing and retrieving details.

Klunder, Frederick. "Managing Maps and Engineering Drawings," in *Taking Control of Your Office Records: A Manager's Guide,* ed. Katherine Aschner. White Plains, NY: Knowledge Industry Publications, 1983.

Powers, Edgar Jr. *Unigrafs.* Nashville, TN: Gresham, Smith and Partners, 1981.

Stitt, Fred A. *Systems Graphics.* New York: McGraw-Hill Book Company, 1984.

This book includes ideas for a standard detail numbering system based on the Construction Specification Institute's *Masterformat* system. One appendix gives a complete list of a recommended detail file numbering system while another appendix suggests a cross-index list of numbering systems listed according to five phases of constructions with subsections listed alphabetically.

CHAPTER 6

Streamlining Project Management

Project management is one of the most important and information-intensive tasks in any design office. A successful firm is one with a well-developed project management system that provides tight control on scheduling, time and resource allocation and daily progress of all jobs in the office. Low-cost computers can vastly improve the handling of the thousands of pieces of data that a project manager must deal with, eliminating much of the drudgery so the manager can concentrate on actually running the job rather than on clerical details.

The applications in this chapter include some of the most common project management tasks and show how computers can make it easier to complete them. Refer to Section 1.2 for suggestions on how to maintain project histories, a common responsibility of the project manager. In addition, review Sections 1.6 and 2.3 for ways to make fee estimates, also an activity the project manager should be involved with.

6.1

STAFF TIME PROJECTIONS AND TIME MONITORING

Two of the most important aspects of project management are accurate estimation of the time needed to complete a job and rigorous monitoring of the actual time expended compared to the estimated time. Most of the project and financial management software packages developed for architects include these features, but in many cases the expensive, complicated applications packages are not necessary. You may find that they provide you with *too much* information. Since they are also closely tied to the overall financial picture of the office (see Section 2.4, Financial Management Simplified), the input, output and review of information may be delegated to the bookkeeper or someone other than the project manager. In this case, the project manager may not receive the information in a timely manner.

Separating time monitoring from detailed financial management has the advantage of putting the information directly into the hands of the project manager who can develop staff time projections and keep track of each job in as much detail as required. Since the original estimate of fee (and therefore, time) is part of your office's financial management system, don't worry about project managers working in a vacuum—the data they use to set up this application are directly tied to the overall financial picture of the office. This section will discuss ways to use simple, off-the-shelf software to implement this aspect of project management.

Basic Application Requirements

Using a computer to monitor time expended on a project is similar to using a paper form. You must be able to list either phases of a job or individual staff members and track these over a period of time, either in days, weeks, months or pay periods. For any given phase and time period, you must be able to compare the estimated with the actual time expended so corrective action can be taken if necessary.

Since monitoring is done on a regular basis for a particular time period (weekly, for example), you must also be able to accumulate hours and dollars to get a "period-to-date" total. You should be able to convert this cumulative subtotal to a percent of the total estimated hours and dollars that can then be compared to the project manager's estimate of what percentage of the actual work is complete at that same time. For example, if 75 percent of the time allowed has been used and only 50 percent of the job is completed, corrective action would clearly be warranted.

Additional Application Requirements

In addition to simply comparing actual time expended with budgeted time, you may also want to be able to perform "what-if" calculations. These may be to study the effects on the job if you add more people or how the time period must be extended if you cannot commit the number of staff to a project you originally planned.

Other useful application requirements include the following:

1. The ability to retrieve data from other files. This is especially beneficial if you want to relate the information to time sheet summaries, overall office financial management or individual personnel productivity summaries.

2. Graphic capabilities to produce bar charts or line graphs illustrating the relationship between estimated time budgeted, actual time expended, and

estimated percent complete as the job progresses. Many of the integrated packages have this ability.

3. Relational functions such as "greater than," "less than," and "if-then-else" to compare actual amounts to budgeted amounts. These can be used to avoid mistakes due to visual comparison of numbers and to alert the project manager when an amount exceeds a certain percentage over that budgeted.

Requirements of Software

A spreadsheet program is best if this application is separate from other financial management functions. The program you select should have the following minimum characteristics.

1. the standard row and column format with four-function mathematical functions

2. the ability to add rows and columns to the matrix if the project time period is extended

3. the ability to vary column widths

4. the ability to format columns for right justification, decimal point location, comma location and percentages

5. the ability to print only selected portions of the matrix

6. the additional mathematical functions of percentage, average, count, maximum and minimum

Refer to the Additional Application Requirements listed above for other software features you might find useful.

Requirements of Hardware

RAM. Many stand-alone spreadsheet programs can operate on hardware with minimal RAM (64K or less), but if you want integrated software to allow you to draw graphs of your data you will need 128K, 256K or more depending on the program.

Disks. For many programs, a single disk drive is all that is necessary, but you will most likely want at least two. A hard disk is desirable for faster operation of integrated software packages, and is necessary if you want a multiuser system.

Printer. A low-cost dot-matrix printer is the minimum requirement. If you are using an integrated software package with graphic capabilities, a printer or plotter capable of producing graphs and charts is necessary.

Cost Variables

Hardware. A minimal setup with two disk drives and a dot-matrix printer can be purchased for $2,000 or less.

Software. Simple spreadsheet programs are available from about $100 to $400.

Setup. Spreadsheet templates are easy to set up. Your first layout may take anywhere from two to eight hours depending on its complexity, but once that is done it can be reused for other jobs or easily modified to accommodate projects with slightly different requirements. If you want to set up a system of several related spreadsheets (assuming your software is capable) additional time may be required.

Data entry. Since the idea of this application is to put the responsibility of data entry and review into the hands of the project manager on a regular basis (weekly, biweekly or whatever you select) the actual time for data entry at each session may run from a few minutes for one job to an hour or more for several large jobs.

Implementation Procedures

The following steps illustrate one method of using a generic spreadsheet program for staff time projections.

1. Beginning with the required completion date and starting date, estimate how much calendar time each phase of the job will (or must) require.

2. Using your spreadsheet program set up a layout similar to that shown in Figure 6.1-1. Subtract consultant fees, nonreimbursable direct expenses, estimated reimbursable expenses (if they are part of your fee quote) and a contingency, if desired, from the fee you quoted to the client. The remaining dollar amount is the "working fee" that the project manager must use to produce the job. This is entered on the spreadsheet. Depending on how you estimate fees for a proposal and how you keep accounting records, this dollar amount will represent either billing rates (including direct labor costs, direct personnel expenses, overhead and profit) or direct labor costs (with an overhead allocation amount and profit separate). Refer to Section 2.3 for more information on how to estimate fees using these two methods.

3. Set up the spreadsheet so this total "working fee" is allocated to the various phases of the job by multiplying it by the percentage of the total job you think each phase will require.

These percentages may be based on the standard AIA amounts of 15 percent for schematic design, 20 percent for design development, 40 percent for construction documents, 5 percent for bidding and 20 percent for construction administration, or by other percentages based on your own experience. For example, if part of the total fee included programming as an additional service the percentages would be different. If you did a detailed estimate in the first place to determine your fee, simply use the amounts from that estimate. If your program is able to

ABC Corporation
Project # 8621
Project Mgr.: Todd Brent
4/23/86

Working Fee ====>> 120,000

Phase	% of Total	$ Allotted	Est. Wks	$/ Week	Ave. Bill.Rt	1 $	1 Hrs.	2 $	2 Hrs.	3 $	3 Hrs.	4 $	4 Hrs.	5 $	5 Hrs.	6 $	6 Hrs.	16 $	16 Hrs.	17 $	17 Hrs.	18 $	18 Hrs.
Programming	8%	9,600	2	4,800	47.50	4,800	101	4,800	101	0	0	0	0	0	0	0	0	0	0	0	0	0	0
S. Design	14%	16,800	4	4,200	53.75	0	0	0	0	4,200	78	4,200	78	4,200	78	4,200	78	0	0	0	0	0	0
Design Dev.	20%	24,000	4	6,000	45.85	0	0	0	0	0	0	0	0	0	0	6,000	131	0	0	0	0	0	0
Const. Doc.	35%	42,000	7	6,000	41.50	0	0	0	0	0	0	0	0	0	0	6,0		0	0	0	0	0	0
Bidding	3%	3,600	1	3,600	45.00	0	0	0	0	0	0	0	0	0	0	0	0	0	0	0	0	0	0
Const. Admin	20%	24,000	16	1,500	44.25	0	0	0	0	0	0	0	0	0	0	0	0	0	80	1,500	34	0	0
TOTAL	100	120,000				4,800	101	4,800	101	4,200	78	4,200	78	4,200	78	10,200	209	80		1,500	34	0	0

Figure 6.1-1
Fee Allocation Worksheet

163

retrieve data from other files and you have used the spreadsheet approach to determine your fees, this step can be completed with a few keystrokes.

4. Enter the number of weeks (or other appropriate time period you estimated in Step 1) that each phase will require. Your program uses this number to divide into each fee allocation amount that was previously calculated. This gives you a fee amount per time period (weeks in the example shown in Figure 6.1-1) to enter into the "dollars" ($) columns.

At this point, the project manager can compare budgeted dollars per time period with the total of actual fee dollars spent. The actual fee dollars amount will come from the bookkeeper or someone else who is totaling time sheets weekly and multiplying hours by billing rates.

The problem with this approach is that it is usually not as meaningful to the project manager or the staff as is "hours." For this reason you should convert dollars to hours and continue with the following implementation steps.

5. Convert the working fee dollars per time period into hours by dividing the average billing rate (or the direct personnel costs if you use that method) into the fee dollars. These hours are transferred to a time-monitoring spreadsheet similar to that shown in Figure 6.1-2.

For example, if you budgeted $4,000 for one week and your average billing rate was $40 per hour, you could allocate 100 hours for that week. For the standard 40-hour workweek, this would be 2.5 person-weeks. With this hourly information, the project manager can easily compare what is actually happening on the job against the budget. Having the information in hours also makes it easier to assign work based on hours; trying to do this with fee dollars is difficult.

Determining the *average* billing rate is the only tricky part of this step. If the people working on a phase have the same billing rate you can proceed as mentioned in the previous paragraph. Generally, however, the average billing rate will vary from phase to phase depending on who is working on the project. Your calculations should reflect this to more accurately convert fee dollars to hours. For example, early in a project there may be much more involvement by firm principals and project managers with a higher billing rate than later in the job when lower billing rate drafters are working.

One way to account for this is to weight the billing rates of each person according to the percentage of involvement he or she will have. Figure 6.1-3 shows an example of this calculated manually. This kind of table can easily be made part of the spreadsheet. The straight average is different from the weighted average. Where there is a wide variation among billing rates or on long-duration projects this difference can become significant when making time allocations. Once you enter the average billing rate for each phase, the program uses this number to divide into the dollars allocated per time period to give you *hours* per time period.

6. These hours are transferred to a spreadsheet similar to Figure 6.1-2 if your program has the ability to read data from other files. If not, combine Figures 6.1-1 and 6.1-2 onto one large spreadsheet.

ABC Corporation
Project # 8621
Project Mgr.: Todd Brent
4/23/86

Total budgeted hours ===> 2,596

Phase		1	2	3	4	5	6	7	8	9	10	11	12	13	14	15
Programming	Budgeted	101	101	0												
	Actual	98	123													
	Cumulative	98	221	221	221	221	221	221	221	221	221	221	221	221	221	221
S. Design	Budgeted			78	78	78	78									
	Actual			60	88	75	90									
	Cumulative	0	0	60	148	223	313	313	313	313	313	313	313	313	313	313
Design Dev.	Budgeted						131	131	131	131						
	Actual						87	115	120	114						
	Cumulative	0	0	0	0	0	87	202	322	436	436	436	436	436	436	436
Const. Doc.	Budgeted									145	145	145	145	145	145	145
	Actual									132	150	156	142	130	165	153
	Cumulative	0	0	0	0	0	0	0	0	132	282	438	580	710	875	1,028
Bidding	Budgeted															
	Actual															
	Cumulative	0	0	0	0	0	0	0	0	0	0	0	0	0	0	0
Const. Admin	Budgeted															
	Actual															
	Cumulative	0	0	0	0	0	0	0	0	0	0	0	0	0	0	0
TOTAL	Budgeted	101	101	78	78	78	209	131	131	275	145	145	145	145	145	145
	Actual	98	123	60	88	75	177	115	120	246	150	156	142	130	165	153
	Cumulative	98	221	281	369	444	621	736	856	1,102	1,252	1,408	1,550	1,680	1,845	1,998
	% of Total	4	8	11	14	17	23	28	32	41	47	53	58	63	69	75

Figure 6.1-2
Time Monitoring Spreadsheet

Staff Time Projections and Time Monitoring

Phase <u>DESIGN DEVELOPMENT</u>

Staff	% involvement	Billing rate	Hourly rate for average
PRINCIPAL	3%	75.00	2.25
PROJECT MGR.	15	60.00	9.00
DESIGNER	50	50.00	25.00
DRAFTING	32	30.00	9.60
TOTAL	100%	53.75	45.85

Figure 6.1-3
Weighted Average Billing Rates

7. At the end of every time period (weekly, biweekly, monthly) enter the total number of hours spent on the project by everyone in the office in the appropriate "Actual" rows. This information can come directly off the time sheets either through the bookkeeper or by the project manager quickly scanning the time sheets of those people working on his or her job.

8. Have the program perform the calculations built into your spreadsheet and review the current status of the project. As a minimum, you would want to calculate cumulative totals by phase and by time period. If you are using an integrated software program, you can plot the budgeted versus actual hours spent and compare them with the percentage complete of the job.

How detailed you want to get in breakdown of the job by task and staff member, subtotals and other calculations is up to you. Make the spreadsheet format complete enough to give you the information you need to control the job, but not so much that you get buried in detail. Figure 6.1-2 shows one format where the cumulative hours are calculated each time you work with the spreadsheet. They are carried out to the end of the job for comparison with the total budgeted hours for each phase.

Additional Tips

- Make sure your financial management system is in order before you implement this application. Since you will be monitoring time based on your contract fees, these must be accurately estimated to cover indirect costs, nonreimbursable expenses, contingencies and allowances for consultants fees if these are built into your total fee.

166

- The minimum level of detail should track phases of the job weekly. The project manager may want to subdivide phases into more detailed tasks, especially if the duration of a phase is long, or there are several staff members assigned to the phase.

Sources for More Information

Ballast, David Kent. *The Architect's Handbook.* Englewood Cliffs, NJ: Prentice-Hall, Inc., 1984.

Haviland, David. *Managing Architectural Projects: The Process.* Washington: The American Institute of Architects, 1981.

Mattox, Robert F. *Financial Management for Architects: A Guide to Understanding, Planning and Controlling the Firms Finances.* Washington: The American Institute of Architects, 1980.

Professional Services Management Journal. *Project Management for the Design Professional.* Brookline, MA: Professional Services Management Journal.

6.2

MONEY-SAVING JOB SCHEDULING APPLICATIONS

Staff time projections and time monitoring discussed in Section 6.1 involve simple comparisons of time budgeted to actual time expended. When a project becomes more complicated with many individual activities closely interrelated such that one may not begin until another is finished you may want to consider using a more comprehensive scheduling technique such as a Critical Path Method (CPM) network or a Program Evaluation and Review Technique (PERT). These scheduling techniques have been used for years by contractors to coordinate large construction projects, but their use by architects has been limited, partially due to the complex nature of setting them up and the previous requirement of large mini- or mainframe computers to use them effectively.

However, with increasing microcomputer capacity and the availability of many usable software packages you may find it cost effective to add this application to your arsenal of computer power to efficiently organize your work and save your limited fee dollars. Refer to the references listed at the end of this section if you are unfamiliar with these scheduling techniques since it is beyond the scope of this section to describe the intricacies of network scheduling.

Basic Application Requirements

In its most basic form, project management using a network-type of scheduling program involves "thinking through" a job and listing all the individual tasks needed to complete it along with their interdependencies. An estimate of time duration for each task is assigned and optional resource constraints (money, time or people) are included.

These data are entered into the program that performs various calculations, manipulates the data, and produces a variety of reports on the status of the project at any desired time.

Every software program of this type performs these basic tasks with varying degrees of sophistication and ease—some doing very little with the data and others providing the project manager with a vast array of reports and useful means of tracking a project.

To be useful, an application program for scheduling architectural design projects should have the following minimum attributes. Of course, for your office's use, you may want to include some of the Additional Application Requirements to this list to set up your own minimum requirements when you evaluate software. Also, refer to Requirements of Software for additional attributes.

A good project scheduling program should have:

1. Flexibility to allow for scheduling periods in days, weeks or months. Some programs limit the period to days, others allow hours, quarters and years.

2. A calendar to allow for weekends, holidays and variable length of work week.

3. The ability to display on-screen reports as well as printed reports.

4. Report formats that include, at a minimum, task lists, Gantt charts and network analysis. Gantt charts are simple, time-based bar charts showing start and end times of activities. The activities that make up the "critical path" should be able to be highlighted in this type of chart, but the relationships and dependencies of activities common to CPM diagrams are not shown. A network analysis is a listing of the individual activities with start and end dates, dependencies, float time and other data concerning each activity.

5. The ability to accommodate the number of tasks per project that you typically deal with. Most design projects can be handled with less than 200 separate activities, many with less than 100.

6. The ability to accommodate the number of time periods your projects will require. If you are planning by weeks and expect the job to last a year and a half you would need at least 78 time periods.

7. The ability to sort the data in various ways. For example, it is useful to sort by critical activities, by start date, by finish date, by resources and alphabetically by task name.

8. The ability to have updated reports on the screen and in printed form based on periodic revisions to the original schedule.

Additional Application Requirements

Beyond the basic requirements mentioned above, you may find the following features of a project scheduling program useful:

1. The ability to supply an updated version of the network and other reports that display actual progress against your original plan. This is one of the most useful features of the better programs and usually adds considerably to the cost, but is well worth the extra price. Consider this feature carefully when you are evaluating application software.

2. The ability to coordinate several projects sharing the same resources of time, money or people.

3. The ability to draw CPM charts or PERT charts. Many programs do not do this, relying instead on the highlighted critical path activities of a Gantt chart to show critical job tasks. This may not be an important feature for you since you will already have worked out a network diagram in your initial preparation for using the program. This feature is useful if you will be making many changes during a project and want to keep an updated chart showing an overall view of the job.

4. The ability to display on the screen and print additional reports such as network analysis charts, listings of resources (money, time, people), manpower loading charts, cash requirements charts and similar outputs sorted in an order defined by the project manager.

5. The ability to include subprojects as part of the main schedule. This is useful for both enlarging the capacity of a program and generating separate files that can be reused for other schedules.

6. The ability to deal with activities based on the PERT techniques of pessimistic, optimistic and most likely activity durations. Additionally, you may want the ability to define two tasks on a finish-to-start, start-to-start or finish-to-finish relationship.

7. The ability to support the use of a color screen. This is useful if the software can highlight the critical path in color.

Requirements of Software

In addition to the basic application requirements previously listed, a good project scheduling program should provide you with most of the following features:

1. Calculation of critical path with early and late start dates, early and late finish dates and float.

2. The ability to allow input of various kinds of resources such as people, time and money.

3. Calculation and summary of resources by designated time periods so that you can review, for example, how many people will be needed in any given work period.

4. Sufficient character spaces for entry of task names; 30 characters is about right, but you may be able to live with less.

5. Ability to insert and delete tasks after initial entry.

6. Ability to readjust dependencies after changes are made.

7. On-line help screens.

8. A suitable maximum range for dollar amounts as determined by the size of projects you do. This value may range from $999,999.99 to $999,-999,999.99.

Requirements of Hardware

RAM.   Many programs can run with 128K, others require 256K. A few can operate with as little as 64K but these are limited in their capabilities.

Disks.   Most can be run on one disk, but two are recommended. Hard disks are usually not required.

Printer.   A dot-matrix printer is the minimum requirement. Some programs require a printer capable of printing 132 columns. Many programs also require a plotter because of the type of output they provide.

Screen.   A monochrome screen is all that is required although some programs support color monitors.

Cost Variables

Hardware.   A complete setup with two disk drives and a dot-matrix printer can be purchased for as little as $2,000 or less. A hard disk will add about $800 to $1,300.

Software.   Project scheduling software that can handle one project at a time and does not provide updating is usually under $500. More sophisticated programs run from $500 to $1,000 with a few over $1,000.

Setup.   Project scheduling application software comes ready to run after the normal installation procedures for your system. Depending on the software and the quality of its documentation, this may take from 15 minutes to an hour.

Data entry.   The big variable here is thinking through your job, listing the tasks that are needed, determining durations and setting up a precedence diagram so you can enter the information. For large projects, after this is done, the actual data entry may take an hour or more.

170

Output. The most time-consuming output is printing network diagrams and long lists. Software that can be used with a multitasking operating system is helpful so you can proceed with other work while your scheduling information is being printed.

Implementation Procedures

1. As with any network analysis problem, you must first list the individual tasks required to complete the project, assign duration times in whatever unit you want (days, weeks or months) and create a chart showing interdependencies. Refer to the references at the end of this section if you are unfamiliar with preparing CPM or PERT charts.

2. Using the procedures dictated by the program you have, enter the task name, duration, prerequisite tasks, start dates, resources allocated and other inputs the program uses. Part of the data entry also involves establishing work periods, holidays and other parameters related to the calendar function.

3. Run the program to calculate the critical path and any of the reports that the software provides.

4. If your software provides for comparison of actual progress with your original plan, enter the actual progress of the job on whatever schedule is appropriate for your job. This may be weekly for complex, short-duration projects or biweekly for longer projects.

Additional Tips

- Analyze exactly what your needs are before proceeding with setting up a network schedule. Avoid planning in too much detail as well as in too little detail.

- Before purchasing a program, determine what features you think are absolutely necessary, which ones would be helpful and those you can live without. Every program has a different set of capabilities—good and bad points— and knowing what you need is essential to selection.

Sources for More Information

Antill, James. *Critical Path Methods in Construction Practice, 3rd ed.* New York: John Wiley & Sons, 1982.

Bennett, F. Lawrence. *Critical Path Precedence Networks: A Handbook on Activity-on-Node Networking for the Construction Industry.* New York: Van Nostrand Reinhold, 1977.

Grant, Donald P. *PERT and CPM: Network Methods for Project Planning, Scheduling and Control.* San Luis Obispo: The Small Scale Master Builder, 1983.

Moder, Joseph J.; Phillips, Cecil R.; Davis, Edward W. *Project Management with CPM, PERT, and Precedence Diagramming, 3rd ed.* New York: Van Nostrand Reinhold, 1983.

R. S. Means Co., Inc. *Means Scheduling Manual, 2nd ed.* 538 Construction Plaza, P.O. Box 800, Kingston, MA 02364–9988.

Stasiowski, Frank, ed. *Project Scheduling and Budgeting.* Professional Services Management Journal, 126 Harvard Street, Brookline, MA 02146.

Application Software Available

There are dozens of project scheduling software packages available. The following list includes those that can be used for architectural applications on microcomputers. The list is by no means complete and is current at the time of this writing. Refer to the directory sources listed in Appendix C for other software available and for current addresses.

CPM/PERT
Elite Software Development, Inc.
P.O. Box 1194
Bryan, TX 77806

Decision Support System
General Software Corporation
8401 Corporate Drive, 502
Landover, MD 20785

EMPACT
Applied MicroSystems, Inc.
P.O. Box 832
Roswell, GA 30077

Gantt-It, Schedule-It, Under-Control
A+ Software, Inc.
16 Academy Street
Skaneateles, NY 13152

Pathfinder
Garland Publishing, Inc.
136 Madison Ave.
New York, NY 10016

The Harvard Total Project Manager
Harvard Software, Inc.
521 Great Road
Littleton, MA 01460

172

IntePert
Schuchardt Software Systems
515 Northgate Drive
San Rafael, CA 94903

MicroGANTT
Earth Data Corporation
P. O. Box 13168
Richmond, VA 23225

MicroPERT
Sheppard Software Co.
4750 Clough Creek Road
Reading, CA 96002

Microsoft Project
Microsoft Corporation
10700 Northup Way
Box 97200
Bellevue, WA 98009

MicroTrak
SofTrak Systems
P. O. Box 22156 AMF
Salt Lake City, UT 84122

Milestone
Digital Marketing Corporation
2363 Boulevard Circle
Walnut Creek, CA 94595

PAC MICRO
AGS Management Systems, Inc.
880 First Avenue
King of Prussia, PA 19406

PertMaster
Westminister Software Inc.
3000 Sand Hill Road
Building 4, 242
Menlo Park, CA 94025

PLAN/TRAX
Engineering-Science, Inc.
57 Executive Park South, NE, 590
Atlanta, GA 30329

PMS-II
Aha, Inc.
147 South River Street
P. O. Box 8405
Santa Cruz, CA 95061–8405

PRO-JECT 6
SoftCorp, Inc.
2340 State Road 580, 244
Clearwater, FL 33575

Project Manager Workbench
Applied Business Technology Corporation
365 Broadway
New York, NY 10013

Project Scheduler 5000
Scitor Corporation
256 Gibraltar Drive, Bldg. D7
Sunnyvale, CA 94089

TARGET TASK
Comshare, Inc.
5901 B Peachtree Dunwoodie Rd. 275
Atlanta, GA 30328

Task Manager
Quala
23026 Frisca Drive
Valencia, CA 91355

The Confidence Factor
Simple Software Inc.
2 Pinewood
Irvine, CA 92714

Time-Plan
Mitchell Management Systems, Inc.
Westborough Office Park
2000 West Park Drive
Westborough, MA 01581

VisiSchedule
VisiCorp
1953 Lindy Avenue
San Jose, CA 95131

PRIMAVERA PROJECT PLANNER & PRIMAVISION
Primavera Systems, Inc.
Two Bala Plaza Suite 925
Bala Cynwyd, PA 19004

SuperProject
Sorcim/IUS
2195 Fortune Drive
San Jose, CA 95131

Timeline
Breakthrough Software Corp.
505 San Mann Drive
Novato, CA 94947

Promis
Strategic Software Planning, Corp.
222 Third Street
Cambridge, MA 02142

6.3

PRACTICAL IDEAS
FOR PROJECT MANAGEMENT CHECKLISTS

A project management checklist is a valuable tool for any office interested in maintaining quality control over their jobs. It helps structure a consistent approach regardless of who is managing, and can insure that the hundreds of tasks required to successfully complete a project are not forgotten. In addition, it provides an easy-to-use format for recording knowledge gained by doing a job. With it, you can amass a collective body of information about project management that is unique to your office and your way of doing business.

A project management checklist can be established manually, but using a computer can make it easier to change and update, more flexible for different types of projects and can make it possible for you to coordinate the list with other computerized applications. This section discusses two ways to apply low-cost software to strengthen your project management.

Basic Application Requirements

Checklists deal primarily with words so any program that has basic text editing capabilities will work. In addition, you need flexibility in formatting the list so it can be customized for different project types and for various scopes of work.

Although a word processing program will meet these requirements, spreadsheets and data base management systems offer certain advantages.

Spreadsheet programs, for example, provide an easy way to list many tasks and relate each task to other factors, such as who is assigned responsibility to complete the task, dates for starting and finishing the task, and similar requirements. All these fit in a matrix format for which spreadsheets are ideally suited.

A database management approach offers the advantages of being able to select various combinations of checklist tasks for a particular type of job from a "master list" and to sort the list in various ways such as chronologically, by person responsible, by phase and so on.

Both of these approaches will be discussed in the Implementation Procedures of this section.

Requirements of Software

Since this application is straightforward the software attributes of any spreadsheet package will satisfy the requirements. For applying data base software a simple file management systems will serve your needs. Refer to Appendix A, Fundamentals of Data Base Management Systems, for a more complex description of this type of software.

Requirements of Hardware

RAM. Many spreadsheets and file management systems will work with as little as 64K of RAM. The ones that are part of an integrated package require more, usually 128K or greater.

Disks. For many programs, a single disk drive is sufficient, but you should have two, one for the program and one for the data. One disk can be dedicated to a particular job including this application and others described in this book.

Printer. A dot-matrix printer is the minimum requirement for this application.

Cost Variables

Hardware. A complete setup with two disk drives and a dot-matrix printer can be purchased for as little as $2,000 or less.

Software. Spreadsheet programs may range from about $100 to $400. Simple file management programs range from under $100 to $400 with a few costing more than $400.

Setup. Initial outlining of your project management checklist will be the most labor intensive part of this application. The type of program you decide to use will determine how complicated the setup is.

176

Data entry. If you are already using a checklist, most of the work will be typing it into your system in whatever format you select. Of course, if you are starting from scratch you will need to develop the individual checklist items.

Output. Cost of output is minimal once you have modified your master list.

Implementation Procedures

1. If you do not already have a project management checklist you will need to develop one. This should be done with the aid of firm principals, managers, job captains and others who will be involved in its use. You can have one extensive list or several coordinated lists. For example, one could be an overall checklist for the project manager while another could focus just on the production of working drawings for a job captain. Refer to Sections 4.3, 4.4 and 5.2 for guidelines on how to set up other types of checklists.

2. Decide if you want to maintain your list with a spreadsheet program or a data base management system. A spreadsheet is easier to set up since it is simply a listing of tasks, numbers and spaces for checking off when the tasks are completed—no formulas are involved. If your spreadsheet program has a sorting feature you can arrange tasks alphabetically, by the date tasks must be completed and similar criteria. Figure 6.3-1 shows one type of template with spaces for noting which member of the team is responsible for a particular task.

A data base management system takes a little longer to design, but gives you greater flexibility. For example, Figure 6.3-2 shows one record from a master checklist. The office that maintains it does architectural projects, interior design projects, and programming as basic services. This particular record (initiate work on project manual) would apply to architectural and interior design projects but not to programming work. This is indicated by filling in the appropriate fields with a "Y" for yes and "N" for no. To create a checklist for an interiors job, you would simply ask the data base to extract all the records from the master list for which the INTERIORS field was equal to "Y" and place them in a new file. You would then proceed to fill in the dates, and make other changes that were unique to the job for which you were creating the new checklist. Checklists can be printed out sorted by task number, phase, by person responsible or chronologically by date the task must be completed.

3. Set up the list on your computer using the program of your choice. For your first try, don't worry about getting the numbering system perfect. Concentrate on the task, the phase, and the person responsible. When you print out the first trial list, you can work on rearranging the tasks in the order you want.

4. Test the adequacy of your list by using it on one or two jobs. Revise and refine it as necessary based on feedback from project managers.

5. As your office uses the checklist, update it as required to reflect in-service use and lessons you learn from completing projects.

Task #	Task (Design Development phase)	PM	Job Captain	Consult.	Client	Date Complete
5.12	Project team meeting at beginning of phase	✓	✓			
5.13	Monitor work for conformance to contract	✓				
5.14	Coordinate work by consultants	✓				
5.15	Prepare 50% DD mechanical drawings			✓		
5.16	Prepare 50% DD electrical drawings			✓		
5.17	Prepare 50% DD structural drawings			✓		
5.18	Initiate work on project manual	✓				
5.19	Complete 50% design drawings		✓	✓		
5.20	Hold-in house design review	✓	✓			
5.21	Complete work authorizations	✓				
5.22	Hold progress meeting with client	✓	✓		✓	
5.23	Final design development presentation	✓	✓		✓	
5.24	Obtain and file written client approval	✓			✓	
5.25	Monitor fees and hours expended	✓				
5.26	Review invoicing to client	✓				
5.27	Review and approve consultant's invoices	✓				

Figure 6.3-1
Spreadsheet Type of Project Management Checklist

Additional Tips

- Make sure the people who will be using the checklist are involved in its creation. Whatever system you set up will have a better chance for success if this kind of participation is encouraged.
- Make each task on the checklist represent work that can be completed by itself so it can, indeed, be "checked off."

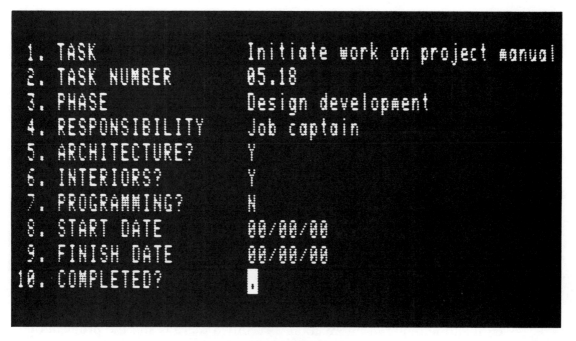

Figure 6.3-2
Data Base Management Record

- Be diligent about keeping your list updated based on what you learn from each job your office completes. A checklist is one of the easiest ways to build up an invaluable storehouse of knowledge unique to your practice.

- With a data base management system, establish a task numbering system that allows you to add records between two existing records without disrupting the sequence. One way is to allow for an extra decimal and digit.

Sources for More Information

Ballast, David Kent. *The Architect's Handbook.* Englewood Cliffs, NJ: Prentice-Hall, Inc., 1984.

Haviland, David. *Managing Architectural Projects: The Process.* Washington: The American Institute of Architects, 1981.

———*Managing Architectural Projects: The Project Management Manual.* Washington: The American Institute of Architects, 1984.

Guidelines, P.O. Box 456, Orinda, CA 94563. *The Guidelines Predesign and Planning Manual. The Guidelines Project Management Task Module Manual.*

Stasiowski, Frank A., and Burstein, David. *Project Management for the Design Professional.* New York: Whitney Library of Design, 1982.

6.4

HOW TO MAINTAIN COMPLETE CONTROL
OVER PROJECT TRANSACTIONS

During a project thousands of decisions are made by dozens of people, and hundreds of documents are exchanged as part of the design and construction process. The project manager is responsible for making sure the myriad verbal and written transactions are communicated to the right person at the right time, and that they are documented for the permanent job record.

Traditionally, standard forms are used to record the more important pieces of information. These include field reports, transmittals, shop drawing logs, change orders and the like. Often, however, other decisions and communications are not recorded—telephone calls, parting comments made as the client is leaving the office, last-minute transmittals of drawings and similar transactions that are a part of any job. There are any number of reasons why these transactions "fall through the cracks," but what may seem like an insignificant decision at the time may later become a major point of contention in litigation.

Even if all the required information is recorded there is still the problem of retrieving all or selective parts of it. For example, if an architectural office becomes involved in a law suit over a leaky roof, it is vital to the defense to have all documents relating to that problem, and to know the who, what, when, where and how of the situation. Information concerning the design of the roof will be spread out from the beginning to the end of the project and will involve letters, meeting notes, drawings, transmittals, telephone calls, design decisions and dozens of other transactions. Often, the only way to retrieve the information is to go through every piece of paper looking for what you need. Any architect who has had to reconstruct a job or a portion of a job knows what a nightmare it can be and the serious consequences of not being able to find the necessary documentation.

The prudent project manager should have a system to record and recall this kind of project information. Manual systems are possible but cannot be as complete and flexible as a computer-based system. A computerized system can easily handle the voluminous amount of project communication, organize it and retrieve it on demand.

Basic Application Requirements

To successfully implement this application you need to be able to record an ongoing collection of information, organize it and retrieve all or selective parts of it. A data base management system is the only reasonable way to handle the volume of data this application generates.

The number and types of transactions that you keep track of will depend

180

on how dedicated you are to this kind of record keeping, your project management system, the capacity of your computer system and how you organize other records. (See Section 2.1 for a discussion of record keeping.) You may want to limit this application to those items that only the project manager is directly involved with (such as change orders, field reports, etc.) and leave correspondence, contracts and transmittals to the secretary for organization.

A more comprehensive system will include *all* documents and decisions related to a job. Either way, the principles are the same. The only major differences are the kinds of hardware and sophistication of software you need, who enters the data and the amount of time to set up the application.

For this application it is not necessary to have the full text of your forms and verbatim accounts of meetings, but simply references to them with enough information to access the paper forms from different points of view—for example, by subject, date, people involved, phase of job and the like. Full text files may become economically possible in the future with improved laser disk storage, but for now all you need is an improved index to your records.

The basic data fields for this kind of application are:

1. project name

2. project number (If you maintain one disk per project you can omit the project name and number.)

3. document identifying number or some way to refer to the full text document and location that the computerized record references

4. date

5. record type (transmittal, meeting minutes, letter, telephone call, change order, etc.)

6. phase of service

7. name of originator of record

8. name of receiver of record

9. subjects of the record (Depending on your data base management software, this may be one field or it may have to be several fields if there are multiple subjects. Being able to selectively search records based on keywords is really the key to the success of this application. The most difficult part of the implementation is planning how to categorize your records. For instance, do you allow any word to be used to describe the document or do you develop a fixed list (controlled vocabulary) of words to assign to each document. Another question is how specific do you need to get? Is it sufficient to categorize a document as relating to "design decisions" or to a more specific "wall fabric selection"?

10. date of follow-up

11. action taken

Additional Application Requirements

Additional data fields you may want to include are:

1. names of people mentioned in a record
2. names of people receiving copies of a record
3. time of the transaction (This could be important for telephone conversations, receiving of bids and transmittals to meet deadlines.)
4. references to other documents that prompted the current record to be generated (For example, a letter received by the client might prompt you to send a letter to the contractor and make a telephone call to the consulting engineer.)
5. references to other computerized records and paper documents that were necessitated by the current transaction
6. an identifying number for the computerized record (Since you need some way of uniquely labeling each record in a data base (the primary key) this may be easier than using other fields in the record as keys. In a relational data base management system it is also easier and faster to use this kind of record number as the link with another record instead of a longer, text field.)
7. a field for general comments about the transaction or for a brief summary of the form or text that the computerized record refers to

Requirements of Software

This application can be implemented with either a file management system (FMS) or relational data base management system (RDBMS). If you are not familiar with these types of programs refer to Appendix A, Fundamentals of Data Base Management Systems. A file management system will present some limitations, but the better FMS programs that allow multiple indexes and sorting capabilities will work well. However, if you want to integrate this project management application with office record keeping and some of the other applications discussed in this chapter, you will have to use one of the relational data base management systems.

Refer to Appendix A for general software selection criteria you should consider. For this application the following software features are critical:

1. at least 30 fields per record (This usually is not a problem except with the very low-cost file management systems.)
2. the ability to have multiple indexes—at least 8, but being able to index

182

on all fields in the record is better (This is what makes an inexpensive FMS usable for this application.)

3. the ability to have more than one "screenfull" of information per record in case you have many data fields

4. an easy method of query either for on-screen retrieval of information or for printed reports (The query method should be tied with complete selections so you can, for example, ask to see all records that occurred before a certain date in which "brick" was a subject and which included contractor "Smith's" name.)

It is helpful to have software that can search for partial strings (groupings of characters) anywhere in a data field. With this feature you can list several subjects in one field and be able to retrieve records based on just one search of one field instead of several searches of several data fields, each containing only one word.

Requirements of Hardware

RAM. Many file management systems will work with as little as 48K of RAM, most with 64K and practically all with 128K. The more sophisticated relational data base management systems usually require 128K or more.

Disks. Two floppy disk drives are usually sufficient, one for the program and one for the data. If one disk is dedicated to only one project, archiving is a simple procedure. There is the additional advantage of not having to enter the project name and number on each record—a real savings in time.

Printer. Any kind of printer will work for this application although you may want a fast, dot-matrix printer for quick in-house reports.

Cost Variables

Hardware. A complete setup with two disk drives and a dot-matrix printer can be purchased for $2,000 or less. A ten-megabyte hard disk drive will add about $800 to $1,300.

Software. Simple file management programs range from under $100 to $400 with a few costing more than $400. Relational data base management programs range from about $400 to over $1,000, but with many very good programs under $800.

Setup. Setup cost depends on the complexity of your application. For a use as important as this, you should spend considerable time thinking about how you want to maintain the information, how to retrieve it and how this application will be integrated with other office functions.

Data entry. Data entry can be done directly by the project manager at the terminal either working directly from memory as soon after the transaction has occurred or from notes. Data entry from printed forms such as meeting minutes, change orders and the like can be saved in a temporary paper file and entered weekly by clerical staff.

Implementation Procedures

1. Decide on what kinds of project transactions you want to record. For very simple applications you can list just those transactions that are not adequately maintained elsewhere such as telephone calls, in-house decisions and the like. With this system, you might decide not to computerize transactions that already have complete paper forms such as transmittals, field reports and change orders, leaving them instead to your existing filing system. However, to get the most use from this application, you should record as many types of transactions as possible.

```
 1. TRANSACTION #      86057
 2. PROJECT NAME       West Side Office Building
 3. PROJECT NUMBER     8631
 4. DATE               11/23/86
 5. RECORD TYPE        Meeting minutes
 6. RECORD LOCATION    Job files
 7. JOB PHASE          Design development
 8. ORIGINATOR         Todd Brent
 9. RECEIVER           J. Smith
10. SUBJECT 1          Ceiling finish
11. SUBJECT 2          Construction schedule
12. SUBJECT 3          Lobby design
13. SUBJECT 4          Roofing
14. COPIES TO          AEA, DKB, CJN, FILE
15. REFERENCE          Letter to AEA, 11/20/86
16. COMMENTS           AEA insisted on drywall ceiling
```

Figure 6.4-1
Project Transaction Record

2. Set up the data fields that will be of most use to you. Use the lists given in the Basic and Advanced Application Requirements of this section as a starting point. Figure 6.4-1 shows an example of one kind of record.

3. Determine if you can use a file management system or need the added flexibility and power of a relational data base management system. A relational system will be necessary if you want to link project management records with records maintained by the clerical staff. This is especially critical if you have or plan on purchasing a multiuser hardware configuration in which several people can access the same data base.

4. Based on the most likely number of records you will have for each project as determined in Step 1 and the size of the record you estimated in Step 2, calculate the maximum file size in both records and bytes (characters). If you don't already have a program or hardware, this calculation will help you purchase the right software and the capacity of storage you need.

5. Following the instructions of your DBMS, set up data entry formats and begin entering information starting from the first day of the project. Establish a clear office policy concerning who does the data entry and when it is to be done. Being diligent about data entry is critical to the success of this application.

Additional Tips

The types of transactions on a typical job are extensive. Consider the following list when deciding on what transactions to record:

meeting minutes

memos

letters (see Section 2.1)

transmittals (see Section 2.1)

telephone conversations

design notes

programming forms or notes

change orders (see Section 6.5)

work authorizations

field reports

field orders (see Section 6.5)

shop drawing and sample logs

contracts

bid log

application and certificate for payment

punch list

bonds and insurance documents

6.5

TRACKING CHANGE ORDERS AND FIELD ORDERS

Keeping track of change orders and field orders is part of the larger task of construction administration. Although this phase of the project manager's duties can be included with other computerized management (see Section 6.4) there are several reasons why change order tracking should be kept separate.

First, change orders always deal with cost and time so any application software needs to have mathematical capabilities. For many other project management activities this feature is not as important.

Second, change orders and field orders are always in hardcopy; that is, there is a form that is filled out and sent to all the appropriate parties: architect, contractor and owner. The paper form, however, does not include information that is valuable to the project manager. Such information includes who initiated the change and why, reference to proposal requests, when copies were sent to the various parties and reference to meeting minutes, correspondence and other communications. This is important data for both managing the job and reconstructing it if disputes arise. A computerized log gives the project manager easy access to the necessary information while the paper form is safely stored in the office files.

Third, the number of individual entries related to change orders and field orders can grow rapidly, even on medium-size jobs. Trying to include these in a larger construction administration file with meeting minutes, telephone logs and other activities can quickly become confusing. However, the two can still be related by including cross-references in each file.

Basic Application Requirements

The basic information in a change and field order log that you should keep track of include the following:

1. change order or field order number (These will correspond to the numbers on the paper form. For easy reference on the computer log, each can be preceded by "CO" or "FO" to differentiate between the two types.)
2. description of changes
3. reference to drawings or other attachments
4. cost of the change (add or deduct); "0" if a field order

186

5. change in contract time (if any) and current contract completion date

6. cumulative dollar change caused by change orders and current contract amount

7. date of change or field order

8. who initiated the change or field order and why (This data field can be split into who and why. Used with a data base management program, a search can be made on names to identify what changes were made by a particular person (for example, architect, contractor or more specifically, "Joe Smith"). Searching on keywords can pull out changes made related to a particular part of the project; for example, "roofing.")

These data fields can be pulled out of the change order and field order file and combined with keyword data fields from other files you set up as part of your "project transactions" application system (See Section 6.4) to make a master subject file. If, at some point, it was necessary to find all references to "roofing," the master file could be searched and those records relating to roofing identified.

Note: The project name, number, address, and so forth does not have to be part of the file since presumably the Change Order and Field Order log is on the same disk as other files devoted solely to one project.

Additional Application Requirements

In addition to the data fields outlined above, you may want to include more information:

1. reference to proposal requests that were sent to the contractor for pricing before the change order was written

2. reference to meeting minutes, phone conversations, letters or other communications that led to the decision to issue a change order or make a field order necessary

3. reference to the application and certificate for payment that includes the change order

4. dates when the change order was sent to the owner and contractor and when they were returned

5. date when the change order or field order was received at the job site

Requirements of Software

Software for this application needs to have basic text-editing capabilities, four-function arithmetic, and the ability to search for requested words. The two types of off-the-shelf generic software best suited for this application are spreadsheets and data base management systems (DBMS), or integrated packages with these two applications. Each has its advantages and disadvantages. Your particular needs and the amount of effort you want put into this application will determine which is best for you.

Spreadsheet Program Advantages

most closely emulates the matrix-type of change order log many project managers keep manually

quick to set up and the template can be copied and reused for other jobs

easy to set up math formulas and keep track of dollars

printed reports often easier to make than with DBMS reports

Spreadsheet Program Disadvantages

search capabilities limited or nonexistent (For a small number of entries, this is not a problem since a printout can be visually scanned for keywords.)

does not handle long strings of text as well as a data base management system (In an integrated package this is less of a disadvantage.)

Data Base Management System Advantages

can easily handle a large number of records

extensive search capabilities

more capacity to handle long data fields for text

if a relational data base, can be integrated with other project management files

Data Base Management System Disadvantages

sometimes more difficult to set up, especially if you are working with a relational data base

more difficult to set up and print reports

on-screen review of information more difficult than with spreadsheet type of program

Requirements of Hardware

RAM. Since the total amount of data in any one project file related to change orders and field orders is minimal from the standpoint of a computer (even large jobs will not require much storage), disk capacity and RAM capacity is not a problem. Even most of the portables have enough capacity to handle this kind of file. Greater RAM and storage is only necessary if you are using an integrated package or want to set up a relational data base with other project management files.

188

Disks. For this application one floppy disk will work, but you should consider two.

Printer. Any kind of printer will work for this application.

Cost Variables

Hardware. Hardware costs for this application are minimal due to limited requirements for RAM and disk storage. A complete setup with two disk drives and a dot-matrix printer can be purchased for $2,000 or less.

Software. Spreadsheet programs may range from about $100 to $400. Simple file management programs range from under $100 to $400 with a few costing more than $400. Relational data base management programs range from about $400 to over $1,000, but with many very good programs under $800.

Setup. Spreadsheet templates are quick to set up. Designing forms and report formats for a DBMS may take some time depending on the complexity of the DBMS. Once either is set up, however, they can be reused for other jobs.

Data entry. Minimal time is required. Data can either be input by the project manager (preferred) or by clerical staff working from the change order form and additional notes written by the project manager.

Implementation Procedures

1. Work with your staff and project managers to determine the particular information your office needs to keep track of and the kind of output it needs related to change orders and field orders. Use the Basic and Advanced Application Requirements outlined above as a starting point for discussion.

2. Decide whether to use a spreadsheet program or data base management program based on the advantages and disadvantages listed and an evaluation of your office's needs and the complexity of the jobs you do.

3. Review how this computerized application relates to other project management activities. Refer to the other applications in this chapter and analyze your current project management procedures. Decide whether change order and field order logs can be a helpful add-on or whether you need to revise your entire office's method for project management.

4. Establish an office policy for using this computer application. Consider such things as who completes the forms, who does data entry, when the various activities are done and how they are communicated to the client. Include this information in your office manual and project management checklist.

5. Review your existing change order and field order forms to see if revisions are necessary to include information that is generally not included. A two-part form may be necessary. The traditional information can be on one form for legal purposes and to simplify it for the owner and contractor (such as AIA form G701).

189

Change Order Log
ABC Corporation
Project # 85-321

Original contract sum: 3,765,400

Original completion date: 07/01/86

No.	Description	Date	Cost	Cumulative	Time change	New comp. date	Initiated by	Reason for change
CO-1	Modify N. foundation wall	08/16/85	3,450.00	3,768,850.00	+ 4	07/07/86	Contractor	Rock obstruction
CO-2	Relocate door # 105	09/23/85	327.00	3,769,180.00	0		Client	Program change
CO-3	Add brick around col G-5	11/21/85	1,200.00	3,770,377.00	0		Client	Client request
CO-4	Lower ceiling, Rm. 203	12/03/85	250.00	3,770,630.00	0		Mech. Eng.	Ductwork too large
CO-5	Move windows, Rm. 300	01/13/86	2,597.00	3,773,220.00	+ 2	07/09/86	Architect	Improve view
CO-6	Delete basement gyp. bd.	01/15/86	-4,328.00	3,768,900.00	0		Client	Cost savings measure
CO-7	Relocate penthouse entry	02/18/86	9,400.00	3,778,300.00	+ 5	07/16/86	Contractor	Piping conflict
CO-8	Delete landscape. n. side	04/10/86	-2,500.00	3,775,800.00	0		Client	Cost savings measure

No.	Reference	Date sent to Owner	Date rtnd. from Owner	Sent to Contractor	App. Pmt. #	Proposal Ref.
CO-1	Dwg R-01, letter 8/14/85	08/16/85	08/20/85	08/20/85	1	B-1
CO-2	Dwg R-02, memo 9/24/85	09/24/85	09/30/85	09/30/85	3	B-2
CO-3	Dwgs R-03, R-04	11/22/85	11/28/85	11/29/85	5	B-3
CO-4	Letter 12/01/84	12/03/85	12/08/85	12/08/85	6	B-4
CO-5	Dwg R-05	01/15/86	01/20/86	01/20/86	7	B-5
CO-6	Dwg R-06	01/15/86	01/20/86	01/20/86	7	B-5
CO-7	Dwgs R-07, R-08, letter	02/19/86	02/21/86	02/24/86	8	B-6
CO-8	Letter: 04/13/86	04/12/86	04/16/86	04/19/86	11	B-7

Figure 6.5-1
Spreadsheet Format for Change Order

The additional data (why the change was initiated, reference to correspondence and so forth) can be on another part for data entry by someone other than the project manager. The advantage of having the project manager do the data entry is that the additional data does not have to be first written down, *then* entered into the computer. The additional information can be entered directly when it is fresh in the project manager's mind without extra paperwork.

6. Set up the spreadsheet template or data base management system according the software instructions. Consider that it should be able to work with any of your jobs or project types so some extra data fields may be necessary to allow it to accommodate minor variations in project types. Remember, the more reuse you can get from any one program application the more cost-effective it is.

7. Enter data on a timely basis. Putting off entering the who, what and why of change orders and field orders may result in forgetting the particulars of the situation.

8. Print out reports for you, the contractor and your client based on a schedule you determine when you set policy for the use of this application. Generally, the more changes occurring on a job, the more often you should be informing everyone of them and their cost implications.

Examples

Any of the standard change order and field order forms can be used for the hardcopy portion of this application (such as AIA form G701 and G708). Many offices design their own, but remember that they have legal implications so a review by your attorney may be a good idea.

Whether you design and print an additional form for the other data fields that are not a part of standard forms depends on whether you plan to split the tasks of recording the information and entering the information between two people. It is preferable to put the tool of the computer directly into the hands of the office staff and take advantage of the computer's ability to reduce paperwork and increase accuracy and completeness. Figures 6.5-1 and 6.5-2 show how a spreadsheet layout and a data base management record might look. Figure 6.5-2 is a data entry screen for only one record of a DBMS. All the individual records are printed in any desired format when a report is needed.

Additional Tips

- Print out your reports whenever you have to approve an application and certificate for payment to verify that your information corresponds to the cumulative costs listed by the contractor.
- Always send a copy of a field order or a list of field orders to the client to keep him or her informed of job progress.

```
 1. Change order #     CO-2
 2. Description        Relocate door # 105
 3. Date of CO or FO   9/23/85
 4. Cost of CO              $327.00
 5. Time chg. (days)   0
 6. New comp. date
 7. Initiated by       Client
 8. Reason for chg.    Program change made by client
 9. Keyword 1          Plan modification
10. Keyword 2
11. Document ref.      R-02
12. App. for pmt. #    03
13. Proposal ref. #    02
14. Sent to           Al Smith
15. Date sent owner    9/24/85
16. Date received      9/30/85
17. Date sent cont.    9/30/85
18. Date received     10/05/85
19. Job site date     10/06/85
20. Sort field
```

Figure 6.5-2
Data Base Management Record for Change Order Log

Sources for More Information

Ballast, David Kent. *The Architect's Handbook.* Englewood Cliffs, NJ: Prentice-Hall, Inc., 1984.

Haviland, David. *Managing Architectural Projects: The Process.* Washington: The American Institute of Architects, 1981.

————*Managing Architectural Projects: The Project Management Manual.* Washington: The American Institute of Architects, 1984.

Stasiowski, Frank A., and Burstein, David. *Project Management for the Design Professional.* New York: Whitney Library of Design, 1982.

CHAPTER 7

Easy-to-Use Cost Budgeting and Control Techniques

Cost estimating is a natural use for microcomputers. With the availability of spreadsheet software and specialized programs every architect and interior designer should be taking advantage of this application. You can use computers for cost estimating at several levels of detail, from preliminary budgeting to very detailed quantity take-offs and pricing. Other money-related applications include feasibility analyses, bid review, and life cycle cost analyses.

This chapter sets forth methods of using simple spreadsheet programs for several budgeting tasks as well as how to use more advanced programs that include data bases of unit cost information. It also demonstrates life cycle costing—one of the most powerful economic applications you can use to improve your decision making. You will find the ideas in this chapter useful in stimulating your own thoughts concerning the myriad ways computers can help with your particular cost-related applications.

7.1

EASY PROJECT BUDGETING WITH A SPREADSHEET

Estimating costs for a project is one of the most difficult tasks an architect or interior designer faces. It is also one that is laced with potential legal problems; if the final project cost is too far from the professional's estimate the designer may be liable. Although computers cannot solve *all* the problems inherent in cost estimating they can make it much easier to deal with more information in greater detail and to update this information as the project progresses.

In concept, construction cost estimating is simple. All projects represent a certain quantity of materials, labor, equipment and overhead. Each of these items costs a certain amount of money per unit (or percentage). Estimating is simply a matter of multiplying one by the other and adding up the results. Unfortunately, things are not quite that simple in practice. Unit costs vary considerably with

193

time, contractor, geographical location, economic conditions and the competitive nature of the industry. Even material and labor quantities change as a particular project progresses from initial concept to final move-in.

For cost estimating (or budgeting, if you prefer) computers are very good at maintaining records of many unit costs and doing the arithmetic necessary to apply them to changing quantities. Many large contracting firms, construction management companies and independent cost estimating services have developed very sophisticated data bases of cost information, and can quickly and accurately apply them to specific project variables. Using these systems, either on a consulting or time-sharing basis, is appropriate for some estimating, but small and large offices alike can make valuable use of microcomputers for much of the estimating they do.

This section describes the use of spreadsheet software to complete some of the basic kinds of cost estimates. Section 7.2 will describe other applications.

Basic Application Requirements

Since cost estimating deals primarily with numbers this application will use the full power of a spreadsheet program. At its most basic, this application lists line items in your budget (in whatever level of detail you select), the quantity of those items, their unit cost, an extension column multiplying the two, totals and additional add-on costs such as contingency, contractor profit and fees. Beyond this, you may want to coordinate the format so you can use the same spreadsheet for monitoring applications for payment and change orders. Of course, this would require *your* setup to be consistent with the contractor's cost summary.

Because accurate information on unit costs is the key to good estimating part of this application should be a separate file in which you record unit costs available to you. These may come from past jobs your office has done, commercially published costs and specific pricing you receive from contractors and vendors. For each line item, you can record the cost, its source, the date and any unusual factors related to it. For each group of line item costs, the spreadsheet can figure an average. You can also have places to enter update factors to account for inflation or geographic location.

When you get ready to do an estimate you select the most appropriate unit cost from your reference file or have the computer do it if your spreadsheet software can call data from one file into another.

Additional Application Requirements

Recording unit cost information in a spreadsheet format as suggested above is not the most efficient way to handle this type of data, but it is possible if your estimating needs are fairly simple. Another alternative is to use an integrated program that has both spreadsheet *and* data base management capabilities. With it you can maintain unit costs easier with the DBMS and have your spreadsheet read in the values as required. Your system would then emulate some of the larger, more sophisticated services and would be customized to the kinds of projects and costs your office deals with daily.

Requirements of Software

The spreadsheet program you select for this application should have the following minimum characteristics:

1. the standard mathematical functions in addition to percentages and averages
2. the ability to vary column widths
3. the ability to add rows and columns at the end and in the middle of the matrix if you need to expand the template once it is set up
4. a column formatting capability to allow right justification, decimal point location, comma location and percentages
5. the ability to print selected portions of the matrix
6. the ability to retrieve data from other files
7. conditional math formulas such as "greater than," "less than" and "equal to" as well as "if-then-else." These are extremely valuable for estimating if a unit price used in a formula depends on the quantity for a particular line item. You can have two or more unit prices and the computer will compare the quantity listed and decide which one to use in the calculation.

Requirements of Hardware

RAM. Many stand-alone spreadsheet programs can operate on hardware with a minimum amount of RAM (64K or less), but if you want integrated software to allow you to draw graphs of your data you will need 128K, 256K or more depending on the program.

Disks. For many programs, a single disk drive is sufficient, but you will most likely want at least two. A hard disk is desirable for faster operation of some of the integrated software packages.

Printer. A dot-matrix printer is the minimum requirement, but if you want to include an estimate in a report to a client, you may want a daisywheel, laser or ink-jet printer. Since many estimate spreadsheets may take up more than a typical 80-column format, your printer should be capable of printing 132 columns or printing in condensed type.

Cost Variables

Hardware.   A complete setup with two disk drives and a dot-matrix printer can be purchased for $2,000 or less. A ten-megabyte hard disk drive will add from $800 to $1,300.

Software.   Spreadsheet programs may range from about $100 to $400.

Setup.   Depending on the complexity of the template you want for this application, setup time may range from two to eight hours. It will be well worth your time to spend extra effort in working out the spreadsheet template. The real cost benefits come from being able to reuse the same format for many jobs.

Implementation Procedures

1. Decide on the various types of formats you will need. Chances are that one spreadsheet template will not serve all your estimating requirements. You may want one for very preliminary estimating based on basic construction components, one for remodeling work and another for detailed take-offs.

2. Estimate your most likely kinds of reports. Will they be on 8½ x 11 inch paper or larger? Will they typically be on one sheet or several?

3. Lay out your spreadsheet on paper. It will certainly occupy more than one screen and preplanning makes it easier to see the big picture and results in a better application. Some of the things you should decide include:

   a. where the variables will be entered (These should be at the beginning of the template.)

   b. how many instructions you need and where they will be placed

   c. what the column widths will be (If you "stack" different information in the same column on different rows (from the spreadsheet's point of view) there can be conflicts with how wide a column needs to be and how it is formatted.)

   d. how you want the various groups of data to be clustered (For printing, it is helpful if you can easily define the first and last rows and columns of a related group of figures to give you a complete report.)

   e. what you want to be able to see on the screen at any one time (Some columns should be placed next to each other so you can see the relation between them while looking at the screen. If your software has a split screen option this is not quite as critical.)

4. Following the instructions of your software, set up the template. Be sure to leave plenty of extra space for adding extra line items dictated by special projects or second thoughts you may have once you start using the program. Partition

Revised Preliminary Cost Budget   September 6, 1983

Section	Description	Unit	Quan.	$/Unit	Extend	Sub-total
02070	Remove plants and planters	days	1	550.00	550	
02070	Remove storefront above base	sf	279	6.00	1,674	
02070	Remove atrium base	lf	31	2.50	78	
02070	Remove ext. terrazzo	sf	500	6.00	3,000	
02070	Remove revolving doors, glass	days	2	700.00	1,400	
02070	Remove drywall on columns	sf	1,085	0.25	271	
01525	Scaffolding for drywall removal on interior columns	csf	14	45.00	630	
	Sub-total Demolition					$7,603
04465	Reinstall granite at openings	sf	150	35.00	5,250	
04465	Remove granite at openings	sf	124	35.00	4,340	
	Sub-total Granite					$9,590
05400	Framing for new atrium base	lf	26	15.00	390	
05400	Misc. frame above revolving door	ea	2	400.00	800	
05400	Framing for new wall	lf	9	35.00	315	
05730	Stainless steel spandrel panels	lf	50	40.00	2,000	
05730	Quirk detail at columns	lf	580	4.00	2,320	
05730	Stainless steel base at columns	lf	35	25.00	875	
	Sub-total Metals					$6,700
06420	Plastic laminate column panels	sf	1,085	15.00	16,275	
	Sub-total Wood and plastics					$16,275
07160	Dampproof at new atrium base and at revolving doors	sf	220	3.00	660	
07210	Misc. insulation and flashing at atrium base	lf	26	5.00	130	
	Sub-total Flashing & Insulation					$790
08450	New glass doors	sf	63	55.00	3,465	
08470	New revolving doors	ea.	2	47,500.00	95,000	
08810	Glazing at revolving doors	sf	245	33.00	8,085	
08920	Move 1st fl curtain wall glazing	sf	234	6.00	1,404	
08120	Move door into retail space	sf	42	7.00	294	
12500	Tinted film on glass in atrium	sf	1,814	2.50	4,535	
	Sub-total Doors and windows					$112,783
09250	Drywall at new atrium base	tot.	1	100.00	100	
09410	New terrazzo where doors removed	sf	360	20.00	7,200	
09410	Terrazzo (ext) at new doors	sf	140	20.00	2,800	
09420	Terrazzo benches, planters, and guard station	tot.	1	8,000.00	8,000	
09920	Paint drywall in atrium (includes scaffolding)	sf	4,553	0.65	2,959	
09950	New fabric on new wall between column 2 and shuttle elevator	sf	104	10.00	1,040	
	Sub-total Finishes					$22,099
12100	Hanging sculpture (no G.C. mark-up on this item)	tot.	1	30,000.00		
12300	Guard station, terrazzo excluded	tot.	1	1,500.00	1,500	
12810	Plants	ea	2	3,000.00	6,000	
12815	Planters, terrazzo excluded	ea	2	75.00	150	
12600	Cushions for benches	ea	6	60.00	360	
12510	Levolor blinds	sf	1,814	2.50	4,535	
	Sub-total Furnishings					$12,545
16050	Power for artwork lighting	tot.	1	5,000.00	5,000	
16050	Power to guard station	lf	60	3.50	210	
16510	Lighting for artwork	tot.	1	2,000.00	2,000	
16510	Lighting for guard station	tot.	1	300.00	300	
16510	Lobby and atrium lighting	tot.	1	3,000.00	3,000	
16700	Communications to guard station	lf	140	6.00	840	
16865	Relocate electric baseboard heat	days	2	250.00	500	
	Relocate night bell	days	1	250.00	250	
	Sub-total Electrical					$12,100

Total	$200,485
Contingency at 15%	$30,073
General conditions at 5%	$11,528
Contractor's O & P at 20%	$48,417
Hanging sculpture (budgeted)	$30,000
TOTAL BUDGET FIGURE *****	$320,503

197

Figure 7.1-1
Cost Budget for Remodel

SECTION	ITEM	QUANTITY/UNIT	UNIT PRICE	AMOUNT	SUBTOTAL
100	DEMOLITION				
100.01	PARTITIONS	3600 SF	2.00	7200	
100.02	CEILINGS	3700 SF	0.25	925	
100.03	CARPET	3700 SF	0.25	925	
100.04	RELOCATE ENTRY	1 ALLOWANCE	7200.00	7200	
					16250
200	PARTITIONS				
200.01	FULL HEIGHT	225 LF	27.00	6075	
200.02	PARTIAL HEIGHT	24 LF	21.00	504	
200.03	PARTIAL GLASS	44 LF	100.00	4400	
200.04	OPERABLE PARTITIONS	50 LF	175.00	8750	
200.05	DRYWALL FACING	124 LF	20.00	2480	
					22209
300	DOORS/FRAMES/HARDWARE				
300.01	ENTRY	5 EA	600.00	3000	
300.02	INTERIOR-SINGLES	3 EA	500.00	1500	
300.03	INTERIOR-PAIRS	2 EA	900.00	1800	
300.04	SLIDING	4 EA	800.00	3200	
300.05	CLOSET-PAIRS	5 EA	1000.00	5000	
					14500
400	FINISHES				
400.01	WALLS-PAINT	(INCLUDED IN PARTITIONS)		0	
400.02	WALLS-FABRIC TACK PANELS	130 SF	6.00	780	
400.03	WALLS-WALL COVERING	1 ALLOWANCE	2000.00	2000	
400.04	FLOOR-CARPET	450 SY	22.00	9900	
400.05	FLOOR-VINYL TILE	140 SF	1.50	210	
400.06	FLOOR-INSET CARPET	1 ALLOWANCE	1000.00	1000	
400.07	CEILING-	3740 SF	2.25	8415	
400.08	WINDOW COVERINGS	342 SF	3.25	1112	
					23417
500	MILLWORK				
500.01	KITCHEN CABINETS	28 LF	350.00	9800	
500.02	MAIL COUNTER & BOXES	14 LF	400.00	5600	
500.03	OFFICE ALCOVES COUNTERS	130 LF	100.00	13000	
500.04	WALL STORAGE	86 LF	150.00	12900	
500.05	PRESIDENT'S OFFICE	9 LF	250.00	2250	
500.06	WORKROOM	30 LF	200.00	6000	
500.07	DISPLAY	21 LF	300.00	6300	
500.08	SHELVING	30 LF	50.00	1500	
500.09	ADMIN. ASSISTANT	35 LF	300.00	10500	
					67850
600	ELECTRICAL				
600.01	FLUORSCENT LIGHTING	67 EA	175.00	11725	
600.02	INCANDESCENT DOWNLIGHTS	7 EA	125.00	875	
600.03	WALL OUTLETS	36 EA	150.00	5400	
600.04	DEDICATED WALL OUTLET	1 EA	250.00	250	
600.05	FLOOR OUTLETS	4 EA	300.00	1200	
600.06	TELEPHONE OUTLETS	9 EA	100.00	900	
600.07	FIRE/SECURITY SYSTEM	1 ALLOWANCE	10000.00	10000	
600.08	UPGRADE POWER PANEL	1 ALLOWANCE	3500.00	3500	
600.09	UNDERCOUNTER LIGHTS	47 EA	100.00	4700	
600.1	EXIT LIGHTS	6 EA	100.00	600	
					39150
700	PLUMBING				
700.01	KITCHEN SINK	1 EA	3000.00	3000	
					3000
800	HEATING/VENTILATING/A.C.				
800.01	ADDITIONAL ROOF UNIT	1 ALLOWANCE	5000.00	5000	
800.02	SECONDARY DISTRIBUTION	1 ALLOWANCE	3000.00	3000	
800.03	CONTROLS	1 ALLOWANCE	500.00	1000	
					9000
900	EQUIPMENT				
900.01	REFRIGERATOR	1 EA	600.00	1000	
900.02	MICROWAVE	1 EA	400.00	400	
900.03	GARBAGE DISPOSAL	1 EA	300.00	300	
900.04	WATER HEATER(INSTA-HOT)	1 EA	300.00	300	
900.05	DISHWASHER	1 EA	400.00	500	
900.06	PROJECTION SCREEN/MOTOR	1 EA	1600.00	1600	
					4100

```
                                          SUBTOTAL    $    199476
                              10% FOR CONTINGENCY.......      19948
                   10% CONTRACTOR'S OVERHEAD AND PROFIT..     21942
                                                            ------
                                              TOTAL    $    241365
```

Figure 7.1-2
Interiors Cost Budget

A12 PART/9'/1HR/LF TYPE 1		C12 PART/9'/LF TYPE 1		E12 SOUND BATTS/9'/LF		G12 FRAME/WELDED/EA. 3'X 9'		I12 FRAME/RACO/EA 3'X 9'		K12 ENTRY HDWE/EA NON-RATED		M12 INTERIOR HDWE/EA	
0	21.17	0	20.26	0	5.56	0	167.62	0	128.68	0	280.45	0	114.76
151	20.95	151	20.05	151	5.49	51	154.16	51	124.34	21	274.20	51	112.41
261	19.76	261	18.88	261	5.42	151	142.87	151	118.86	31	267.57	151	109.68

A19 PART/9'/1HR/LF A17-TYPE 2		C19 PART/9'/LF TYPE 2		E19 DOOR/EA 3'X 9'		G19 FRAME/WELDED/EA. 3'X 8'		I19 FRAME/RACO/EA 3'X 8'		K19 ENTRY HDWE/EA 20-MINUTE	
0	24.53	0	23.62	0	293.96	0	162.71	0	125.61	0	256.27
151	24.27	151	23.38	51	285.42	51	149.25	51	121.27	11	250.02
261	24.01	261	23.13	151	257.50	151	137.97	151	120.48	31	243.39

A26 PART/9'/1HR/LF TYPE 3		C26 PART/9'/LF TYPE 3		E26 DOOR/EA 3'X 8'	
0	32.92	0	32.01	0	251.99
151	32.56	151	31.66	51	243.45
261	32.19	261	31.31	151	234.54

* *

A36 CEILING TILE/SF INSTALL		C36 DUPLEX RECEPT/EA		E36 EXIT LIGHTS/EA		G36 PAINTING PART/CSF		I36 SPRINKLERS/EA RELOCATE ONLY		K36 CARPET/SY		M36 LIGHT FIXTURE NEW	
0	0.22	0	NA	0	NA	0	27.14	0	82.60	0	12.31	0	86.02
1001	0.20	6	NA	6	NA	13.59	25.96	10	64.90	1000	12.31	16	81.47
2001	0.185	16	108.97	16	206.46	23.5	23.60	100	64.90	5000	12.31	46	78.56

A43 CEILING TILE/SF 1 HR RATED		C43 PHONE OUTLET/EA		E43 COND & WIRE/SF		G43 PAINTING FRAMES/EA.		I43 SPRINKLERS/EA PROVIDE & INSTAL		K43 WINDOW COVRNG/EA		M43 LIGHT FIXTURE INSTALL ONLY	
0	0.85	0	26.24	0	0.00	0	27.14	0	100.30	0	34.00	0	34.93
1001	0.83	6	21.69	3001	0.00	6	25.96	10	73.75	1000	34.00	16	29.52
2001	0.81	16	18.93	8001	0.00	11	24.78	100	73.75	5000	34.00	46	26.40

A50 LIGHT HOOD/EA		C50 LIGHT SWITCH/EA		G50 PAINTING VINYL/SF		I50 HVAC/SF	
0	14.16	0	NA	0	10.09	0	0.50
100	14.16	6	NA	151	9.68	10	0.50
1000	14.16	151	57.50	261	9.15	100	0.50

* *

Figure 7.1-3
Unit Costs Spreadsheet

the various sections of your spreadsheet into groups to accommodate the requirements discussed in Steps 2 and 3 above. For example, the "upper left" portion of the template that you first see on your screen when you start the program may contain all the prompting and data entry cells for the cost variables.

Examples

Figures 7.1-1, 7.1-2 and 7.1-3 show three variations of cost budgeting. Figure 7.1-1 is a preliminary estimate for the remodel of a building lobby. It allowed the designer and developer to quickly see the bottom-line effect of various alternatives that were being considered during schematic design.

Figure 7.1-2 is an interior construction estimate using major cost parameters such as "partitions" and "electrical" and then breaking these down into individual building elements. Figure 7.1-3 shows one method for maintaining unit costs in a separate file. In this case, the contractor's prices varied with the quantities used so there could be as many as three prices for each item. This is an instance where conditional math capabilities are useful. The formula for figuring cost can be written so it retrieves one unit cost if the quantity is over a certain level and another unit cost if the quantity was something else.

Additional Tips

- For easier updating, place all the variables in one group near the "front" of the spreadsheet. Do not put a cost per square foot figure in a formula somewhere or a given percentage such as contractor's profit. When you first enter the data for a particular project you will only have to do it once. All the other formulas in the spreadsheet can then "call" the data from the one cell where it was first entered. This also makes it easier to do "what if" calculations.

- Except for very abbreviated estimates (those with a limited number of line items) try to keep unit costs in a separate spreadsheet if your software can retrieve data from different files. This way a number of different templates can retrieve the same cost figures. For instance, in your unit cost file the price per square foot of a masonry wall may be assigned to cell D47. Any time you do an estimate with this type of wall your program simply calls for the data in that location.

7.2

DETAILED COST ESTIMATING SOFTWARE

Section 7.1 discussed how to set up your own cost budgeting system using a simple spreadsheet system. For most architects and interior designers this is a perfectly adequate way to provide clients with initial estimates. An extreme level of accuracy is only needed by contractors who are actually bidding on or writing a contract for a specific project.

In both cases, however, the key to a good estimate is the unit cost information for each line item. This applies whether an architect is trying to budget dollars per square foot for a given roofing system or a contractor is including the base wage rates for a nonunion roofer in a given city as part of the overall cost of installing the same roof.

The use of a spreadsheet for cost budgeting assumed that you would be maintaining your own "mini-data base" of cost information gathered from contractor's quotes, pricing books like the *Dodge Construction Systems Costs,* previous bids and educated guesses. This section assumes that you want a larger, more accurate and consistently updated data base of unit cost data. Special application programs are available that allow you to generate more detailed cost estimates than those possible with a spreadsheet. The representative list at the end of this section includes software that contain cost data as part of the package and software that require the design firm to supply its own unit costs.

Basic Application Requirements

Many of the special cost estimating software packages are expensive, especially those that provide a continuously updated data base of unit prices. For this reason alone you should carefully review the available packages before buying so you get something that works for you. Keep the following points in mind when reviewing this type of software.

1. The software should provide the level of detail your firm most often requires. Some simply take the square footage, number of stories, geographical region and similar broad criteria and print out a list of ten to fifteen building parameters (such as foundations, HVAC, etc.) with their associated costs. Other software allows you to enter very detailed quantities of labor, material and equipment required and generates an estimate for that data much as a contractor would do in preparing a bid. If all you need is a preliminary budget then the first type will meet your needs.

2. In most cases the program should match your office's established method of estimating. This includes quantity units and how you add for overhead, profit, fees and other soft costs. Trying to force your office staff to follow a new estimating procedure may alienate them to the system.

3. Does the software include access to a unit cost data base that is complete, accurate and reliable? Of course, you will pay extra for this, but maintaining a continuously current cost data base yourself is nearly impossible. If you buy an applications program that requires you to enter your own data, make sure it is compatible with the quantity and type of information your office *can* maintain.

For instance, if you keep track of partitions costs based on a square foot basis and the software requires you to enter the costs of individual items like studs, wallboard and taping and finishing the package will be of little use to you.

4. The unit cost data base needs to be periodically updated. Six-month updating is about the minimum; quarterly is better. When buying software that includes unit costs find out how often it is updated and how extensive the changes are. If you decide to maintain your own costs you must commit yourself to the time and effort required to do it right.

5. Unit prices must reflect costs in the geographical areas in which you practice.

Additional Application Requirements

Extra features you may want to consider include:

1. The ability to access the system from a remote location through a modem. This is especially useful for client demonstrations or work sessions right in their office.

2. The ability of the software to accept actual bidding information so estimated versus actual prices can be compared. This is valuable to have for more accurate estimating on future jobs.

3. The ability to let more than one person work with the system at once. Of course, a multiuser system will cost more and may not be necessary for a small firm, but larger firms will find it useful.

Requirements of Software

Computer estimating programs should make the process easy. Some of the specific software features to look for include the following:

1. ease of use (Are you prompted for the required information without having to learn a complicated set of commands?)

2. minimum keyboard entries (Entering quantities and other variables is time consuming and error prone. The program should require as few keystrokes as possible.)

3. override capabilities (Can you enter a different labor rate or unit cost if the one included with the program is inappropriate for your project?)

4. ability to customize (Can you add special items to the data base that reflect unique aspects of projects you estimate?)

5. flexible report formats (You should be able to print out a summary estimate as well as a detailed breakdown of the entire project. Ideally, the kinds of reports you need to generate are built into the program.)

6. transportability (Can the software be run on several types of hardware.

In case you upgrade or change computers you shouldn't have to purchase a new program.)

Requirements of Hardware

There are no standard guidelines for this application since it depends on the software you purchase and whether or not there is a unit cost data base as part of the system. Some packages will operate with as little as 32K of RAM and one floppy disk while more sophisticated programs require 512K with a 40-megabyte hard disk. However, most of the systems architects and interior designers may want to use require from 64K to 128K of internal memory with two floppy disks. A fast dot-matrix printer is the only requirement for output.

Cost Variables

Like hardware, cost varies considerably. The prices of the software listed at the end of this section ranged from $600 to $17,000 at the time of this writing with most being in the $800 to $3,000 range. Most run on low-cost personal computers.

Additional Tips

- Be sure to talk to other design firms that are using the software to get their evaluation. If the vendor is reluctant to provide you with the names of its customers chances are you shouldn't buy that package.
- Make a commitment to learn and use the system after you buy it. Many times people who do construction cost estimating become fixed in their ways and resist change. As always, there must be encouragement and direction from top management.

Sources for More Information

The following is only a partial list of cost estimating programs available. The list is current at the time of this writing; you should refer to the directory and newsletter sources listed in Appendix C for current addresses and phone numbers and for program updates.

Programs That Have Unit Costs Provided by the Vendor

DESIGN ESTIMATOR
McGraw-Hill Cost Information Systems
P.O. Box 28
Princeton, NJ 08540

Data disks are available for ten regions in the United States and run on Apple or IBM computers. McGraw-Hill also offers various interactive data base cost estimating services at various levels of detail. Write to them for a complete description.

CACTES
E. F. Paynter & Associates, Inc.
6508 Westfield Boulevard
Indianapolis, IN 46220

ESTIMATOR
Disco-Tech/Morton Technologies
600 B Street
P.O. Box 1659
Santa Rosa, Ca 95402

ESTIMATOR PROGRAM-PERSONAL COMPUTER VERSION
Marshall and Swift
1617 Beverly Boulevard
Los Angeles, CA 90026

Produces reports of the estimated replacement and depreciated costs for up to 125 commercial, agricultural and residential occupancy types. Building description consists of 12 items and can include additional items described by the user. Cost includes building cost updates for a 12-month period.

CMS COST MANAGEMENT SYSTEM
Educol, Inc.
P.O. Box 726
San Luis Obispo, CA 93406

Microcomputer-based program with three levels of cost estimating: preliminary cost estimates, approximate quantities cost estimates and detailed quantities.

MICOS
Constech, Inc.
8615 Freeport Parkway
P.O. Box 610663
D.F.W. Airport, TX 75261

Micos is the most recent Orr Cost Management System that incorporates a cost data base of more than 25,000 detailed items, composite systems and buildings. Users may add to the data base or substitute their own.

PRELIMINARY PROJECT COST ESTIMATE
Micro Mode, Inc.
322 Greycliff Drive
San Antonio, TX 78233

This program produces a construction cost estimate broken down into 12 building systems, special building features and site and special outside work. Cost figures are based on Dodge, Means and Marshall & Swift data and cover locations in all 50 states.

Programs That Require the User to Provide Unit Costs

JOB COST & ESTIMATING PROGRAM
Computer Services
P.O. Box 702
Fairmont, N.C. 28340

Keeps track of job costs and allows estimation of similar jobs. Can track job costs for ten projects.

STAR
R. S. Means Co., Inc.
100 Construction Plaza
Kingston, MA 02364

General estimating program using the unit price method. The user must develop his or her own unit cost information.

7.3

FAST AND ACCURATE TENANT FINISH ESTIMATING

For any architect or interior designer involved with tenant finish work in commercial office buildings "over/under" sheets are an important part of the budgeting process. These cost estimates determine what amount of money a new tenant owes to the building owner *above* what the tenant is allowed or what *credit* the building owner must give to the tenant because all the build-out allowances are not used.

In practically all new office development, the developer (owner) figures in a cost allowance to finish out the lease space above the basic shell of the building. This is necessary to make the space attractive to potential tenants. Based on rentable square footage the developer allows a certain amount of partitions, doors, lights, switches and other basic components to make the space habitable so the tenant can move in without worrying about any construction.

The cost of this for the entire building is part of the overall pro forma economic study made before the building is constructed. For example, a tenant may be allowed, as part of the basic rent, one linear foot of partition for every 80 square feet of space leased. Any amount of partitioning used *above* this allowance is an extra cost the tenant must pay. Conversely, for some items, if the allowed quantity is not used the tenant receives a credit.

205

The tool used to figure the final, bottom line amount of credit or amount owed is the over/under sheet. In many cases, if the design professional is performing all or most of the tenant finish work on a building, he or she will complete the over/under sheet based on the space plan worked out with the tenant. This is used to give the tenant an idea of how much money will be owed to the building landlord or how much credit will be given, which in turn can be used by the tenant for additional construction items.

For a building with many tenants there is a great deal of mathematics to do, but most of it is repetitious and based on a few variables, namely the tenant's rentable square footage and the quantity of various items used: partitions, doors, lights, telephone outlets and so forth. The unit prices are fixed and are determined by the tenant finish contractor. Thus, figuring an over/under sheet is an important task, but one ideally suited for a computer application.

Basic Application Requirements

A spreadsheet is most appropriate for this application since most of the work is basic arithmetic. Both the tenant and building owner (or leasing agent) need to see an itemized list of the various standard construction items and the quantity used along with any extra upgrade items. The quantity allowed then needs to be converted to dollars using the allowances based on the amount of square footage the tenant is leasing. Finally, a bottom line extra or credit must be calculated.

Some owners like to see two separate sheets, one for the standard building allowances and one for special construction items. This can easily be accomplished by putting both on the same spreadsheet template and then selectively printing the two matrices on two sheets of paper.

Requirements of Software

Since this application is straightforward the software requirements are minimal. The program you select should have the following minimum characteristics:

1. the standard mathematical functions
2. the ability to vary column widths
3. the ability to add rows and columns at the end and in the middle of the matrix
4. a column formatting capability to allow right justification, decimal point location, comma location and percentages
5. relational functions such as "greater than," "less than" and "equal to" as well as "if-then-else" (This function is helpful if any dollar allowances are based on quantity. *If* a certain quantity is above a particular number *then* one price is used, *else* another price is used.)

206

Requirements of Hardware

RAM. Many stand-alone spreadsheet programs operate on hardware with a minimum amount of RAM (64K or less).

Disks. For many programs, a single disk drive is sufficient, but you will most likely want at least two.

Printer. A dot-matrix printer is the minimum requirement. For final printing to include in a report, you will want a daisywheel, laser or ink-jet printer.

Cost Variables

Hardware. A complete setup with two disk drives and a dot-matrix printer can be purchased for as little as $2,000 or less. If your office does a great deal of tenant finish work you may want to consider purchasing a separate computer for this kind of work. It can also be used for programming (Section 3.2), rentable area leasing studies (Section 3.4) and keynoting for tenant finish production drawings (Section 5.1).

Software. Spreadsheet programs may range from about $100 to $400.

Setup. Depending on the complexity of the template you want for this application, setup time may range from one to three hours.

Implementation Procedures

1. With the building owner or leasing agent, decide on the format that will work for the tenant, owner and tenant finish contractor since all three will need to review the document. Figure 7.3-1 illustrates one type of over/under sheet. In this case, an additional column was added for the total *dollar* allowance in addition to the quantity allowance. This provides the leasing agent and the client with a total figure of what the allowances are worth.

2. Obtain a copy of the lease work letter that describes the kinds and quantities of allowances available. Also, obtain the unit price schedule from the tenant finish contractor. This should include the building standard items as well as "upgrade" items. These upgrade items include such things as kitchen cabinet work, plumbing fixtures, vinyl wall covering and similar improvements. Although *all* tenants will not want these, many do, so the contractor usually develops "standard above-standard" costs to expedite cost estimates.

3. Following the instructions of your software set up the spreadsheet. Provide data entry spaces at the beginning for the tenant name, date, and the square footage of the lease. This is usually based on the rentable square footage rather than the usable square footage.

Since the unit prices and allowances will remain the same throughout the leasing process this is one instance where you can set up variable values *within*

207

Smith Office
Tenant allowance

Rentable sq. ft.: 3894
Date: 3/2/84

Item	Allowance	Unit Pr	Allowed	$ Allowance	Used	Over	Under	Extra	Credit
Partition A 1Side	1/80 SF	28.90	49	1,590.05	197	148	0	4,802.60	0.00
Partition A 2Side	1/80 SF	32.45	371	9,200.80	222	0	(149)	0.00	(3,695.20)
Partition B	1/10.5 SF	24.80							
Interior doors	1/300 SF	473.00	13	6,149.00	9	0	(4)	0.00	(1,892.00)
Entrance doors	1/1813 SF	841.60	2	1,683.20	1	0	(1)	0.00	(841.60)
Duplex outlet	1/150 SF	59.18	26	1,538.68	24	0	(2)	0.00	(118.36)
Telephone outlet	1/200	90.00	19	1,710.00	13	0	(6)	0.00	(540.00)
Wall switch	1/300 SF	92.50	13	1,202.50	15	2	0	185.00	0.00
Light fixture	1/83 SF	99.70	47	4,685.90	23	0	(24)	0.00	(2,392.80)
Exit lights	1/1290	121.00	3	363.00	3	0	0	0.00	0.00
HVAC satellite	1/150	85.00	26	2,210.00	24	0	(2)	0.00	(170.00)
Thermostat	1/744	75.00	5	375.00	6	1	0	75.00	0.00
Carpet, SY	As needed	16.00	433	6,928.00	433	0	0	0.00	0.00
Ceiling tile, SF	As needed	0.20	3,894	778.80	3,894	0	0	0.00	0.00
				38,414.90				5,062.60	(9,649.96)

```
                                      +++++++++++++++++++++++++++++++++++
Building standard                     + Total extra/credit:  -4,587.36 +
allowance per sq ft                   +++++++++++++++++++++++++++++++++++

> > > > >   $9.87
```

Figure 7.3-1
Over/Under Sheet

208

the formulas (rather than in a data entry area at the beginning of the spreadsheet) without too much trouble. Thus, if a tenant is allowed one light switch for every 90 square feet of rentable area, the number "90" can be part of the formula to figure number allowed by dividing 90 into the square footage.

If you want to use the same template for several different buildings, however, you will need to have formulas refer to values placed somewhere else in the spreadsheet. This way, by simply changing the per-square-foot allowances of the various constructions items once, the template is immediately ready for another job.

Additional Tips

- You can also keep a separate spreadsheet with a running total of various tenants' costs as the building leases. This is useful for the leasing agent and building owner. The tally can include the tenant's name, suite number, rentable square footage, lease start and finish date and amount of tenant allowance.

- Be sure to incorporate the unit price figures you get from the contractor into your firm's own data base of cost information that can be used for other budgeting (Section 7.1). Although the costs are based on larger quantities and other market factors, the information is useful for comparison purposes and to keep you current with changing prices in the local market.

7.4

SIMPLIFIED BID REVIEW AND ANALYSIS

One of the architect's responsibilities during the design process is to receive and analyze all bids. This includes checking for completeness, determining that all requirements have been met and reviewing the base bid and all alternates to help the client decide who really has the lowest, valid, *effective* construction cost proposal. This is often not easy because there may be several requested alternates as well as alternate proposals contractors make on their own. Occasionally, the apparent low bid will turn out to be higher than someone else's after all alternates are considered and you determine that every contractor is bidding on a slightly different interpretation of the scope of work.

A simple computer application can take much of the tedium out of analyzing bids. It can help you organize the various pieces of data you get from each contractor, and perform the mathematics quickly and accurately.

Basic Application Requirements

This application is essentially an extension of the bid tally forms many architects use now. You need a space to enter the base bid amounts and alternates of each contractor. In addition, there should be room for any voluntary alternates and comments the contractors make. Where a computer extends the value of such a form is in the analysis it is able to provide, comparing one bid to another and all the bids to the original estimate.

Requirements of Software

A spreadsheet program is perfectly suited for this application because most of the analysis involves a simple listing of the information and arithmetic comparison for analysis. The software you select for this application should have the following minimum characteristics:

1. the standard mathematical functions
2. the ability to vary column widths and the ability to add rows and columns at the end and in the middle of the matrix
3. a column formatting capability to allow right justification, decimal point location, comma location and percentages
4. the ability to print only selected portions of the matrix
5. the additional mathematical functions of percentage and "minimum" so you can easily find the low bid

Requirements of Hardware

RAM. Many stand-alone spreadsheet programs can operate on hardware with a minimum amount of RAM (64K or less). If you are thinking of buying an integrated software package you will need 128K, 256K or more, depending on the program.

Disks. For many programs, a single disk drive is sufficient, but you will most likely want at least two. A hard disk is desirable for faster operation of some of the integrated software packages.

Printer. A dot-matrix printer is the minimum requirement. For final printing to include in a letter or report to your client, you will want a daisywheel, laser or ink-jet printer. You will need a 132-column printer for this application unless your software and dot-matrix printer can produce compressed print. For jobs with six or more contractors you may need *both* a wide printer and compressed type.

Cost Variables

Hardware. A complete setup with two disk drives and a dot-matrix printer can be purchased for as little as $2,000 or less. A letter-quality printer will add about $1,500 to $2,500.

Software. Spreadsheet programs may range from about $100 to $400.

Setup. Depending on the complexity of the template you want for this application, setup time may range from two to four hours.

Data entry. Data entry is very fast. Simply enter the budget amount, project identifying information and the bid amounts from each submittal and you are ready for your analysis and a clearly organized printout of the results.

Implementation Procedures

1. Determine the form of your bid analysis sheet. You may want to follow an existing form you have, or set up an entirely new one. Your decisions must include *how* to tally the data extracted from the bids and *what kind* of analysis you want to perform. Figure 7.4-1 shows one kind of bid analysis form. In this example, "deduct" alternatives are separated from "add" alternatives because you want to start with the base bid (which is usually over budget) and see how far you can reduce it by using the alternatives. Some clients (and architects) prefer to have only deduct alternates. If this is the case simply delete the "add" alternates portion.

2. Leave enough room for the typical number of alternates your office uses. Some firms keep them to a minimum while others create a "shopping list" to choose from. If one bid analysis form uses only a few of many available rows, use your software's nonprint command to delete any blank rows to produce a more compact printout.

3. Following the instruction of your software, set up the template, including formulas and printing commands. You may set up any kind of analysis you think is useful. In the example, the high bids are compared to the low bid on both an actual dollar basis and a percentage basis. The software's "MINIMUM" math function is used to find the low bid and uses that as a basis for other calculations. The base bid is then reduced by the total of the deduct alternatives and the same comparison made. As in Figure 7.4-1, one contractor's bid is less than the low bid *after* the alternates are deducted.

A separate section is also included to compare the bids to the budgeted amount. Of course, you can extend the analysis to show any figures you want.

4. After bid opening, enter the various amounts from each contractor's proposal and perform the calculations. This gives an instant analysis for both you and your client. In the example, the comparison of the different bids is done separately from comparison to the budget. This way you can print a report for the contractors, leaving out the budget information, and another report for your client and in-house use with the budget data.

Additional Tips

- Use the columns of your spreadsheet for the bidders, with the various line items in rows. This way, you only have to use as many columns as you

BID ANALYSIS

Project name: Smith Office Bldg.
Project number: 8628
Bid Date: Nov. 12, 1986
Budget: 2,550,000.00

Item	Bidders		
	Acme Const. Co.	Hammerhead Co.	Lowball, Inc.
Addenda received?	Yes	Yes	Yes
Base bid	$2,774,500.00	$2,602,400.00	2,585,700.00
Amount over low bid	188,800.00	16,700.00	0.00
% over low bid	7.30%	0.65%	0.00%

No.	Deduct Alternates			
1	Substitute alum. windows	35,850.00	43,570.00	23,000.00
2	Delete patio paving	8,000.00	9,500.00	7,900.00
3	P.L. doors	3,900.00	4,750.00	3,700.00
	Total deducts	47,750.00	57,820.00	34,600.00
	Bid with all deducts	2,726,750.00	2,544,580.00	2,551,100.00
	$$ over low bid w/ deducts	182,170.00	0.00	6,520.00
	% over low bid w/ deducts	7.16%	0.00%	0.26%

	Add Alternates			
4	Marble entry floor	8,000.00	8,500.00	8,750.00
	Total adds	8,000.00	8,500.00	8,750.00

ANALYSIS			
Base bid amount over/under budget (+ =over, - =under)	224,500.00	52,400.00	35,700.00
% base bid over/under budget	8.80%	2.05%	1.40%
Base bid with deducts over/under budget	176,750.00	-5,420.00	1,100.00
% base bid with deducts over/under budget	6.93%	-0.21%	0.04%

Comments		Substituted non-spec. flooring	

Figure 7.4-1
Bid Analysis Form

212

have bidders and you can set the limits of printing to the last contractor in the list. You will have many more line items than bidders so this makes more efficient use of the vertical format of the sheet.

• Set up the formulas so you enter *deduct* numbers as positive values. This makes data entry a little faster since you do not have to enter a minus sign. When calculating the amount over or under the budget amount, arrange the arithmetic so that a positive figure indicates you are over budget and a negative figure shows you are under budget.

7.5

IMPROVED SERVICE WITH LIFE CYCLE COST ANALYSIS

Estimating an initial construction budget is only part of determining the true cost of a building project. Over the life of the building there are costs of operating it, paying the employees, taxes, short-term financing, repairs, replacement of major components, energy costs and dozens of others items. In fact, when the expenses of paying the employees who work in a building over a long period of time are considered, the first cost becomes a small fraction of the *total* cost. Life cycle cost analysis is a technique that allows you to consider various fiscal implications of a project over a period of time.

For the architect or interior designer, life cycle costing can help in the decision-making process by adding another dimension to the various criteria used during design. It can also benefit your firm's marketing effort by showing potential clients that you are as concerned with the "bottom line" as with any other aspect of design. In some cases, competence in life cycle costing is a requirement of clients, including state and federal agencies.

Life cycle cost analysis came to many design professionals' attention during the energy "crisis" of the early 1970s. With rapidly rising energy costs it became evident that extra money spent during construction quickly "paid off" by reducing yearly costs for fuel. Since then, more and more building owners and developers have seen this type of economic evaluation as a valuable part of the total development process, not only for making energy-related decisions, but also for other aspects of a project.

Life cycle cost analysis has many uses. It can be used to evaluate site location alternatives, building configurations and mechanical systems. It can also be used to assist with material selection, building component selection and such questions as whether to use an expensive first-cost daylighting configuration instead of standard artificial lighting. Variations of the technique can be used to calculate rates of return, breakeven points and payback periods.

It is beyond the scope of this section to detail all of the principles of life cycle costing, the myriad subtleties of its use, and the entire range of mathematical procedures often required. You should refer to the references listed at the end of this section for more information. However, this part of the chapter will describe the essentials of the technique and how you can use a microcomputer to set up cost models to improve your decision making. The variations of the basic approach and how a personal computer can be used to expedite the analysis are almost limitless. Once you understand the basic principals you can easily set up specific models for your practice and client's needs.

Basis Principles of Life Cycle Cost Analysis

The concept of life cycle costing is simple; it is the application of many variables and accuracy of assumptions that can get complicated. The technique allows you to consider *all* the relevant cost implications of a decision over a particular span of *time* with all the various costs reduced to their true worth at a given time. The last aspect is important. Life cycle costing allows for the time value of money; the fact that today's dollars are worth more than tomorrow's dollars and that money invested today will yield a return tomorrow. In life cycle costing the term "discounting" is used to account for this and the number is a percentage, called the discount rate.

The discount rate is used to manipulate the various costs over time to a single point so you can compare apples with apples. There are two basic methods. The first is to convert all costs to their "present worth" which is the value of money today. The other method is to spread all the costs equally over the life cycle you are considering. The number becomes the "equivalent uniform annual cost" and is useful when you want to look at approximately how much a facility will cost to operate over its life.

The percentage used for the discount rate depends on the type of analysis you are making and the preferences of your client. It is sometimes tied to the cost of borrowing money, the rate of return the client wants, or the return on an alternate investment.

The time span you consider is another important variable. The "life cycle" you select, like the discount rate, depends on many things. It may be tied to the actual expected "life" of the building, the loan period the owner has, how long the owner wants to keep the building before it is sold, the useful life of major components (like HVAC systems) or to tax considerations. Which period you select should be a joint decision between you and your client.

There are several types of costs that can be included in a life cycle cost analysis. Any particular analysis will not include *all* of them, but they serve as a checklist for developing what must be considered under a given condition. In some cases a particular cost will apply, but it will apply *equally* to all the alternatives so it can be excluded from the analysis.

The possible cost factors in a life cycle cost analysis include:

- *First Costs.* These are costs related to the initial construction of the building or item under analysis. If you are doing a present worth analysis, the first costs are used as is, without any discount rate adjustment.

- *Financing Costs.* Short-term financing costs, loan fees, and other kinds of charges related to borrowing money are included.

- *Operating and Maintenance Costs.* These include such things as daily cleaning and maintenance, fuel costs, building security, grounds maintenance and other utility costs.

- *Repair and Replacement Costs.* These costs are major repairs or modifications to a facility or building component that are foreseen. Planned replacement of a roof after ten years is an example of this type of cost.

- *Alteration and Improvement Costs.* These are planned costs associated with making changes to the facility to keep it functionally current.

- *Functional Use Costs.* These include the costs of the people working in the facility such as salaries and benefits. Functional use costs can also include taxes, insurance and other recurring costs related to the occupancy of the facility. They are sometimes considered by the designer because how a building is designed can affect its use.

- *Salvage Costs.* These are costs (or positive values if money can be gained in salvage) related to demolition during or at the end of the life cycle.

Basic Application Requirements

The value of a microcomputer in life cycle cost analysis is its ability to perform complex mathematics quickly and accurately, and to allow changing the variables to analyze various options. A computer also makes it easy to produce consistent, organized reports for review by you and your client. For most analyses, a good spreadsheet program is ideal for this application.

One warning: Although a computer makes the arithmetic easy, it cannot make the correct assumptions, select the proper cost factors, determine the best discount rate or check to make sure your procedures are accurate. If you are not familiar with life cycle costing, study the references listed at the end of this section.

Additional Application Requirements

If you set up a spreadsheet to track costs of several alternatives year by year, an integrated software package with graphics capabilities is useful to give you a visual picture of your numbers. It is also possible to write your own program in BASIC or some other high-level language to solve a specific problem that includes variables other than time and money. Examples are programs that calculate life cycle energy costs based on insulation values, fuel costs, building orientation and other factors.

Requirements of Software

The spreadsheet program you select for this application should have the following minimum characteristics:

1. the standard mathematical functions including exponential functions (Since some of the formulas are lengthy, make sure the software can handle all your requirements. If not, you can sometimes get around this by setting up a "scratch pad" section on your spreadsheet to do preliminary calculations that are then used to put in the final formula. You thus reduce one very long formula to two shorter ones.)
2. the ability to vary column widths
3. a column formatting capability to allow right justification, decimal point location, comma location and percentages.
5. the ability to print only selected portions of the matrix
6. the ability to retrieve data from other files

Requirements of Hardware

RAM.   Many stand-alone spreadsheet programs can operate on hardware with a minimum amount of RAM (64K or less), but if you want integrated software to allow you to draw graphs of your data you will need 128K, 256K or more, depending on the program.

Disks.   For many programs, a single disk drive is sufficient, but you will most likely want at least two. A hard disk is desirable for faster operation of some of the integrated software packages.

Printer.   A dot-matrix printer is the minimum requirement. For final printing to include in a report to your client, you may want a daisywheel, laser or ink-jet printer.

Plotter.   If your program can produce charts from the data you will need a plotter capable of supporting the output.

Cost Variables

Hardware.   A complete setup with two disk drives and a dot-matrix printer can be purchased for as little as $2,000 or less.

Software.   Spreadsheet programs may range from about $100 to $400.

Setup.   Depending on the complexity of the template you want for this application, setup time may range from four to sixteen hours. Some life cycle cost analysis formats can be very complicated and it may take you several days to design the format, test the formulas and make revisions.

Life Cycle Cost Formulas

As stated in the first part of this section, life cycle costing requires that you convert the various costs to one point in time, either current costs (present worth) or recurring annual costs. You can also convert a single present amount or several annual amounts to a *future* cost, but this is not used as much as the other methods. When you perform the calculations manually, it is easier to use tables of factors based on the formulas than it is to substitute actual values. You simply find the factor for the number of years in the life cycle and a given discount rate and multiply it by the dollar amount you are analyzing.

When using a spreadsheet, however, it is necessary (and more flexible) to use formulas. You avoid having to interpolate between factors in an abbreviated table. Figure 7.5-1 shows the formulas used to convert costs to present worth and present and future costs to annual amounts. The single present worth (SPW) finds how much money invested today in a single lump sum (P) would earn at some specified time in the future (F). The uniform present worth (UPW) tells you how much a series of uniform annual payments is worth in today's dollars. The modified uniform present worth (UPW*) is similar to the UPW, but takes into account the affect of uniformly escalating annual payments (or inflation) such as with rising energy costs.

The uniform capital recovery (UCR) converts a known present cost to annual payments. This is similar to a home loan where you borrow a given amount today and repay it over a number of years at a constant interest rate. The uniform sinking fund (USF) takes a future amount and determines how much each annual payment will have to be to reach that amount at the end of the life cycle.

Figure 7.5-1 also includes a spreadsheet formula for each of the equations using the familiar one-line format required by all programs and using the arithmetic operators of "+" for addition, "−" for subtraction, "*" for multiplication, "/" for division and "^" for an exponent. References to other cells in the spreadsheet are given in the format [x,y] where x is the row and y is the column. The actual numbers refer to arbitrary cells used for the example. Your spreadsheet program may use different cell referencing so change them accordingly if you use the formulas. If you are using the same formula in several places you will want to use relative references rather than specific cell locations. If so, follow the instructions of your software on how to do this.

Examples

There are many possible formats for a life cycle cost spreadsheet depending on what you are analyzing, whether you are looking at present worth costs or

217

Single Present Worth   (SPW)

$$P = F \left[\frac{1}{(1+i)^n} \right]$$

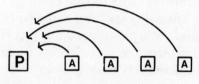

P = [34,2]*(1/((1+[11,3])^[34,3]))

Uniform Present Worth   (UPW)

$$P = A \left[\frac{(1+i)^n - 1}{i(1+i)^n} \right]$$

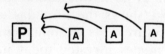

P = [26,2]*(((1+[11,3])^[10,3]-1)/([11,3]*(1+[11,3)^[10,3]))

Uniform Present Worth Modified for Escalation   (UPW*)

$$P = A \left[\frac{1+E}{i-E} \left[1 - \left(\frac{1+E}{1+i} \right)^n \right] \right]$$

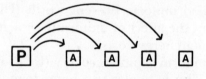

P = [30,2]*((1+[30,3])/([11,3]-[30,3]))*(1-(((1+[30,3])/(1+[11,3]))^[10,3]))

Uniform Capital Recovery   (UCR)

$$A = P \left[\frac{i(1+i)^n}{(1+i)^n - 1} \right]$$

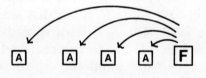

A = [57,2]*(([11,3]*((1+[11,3]^[10,3]))/(((1+[11,3])^[10,3])-1))

Uniform Sinking Fund   (USF)

$$A = F \left[\frac{i}{(1+i)^n - 1} \right]$$

A = [63,2]*([11,3]/(((1+[11,3])^[10,3])-1))

P = Present sum of money
F = Future sum of money
A = End of period payment or receipt for n periods
i = Discount rate (interest rate)
n = Number of periods (years)
E = Escalation rate

Figure 7.5-1
Life Cycle Cost Formulas

Life Cycle Cost Study
August 16, 1987

```
=================================================================
[              Project: Smith Office Bldg.                      ]
[             Project #: 8721                                   ]
[          Item Analyzed: Exterior wall system                 ]
[Alternate Description: Porcelain panel system 'B'             ]
[                                                              ]
[                                                              ]
=================================================================
```

```
          > > >      20  : Enter life cycle in years
          > > > 0.1200  : Enter discount rate in decimal format
```

```
=================================================================
     Variables         LCC Items          Formula      Present
               Years                        used         Worth
  $ $ $         or %
-----------------------------------------------------------------
                    FIRST COSTS             none
   $450,000           Construction costs                450,000
    $31,500           Add. mtl. framing                  31,500

                    FINANCING COSTS          UPW
                      none

                    O & M COSTS--uniform     UPW
    $7,000            Window washing                     52,286


                    O & M COSTS--inflated   UPW*
    $5,000   0.0350   Extra energy costs                 48,324


                    REPAIR & REPLACE COSTS   SPW
   $38,000      10    Replace sealant                    12,235
                      in 10 years


                    ALTERATION/IMPROVEMENT   SPW
                      none

                    SALVAGE/DISPOSAL COSTS   SPW
                      none

-----------------------------------------------------------------
                    TOTAL PRESENT WORTH   > > >          594,345
```

Figure 7.5-2
Life Cycle Cost Analysis

annual costs and how detailed you want to be. Figure 7.5-2 shows a simple setup for studying present worth costs of an exterior wall system.

In the example, one alternative is examined. Other alternatives are examined by substituting different costs for the variables. You can also set up the spreadsheet so all alternatives can be printed on one piece of paper. The example shows a format that can be set up once and reused for any number of analyses for present worth. For this particular example, some of the life cycle cost items were not used because they were not appropriate for this particular study.

At the top of the form are places to enter the life cycle period under study as well as the discount rate. Since a different percentage is used for the modified present worth cost (UPW*) the entry is made next to the line item rather than at the top of the page. The same is done for the years with the line items of repair and replacement, alteration and improvement and salvage and disposal. These are usually not the same as the life cycle for other calculations so putting them next to the costs to which they pertain avoids confusion. The total dollars used for each type of cost is likewise entered on the same line.

If you wanted to set up a standard form for many types of life cycle studies, another screen could contain the numbers and formulas for figuring annual costs. When you had all the information ready, you would simply enter the numbers in the appropriate places, have the computer calculate and print only that part of the template required to show the results.

Additional Tips

- Don't make a life cycle cost analysis more complicated than it has to be. First consider the alternatives that have the most significant cost consequences. These are usually first costs as well as any figures that are subject to compounding or inflation such as financing costs, rising energy costs, salaries and the like.

- Consider the costs that you as a designer have control over. One obvious example of this is the set of design decisions affecting the energy consumption of the building.

- A computer printout always looks precise. Don't give the false impression of precision by using decimals. Have your program round off to at least the nearest dollar.

Sources for More Information

The American Institute of Architects. *Life Cycle Cost Analysis: A Guide for Architects.* Washington: The American Institute of Architects, 1977.

Brown, Robert J., and Yanuck, Rudolph R. *Life Cycle Costing: A Practical Guide for Energy Managers.* Atlanta, GA: Fairmount Press, 1980.

————. *Introduction to Life Cycle Costing.* Atlanta, GA: Fairmont Press; Englewood Cliffs, NJ: Prentice Hall, Inc., 1985.

Grant, E.L., and Ireson, W. Grant. *Principals of Engineering Economy.* New York: The Ronald Press, 1970.

Haviland, David S. *Life Cycle Cost Analysis 2: Using it in Practice.* Washington: The American Institute of Architects, 1978.

Isola, Alphonse Dell, and Kirk, Stephen J. *Life Cycle Costing for Design Professionals.* New York: McGraw-Hill, 1981.

————. *Life Cycle Cost Data.* New York: McGraw-Hill, 1983.

Marshall, Harold E., and Ruegg, Rosalie T. *Energy Conservation in Buildings: An Economics Guidebook for Investment Decisions, NBS Handbook 132.* Washington, DC: U.S. Government Printing Office, May, 1980.

————. "Life-Cycle Costing Guide for Energy Conservation in Buildings." In *Energy Conservation Through Building Design,* edited by Donald Watson, pp. 161–181. New York: McGraw-Hill, Inc., 1979.

Smith, G.W. *Engineering Economy: Analysis of Capital Expenditures, 2nd ed.* Ames, Iowa: Iowa State University Press, 1977.

CHAPTER 8

Building Income
with Facility Management
Services

As the discipline of facility management matures, the architect's and interior designer's potential for expanded service increases. Many very large corporations have had facility management departments for a long time (although not always under that name) to control large quantities of space, furniture and equipment. It is unlikely that any but the very large design firms will capture this particular market. There are, however, innumerable businesses that need some type of facility management assistance, but have neither the staff nor the expertise to do it themselves.

Since the computer can provide the tool to easily handle the quantity and type of data involved with facility management, you may want to consider this service as a way to expand your business and your profits. It is also an excellent way to extend your services for existing clients who have an ongoing building program. In this chapter you will find detailed instructions for implementing various facility management services with computers. Section 8.3 also discusses how to use sophisticated programs that integrate all the various facility management tasks including CAD.

8.1

HOW TO ORGANIZE THE SPACE INVENTORY

In nearly all cases, facility management begins with an accounting of what a company already has—buildings, furniture and equipment. This accounting serves as a baseline from which other decisions concerning expansion, consolidation, reuse, purchasing and disposal are made. However, many companies hire architects, interior designers or space-planning firms to create new quarters for them without even knowing what they currently have and how it is being used. This section

223

describes how to start the inventory by accounting for space. Section 8.2 details a method for keeping track of furniture and equipment. Together, these form two of the key elements of facility management.

Performing a space inventory can either be a valuable first step in programming, or can be marketed as a special service. Either way, it serves several vital functions for your client.

First, it presents an organized list of current space use so efficiency can be determined. For instance, a company may find that the circulation factor for their facility type is well above the average and that more employees can be accommodated without leasing more space.

Second, it forms the basis of developing space standards. These standards can then be used for programming a new facility or expanding an existing one. They can also be used to equitably distribute space among employees of equal job function, title or status in an existing office.

Third, an inventory analysis by a designer can assist in determining the usable and rentable area needed for leasing new space. Quite often, a business doesn't know exactly how much *rentable* space is required to accommodate their operation before they sign the lease and commit themselves to more costly square footage than they need.

Performing space and furniture inventories also benefits the architect or interior designer. It is a good marketing tool to show potential clients that you can help save them money. As you complete several inventories you develop a data base of information concerning typical efficiencies, areas per employee, typical space standards and similar data that further enhance your firm's credibility.

Basic Application Requirements

This application helps your client take a look at what *already exists* as opposed to what *should* exist. Determining what *should* be is part of programming and is discussed in Sections 3.2 and 3.3. However, an inventory is an excellent way to begin the programming process to provide raw data for analysis.

For this application you need to survey each space and measure it. In addition, each space should be assigned a room name (or position title such as "accountant"), a room number (if it already doesn't have one), a person's name if it is occupied and a department or group name. You may also want to give each space a workstation type if one already exists. The data you collect will then have to be manipulated to give department area totals, circulation factors and other ratios.

Additional Application Requirements

Specific application programs are available that integrate inventory functions with sophisticated graphics. These are described in more detail in Section 8.3.

Requirements of Software

Either a spreadsheet or data base management program can be used for this application, but because of the tally and analysis functions required, a spreadsheet is easier and quicker for small to medium-size facilities, less than about 50,000 square feet or for buildings with many spaces (such as offices). More square footage can be handled for facilities with fewer, but larger spaces (such as manufacturing plants, schools, etc.). Section 8.2 discusses how to use a data base management system for conducting and maintaining furniture inventories. If you want to use a DBMS for a space inventory the procedure is similar.

The spreadsheet program you select for this application should have the following minimum characteristics:

1. the standard mathematical functions as well as the functions of "count," "average," "mean," "minimum/maximum," "variance" and "standard deviation" (These are useful for simple statistical analysis of the data such as finding the average square footage of existing office size.)
2. the ability to add rows and columns at the end and in the middle of the matrix
3. a column formatting capability to allow right justification, decimal point location, comma location and percentages as well as the ability to vary column widths
4. the ability to print only selected portions of the matrix
5. the ability to retrieve data from other files
6. relational functions such as "greater than," "less than," and "equal to" as well as "if-then-else"
7. the ability to sort numerically and alphabetically based on defined rows or columns
8. the ability to print in compressed format (Your printer must also have this capability. It is useful to print a wide spreadsheet on 8½ × 11 paper for inclusion into standard-sized reports. The alternate is to use 132 column-wide paper and make a photocopy reduction.

Requirements of Hardware

RAM. Many stand-alone spreadsheet programs can operate on hardware with a minimum amount of RAM (64K or less), but if you want integrated software to allow you to draw graphs of your data you will need 128K, 256K or more, depending on the program.

Disks. For many programs, a single disk drive is sufficient, but you will most likely want at least two. A hard disk is desirable for faster operation of some of the integrated software packages.

Printer. A dot-matrix printer is the minimum requirement, but for final printing to include in a programming report, you will want a daisywheel, laser or ink-jet printer. You will find it useful to have a printer that can print "compressed type" so you can fit larger spreadsheets onto standard-size paper.

Plotter. If your program can produce charts from the data you will need a plotter capable of supporting the output.

Cost Variables

Hardware. A complete setup with two disk drives and a letter-quality printer can be purchased for as little as $3,000 or less. A ten-megabyte hard disk drive will add about $800 to $1,300.

Software. Spreadsheet programs range from about $100 to $400.

Setup. Depending on the complexity of the template, setup time may range from two to eight hours.

Implementation Procedures

1. Decide what data and analysis you need to have when the inventory is complete. Some clients will simply require a listing of existing spaces with areas and a circulation factor calculated while others may want much more detail such as a separate listing of all "offices" or "conference rooms" with the minimum and maximum size, average, standard deviation and other statistical figures. Most client needs should fall somewhere in between these two extremes.

2. Based on the needs developed in Step 1, decide on the overall organization of the information you will gather and the format for the spreadsheet. There are two general methods you can use depending on your preferences and the capabilities of your software. See Figure 8.1-1. The first method sets up several separate spreadsheets as *files*. The first file type is a "worksheet" for each department where you list the spaces, names and sizes and calculate the areas. See Figure 8.1-3. The second file type is a summary of the totals and an analysis sheet. See Figure 8.1-4.

The second method puts all the data, summary and analysis on one large spreadsheet as a single file. Data is transferred from cell to cell as required and separate reports are developed by printing only within certain row and column boundaries.

The single file method is better for smaller jobs. Setting up formulas to get information from one cell to another is a little more convenient. The price you pay is that this method is more difficult to set up because you have to carefully think through how rows and columns are arranged so you can print selected por-

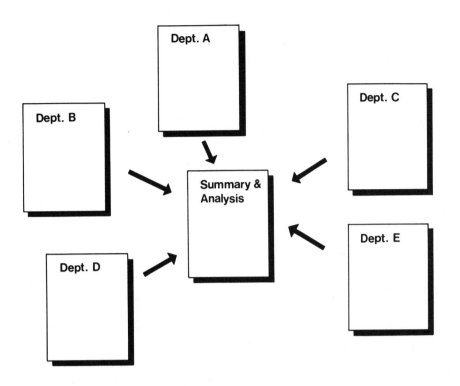

Method 1
Multiple Files

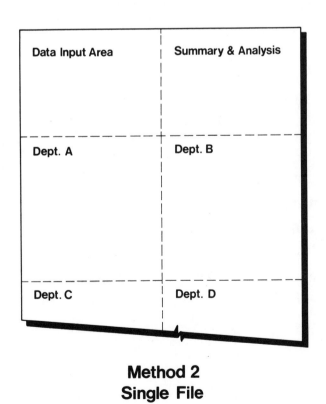

Method 2
Single File

227

Figure 8.1-1
Options for Developing Space Inventory

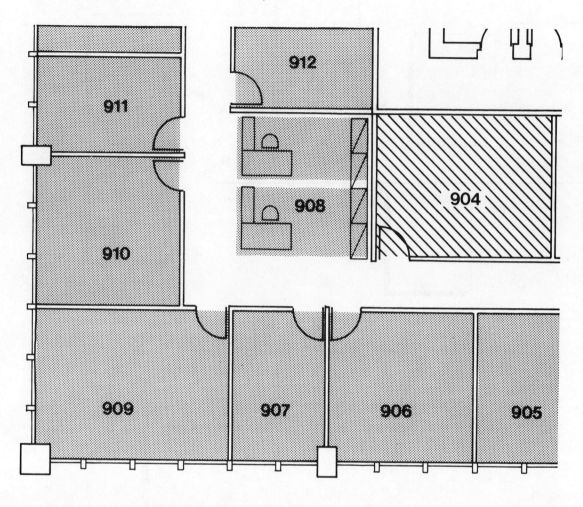

Assignable

Common Areas

Circulation

Figure 8.1-2
Space Inventory Floor Plan

```
SPACE INVENTORY WORKSHEET
Department:  Controller
Date: November 18, 1986
  Note: Does not include circulation


================================================================
Assigned areas:

Space                  Name        Room #   W      L     Area
----------------------------------------------------------------
Controller             Smith, P.    909   14.50  19.75   286
Secretary              Evans, S.    908    6.50  13.00    85
Int. Auditor--Mgr.     French, D.   910   14.50  14.25   207
Auditor 1              Smith, B.    907   14.50   9.50   138
Auditor 2              Jones, Q.    911   14.50   9.50   138
Word processor         Segal, M.    908    6.50  13.00    85
Accountant 1           Frost, S.    906   14.50  14.25   207
Accountant 2           Towne, A.    905   14.50   9.50   138
Accountant 3           Dover, B.    904   14.50   9.50   138
Accountant 4           Jones, A.    903   14.50   9.50   138
Accountant 5           Future       902   14.50   9.50   138
Accts. Payable 1       Swin, C.     912   14.00  12.25   172
Accts. Payable 2       Gary, T.     913   14.00  12.25   172
Data entry 1           Newman, N.   914    8.25   9.00    74
Data entry 2           Beller, D.   915    8.25   9.00    74
Data entry 3           Future       916    8.25   9.00    74
                                                           0
                                                       =======
Total Assigned Area                                     2,261
   Ave. Area for department                               141


Common Areas:

Space                           Room      W      L     Area
----------------------------------------------------------------
Library                          927   14.25  12.25    175
Conference room                  904   14.00  17.75    249
Visiting auditors room           935    8.00  10.25     82
                                                          0
Acct. files, legal               918   15.25  20.50    313
Acct. files, letter              919    9.75  12.75    124
Legal files, legal               922   12.50  14.75    184
                                                          0
Computer                         925   15.75  20.00    315
                                                          0
Storage room                     926    8.75  12.25    107
                                                          0
                                                      =======
                                                       1,549
================================================================

DEPARTMENT TOTAL                                        3,809
```

Figure 8.1-3
Space Inventory Worksheet

How to Organize the Space Inventory

```
EXISTING SPACE SUMMARY AND ANALYSIS
ABC Corporation
Date:  November 18, 1986


Number of employees:            88
BOMA usable:                31,225
Existing rentable Sq. Ft.   32,167


============================================================================
Space                       Area      Remarks
----------------------------------------------------------------------------
Executive group            4,327
Treasurer                    850
Controller                 3,809
Insur. & Employee Benefit  1,252
Industrial relations         435
Minerals exploration       4,327      U.S. operations only
Legal                        983
Traffic                      832
Environ. control           2,350
Public relations             528

General use spaces         2,955      Not off-site storage

----------------------------------------------------------------------------
Total assignable          22,648
Circulation (measured)     7,920
                        ===========
   TOTAL 'actual usable'  30,568

Circulation factor         0.259      Circulation/'actual usable'

============================================================================

BOMA usable               31,225      Includes walls, columns, etc.
Current rentable          32,167      Based on lease
U/R Ratio                  0.971

Usable efficiency          0.725      Total assignable/BOMA usable
Usable area/person           355      BOMA usable per person
Assigned area/person         257

BOMA/ 'actual usable'     1.0215

============================================================================
```

Figure 8.1-4
Existing Space Summary and Analysis

230

tions and not overlap incompatible rows and columns. For example, if you "stack" the analysis area over the summary area a column for one may need to be eight characters wide while a column below may need to be 20 characters wide.

If your software can retrieve data from one spreadsheet file and put it in a selected cell or range of cells in another the multiple file method is preferable. This gives much more flexibility since you can use as many "worksheets" as the size of the project dictates. Simply copy the basic template as many times as necessary, one for each department or functional grouping.

3. Obtain an accurate floor plan of the facility you are surveying. Use this to identify each space in the inventory and as a record of what you measured. Figure 8.1-2 shows a partial floor plan of an office and the various areas measured. Note that several specific types of area are differentiated. Rooms occupied with a person are measured and called "assigned" areas. Workstations in open areas, such as secretarial desks, are also called assigned areas and are measured according to the space devoted to that person, usually an imaginary rectangle defined by the desk, typing return and any file or other furniture within that person's work area.

Common areas such as conference rooms, libraries, storage rooms, and the like are listed separately, either as part of a department's space as shown in Figure 8.1-3 or as part of a separate worksheet you might call "common areas." These would include spaces that are shared by the entire facility, not just one department such as reception areas, lunchrooms, coatrooms and so forth.

4. Measure each room. If the drawing you have is accurate enough you may be able to take the measurements directly off of it. If not, you will have to field measure. In either case, an on-site check should be made to verify existing conditions. If you have a portable computer the measurements, room names and numbers can be entered while you are on site. Otherwise, note the information on a plan for data entry later.

Notice that this type of field measurement (or drawing measurement) does not take into account partition thicknesses, columns or other miscellaneous items that take up floor space, but that are not usable area. However, in terms of leasing or building a new facility, this space is considered *usable* area and should be accounted for. You can do this by taking an overall measurement of the facility (either on site or from accurate drawings). For office space the measurement should be taken from the inside face of the exterior walls to the office side of the corridor walls. This measurement is consistent with the Building Owners and Managers Association (BOMA) *Standard Method for Measuring Floor Area in Office Buildings.* (Also ANSI standard Z65.1) This figure is listed as "BOMA usable" in Figure 8.1-4.

For smaller facilities with few rooms, the difference between the total assignable square footage with circulation and BOMA usable is negligible. As the facility becomes larger and more spaces are divided by fixed partitions it can make a difference. In either case, it is a good idea to have both numbers. By dividing the BOMA usable by the "actual" usable (including circulation) you can establish a ratio that approximately reflects how much additional area you may need to add to any new programmed area. You also need the BOMA usable square footage to calculate the usable/rentable ratio.

5. Enter the measurements on the spreadsheet template you have set up. The computer can do the area calculations, summary and any additional figuring you have established. If you have used the multiple file method and your software can sort, each department worksheet can be arranged according to room number, alphabetically by name of occupant or any way that is most useful to you and your client.

Additional Tips

- If your office does much of this type of work for clients, you may want to develop two or three separate spreadsheet templates to accommodate different sizes and complexities of facilities.

- Establish a consistent method of measuring various elements before you start. Open area workstations, large, free-standing equipment, banks of file cabinets and similar items are particularly troublesome since the line between the space dedicated to the assigned area and general circulation is not always clear.

Sources for More Information

Standard Method for Measuring Floor Area in Office Buildings
(ANSI Z65.1)

Building Owners and Managers Association International
1221 Massachusetts Avenue, N.W.
Washington, DC 20005

8.2

HOW TO MAINTAIN FURNITURE INVENTORIES

With the space inventory (Section 8.1), the furniture and equipment inventory form the basis of a sound facility management program. Like buildings, furniture and equipment represent a substantial capital investment to a company and keeping track of their value, condition and location makes economic sense.

There are several reasons for a company to keep a good inventory of its furniture and equipment. There is the obvious accounting function for the purposes of taxes and insurance. Inventories also assist in developing purchasing strategies and long-term capital investments by giving management an indication of existing quantities and condition of these items. An itemized count of furniture is helpful during a move as well. Each piece can be reviewed for reuse or disposal and moving labels printed with the existing location and the new location. Finally, there is always the matter of equitable distribution of furniture among employees. An inventory can help alleviate this problem by listing the quantities of each type so the facility manager can make informed decisions.

Offering a furniture inventory service can be a bonus for an architectural or interior design firm. Design firms can offer the service as a way of initiating extra business or as part of a programming assignment. The information is required anyway since very few clients will discard *every* piece of furniture and purchase new items.

Basic Application Requirements

This application requires the collection and maintenance of a wide range of information. It needs to be organized separately from the space inventory because of the differences between the two. Some of these differences include:

1. Furniture and equipment is depreciated while space is not. The tax implications are significant.
2. Furniture and equipment is dynamic. It is moved around, lost, traded, and damaged.
3. Furniture and equipment is bought, retired and replaced more often than buildings or space and is therefore more difficult to keep track of.
4. There is a larger quantity of furniture and equipment items than spaces.
5. Furniture (more than one piece) is assigned to a space but space is not assigned to a piece of furniture. This relative position of one to another is important is setting up computer data base management systems.

Because most of the data collected on furniture is qualitative rather than quantitative and because very little mathematics needs to be performed, a data base management system (DBMS) is required rather than a spreadsheet. A DBMS is also required because of the large amount of furniture found in even a small company. Only a DBMS can handle the quantity of records required and allow them to be easily updated.

A file management type of data base management system can keep track of furniture in most applications. If you want to tie in your space inventory with furniture and equipment you will need a relational data base management system. If you are not familiar with these types of software refer to Appendix A, Fundamentals of Data Base Management Systems.

Additional Application Requirements

Furniture and equipment inventories can be part of computer-aided design if the software has the ability. Most large CAD systems have this capability as well as a few low-cost systems. With it, you can assign attributes to a graphic element on the screen, such as a desk. These "attributes" are the same as DBMS data fields in a record. So, for the data base record of the "desk" seen on the screen, the attributes might be such things as size, manufacturer, purchase data and so forth. You can then query the data base or print out reports using the attributes sorted in any way you like.

Requirements of Software

The following are some of the specific software requirements you will need to successfully implement this application. Refer to Appendix A, Fundamentals of Data Base Management Systems, for a complete description of these and other criteria for selecting a DBMS.

1. For a file management system the program should allow at least 30 fields per record. There is a great deal of information that can be assigned to a piece of furniture or equipment so the software should not limit you in this area.
2. For a relational data base management system you will need at least three files open at one time. This would allow you to keep one file for the room to which the furniture was assigned and two files for different kinds of data on the furniture.
3. It is preferable to be able to index on all the data fields in the record. If this is not possible, you should have at least ten indexable fields.
4. The software should allow you to sort on several key fields together instead of just one. For example, you may want a list sorted first by department, then by furniture type, then by age.
5. In addition to numeric and alphanumeric field types the software should have date format fields.
6. Since this application can become complex and each record lengthy, the program should allow more than one "screenfull" of information per record.
7. The program must have flexible methods of querying the data base, both on screen and in printed reports. This includes relational queries, Boolean searches and partial string searches.
8. The program must have a flexible report generator since you will want to print out results in various ways. For a relational data base management

system this includes being able to access more than one file at a time for report generation.

9. The program must have at least basic four-function arithmetic calculation capability. For reports you will need to perform counts of furniture types, add up current values and perform similar simple calculations.

Requirements of Hardware

RAM. Many file management systems will work with as little as 48K of RAM. Some relational data base management programs operate with as little as 64K of RAM with the more sophisticated ones requiring 128K or more.

Disks. You should have at a minimum two disk drives, one for the program and one for your data. Since this application can require a great deal of storage you should estimate your needs prior to buying a system. Hard disks have the advantages of more storage space as well as faster access time, an important consideration when using a FMS or RDBMS.

Printer. Since you will want reports produced quickly in house, but will also want letter-quality output for reports and client use, you should consider having both a dot-matrix printer and daisywheel printer, or a laser or ink-jet printer.

Cost Variables

Hardware. A complete setup with two disk drives and a letter-quality printer can be purchased for as little as $3,000 or less. A ten-megabyte hard disk drive will add about $800 to $1,300.

Software. Simple file management programs range from under $100 to $400 with a few costing more than $400. Relational data base management programs range from about $400 to over $1,000, but with many very good programs under $800.

Setup. Setup costs depend on the complexity of your application. A simple file management system will take from one to two hours to set up while a more complex RDBMS may take from eight to twenty hours. Keep in mind that much of this setup time will include thinking through your method of maintaining the data and reviewing it with your client.

Data entry. Performing the inventory and keyboarding the information will take a considerable amount of time. You should negotiate an hourly rate for this service if at all possible. The big advantage to your client is that once the initial work is complete, updating and adding to the data base is easy.

Implementation Procedures

1. Decide what information, analysis and report formats you will need when the initial inventory is complete. Of course, this should be done in consultation

with your client since he or she will have a better idea of long-term needs. If the inventory is only going to form the basis for programming you will only require a listing of the furniture, its size, what space and department it is assigned to and whether or not it will be reused or discarded. For ongoing facility management you will need more extensive information and more flexible reporting.

2. Following the instruction of your data base management system set up the data entry screens, indexes, report formats and other files as required. The data fields you set up will depend on your work in step one, but you may want to consider the following list as possible furniture and equipment attributes.

item code number (one you assign to uniquely identify the item)

description (for example, "side chair," "four-drawer lateral file" or "desk, executive, with return")

manufacturer

manufacturer's name of the item

manufacturer's serial number

date

photo number (It is helpful to keep a photographic record.)

size

color/finish

condition (This can be descriptive text or based on a coding system you devise.)

department assigned to

person assigned to

location (room number, floor and building as required)

reuse(?)

refinish(?)

discard(?)

furniture or equipment(?) (useful for sorting purposes)

electrical requirements (if equipment requires it)

heat output (if heat-producing equipment)

proposed location (for moving coordination)

original cost

current value

replacement cost

A typical data entry screen for this application is shown in Figure 8.2-1.

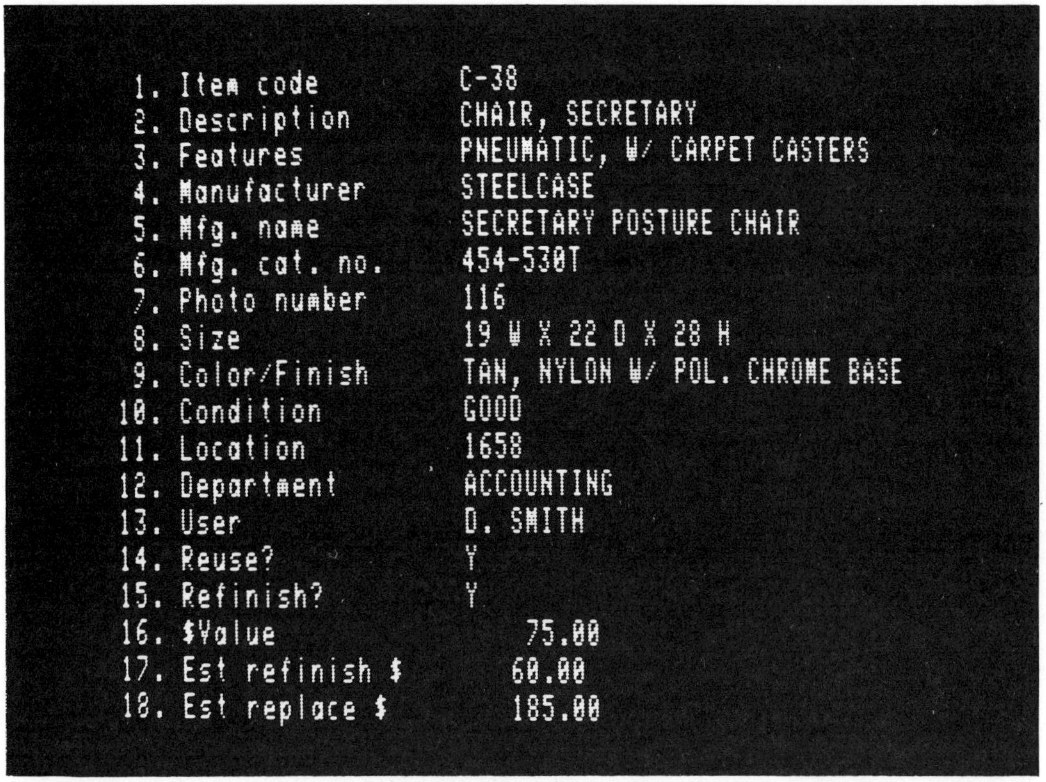

Figure 8.2-1
Furniture Inventory Data Entry Screen

3. Design the forms for data collection. These should be coordinated with the DBMS data entry screen so it is easy for a secretary or clerical help to keyboard the information in with a minimum of mistakes.

4. Collect the information. Use an accurate floor plan of the space so you can reference the location of all equipment and check off the spaces as you complete the work. This is the simplest way to avoid counting the same thing twice.

5. When you have finished the inventory and entered all the information into the data base, print out a list of all information in a format similar to your data collection forms. Use this printout to check for errors. Although tedious, this step is crucial to catch mistakes before anyone starts using the data base.

Examples

Figure 8.2-2 illustrates a portion of one type of furniture inventory report.

PLAN CODE	ITEM	MANUFACTURER	PRESENT FLOOR LOCATION	PRESENT DEPT. LOCATION	NEW LOCATION	SIZE	RETURN SIZE	FINISH	FABRIC	CONDITION	QUANTITY	COST	EXTENDED COST
SD2	SEC CHAIR	SCHAFFER 246SC-R75AB			SAFE DEPOS LWR LVL					NEW	1	230	230
SD3	LOUNGE CHAIR	CARTWRIGHT W20/200			SAFE DEPOS LWR LVL					NEW	4	1000	4,000
SD4	OCC TABLE	METROPOLITAN 91252			SAFE DEPOS LWR LVL					NEW	2	600	1,200
SD5	CONFERENCE TABLE		BASEMENT	SAFE DEPOSIT	SAFE DEPOS LWR LVL	8' x 48"		PLASTIC LAM		EXIST	1	0	0
SD6	CONFERENCE CHAIR	STEELCASE	BASEMENT	SAFE DEPOSIT	SAFE DEPOS LWR LVL			REUPHOLSTER		EXIST	6	0	0
SD7	CHAIR				SAFE DEPOS LWR LVL			REUPHOLSTER		EXIST	8		
E1	WORKSTATION RIGHT RETURN	STEELCASE			ESCROW 1 FLOOR	30" x 60"	74+36x26"	MAHOGANY		NEW	1	5049	5,049
E2	WORKSTATION LEFT RETURN	STEELCASE			ESCROW 1 FLOOR	30" x 60"	74+36x26"	MAHOGANY		NEW	1	5049	5,049
E3	FILE/FIREPROOF	VICTOR FIRE MASTER 764	2 FLOOR	AGRI-BUSINESS	ESCROW 1 FLOOR	30x21x54"	4 DRW	STEEL- REPAINT		EXIST	12	0	0
E4	TABLE - PANEL	STEELCASE			ESCROW 1 FLOOR	30" x 60"		MAHOGANY		NEW	1	606	606
E5	DESK CHAIR	SCHAFER P60-10EP			ESCROW 1 FLOOR			BRONZE		NEW	2	636	1,272
E6	GUEST CHAIR	STEELCASE/SNODGRASS			ESCROW 1 FLOOR			BRONZE		NEW	5	367	1,835
E7	CONFERENCE CHAIR	SCHAFER P60-10EP			ESCROW 1 FLOOR			BRONZE		NEW	5	636	3,180
E8	CONFERENCE TABLE	VECTA 337903			ESCROW 1 FLOOR	54"D		MAHOGANY		NEW	1	803	803
E9	SEC DESK/LEFT RETURN	STEELCASE			ESCROW 1 FLOOR	30" x 60"		MAHOGANY		NEW	1	1965	1,965
E10	SEC CHAIR	SCHAFER 246SC-R75AB			ESCROW 1 FLOOR			BRONZE		NEW	1	230	230
CS1	WORKSTATION RIGHT RETURN	STEELCASE			CUST SERVICE 1 FLR	30x60(72)"	74+36x26"	MAHOGANY		NEW	3	5049	15,147
CS2	FILE/LATERAL	SCHAFER			CUST SERVICE 1 FLR		4 DRW			NEW	5	518	2,590
CS3	DESK CHAIR	SCHAFER			CUST SERVICE 1 FLR			BRONZE		NEW	4	636	2,544
CS4	GUEST CHAIR	STEELCASE/SNODGRASS			CUST SERVICE 1 FLR					NEW	6	367	2,202
CS5	LOUNGE CHAIR	CARTWRIGHT			CUST SERVICE 1 FLR					NEW	4	1000	4,000
CS6	SEC CHAIR	SCHAFFER			CUST SERVICE 1 FLR			BRONZE		NEW	3	230	690
CS7	WARDROBE	STEELCASE			CUST SERVICE 1 FLR					NEW	3		
TV1	STOOL				TELLER VAULT 1 FLR			BRONZE		NEW	9	297	2,673
CV1	TABLE				CASH VAULT 1 FLR	30" x 60"				EXIST	1		
TEL1	STOOL	STEELCASE			TELLER 1 FLOOR					NEW	17	297	5,049
TEL2	EXECUTIVE DESK	STEELCASE	2 FLOOR	AG. BUSINESS	TELLER 1 FLOOR	36" x 72"		OAK		EXIST	1		
TEL3	CREDENZA	STEELCASE	2 FLOOR	AG. BUSINESS	TELLER 1 FLOOR	65" x 19"		OAK		EXIST	1		
TEL4	DESK CHAIR	STEELCASE			TELLER 1 FLOOR			REUPHOLSTER		EXIST	1		
TEL5	GUEST CHAIR				TELLER 1 FLOOR			REUPHOLSTER		EXIST	2		
TEL6	SEC CHAIR				TELLER 1 FLOOR			REUPHOLSTER		EXIST	1		
TEL7	SEC DESK/LEFT RETURN	STEELCASE	1 FLOOR	CUST. SERVICE	TELLER 1 FLOOR	66" x 36"		OAK		EXIST	1		
TEL8	FILE LATERAL				TELLER 1 FLOOR					EXIST	2		

**Figure 8.2-2
Furniture Inventory Report**

8.3

INTEGRATED FACILITY MANAGEMENT SYSTEMS

Microcomputers are ideal for many facility management functions. As described in Sections 8.1 and 8.2 they can maintain data bases of information on furniture and space. They can also be used for cost estimating, programming and scheduling as described elsewhere in this book. There are times, however, when a designer may want to combine all the common facility management tasks (including computer-aided design) into one integrated package. The primary reason for this is to share data between the various individual applications. For example, the spaces developed during programming can be used as the basis of a space, furniture and personnel inventory. Later, the same data can be used to project space needs or help outline a maintenance schedule or moving schedule.

Your judgment will determine whether or not you need a more elaborate integrated software package and the sophisticated hardware to run it. Generally, you will either need a good backlog of work in this area to justify the added expense, or the commitment to make this a significant part of your business. This section will outline some of the basics of this application, what you should look for when shopping for software and what to expect from such software.

Basic Application Requirements

Many components can be built into an integrated facility management program. Generally, the more components the more expensive the software. Not all of them are necessary for every office so you need to decide which ones you need and how much you are willing to pay. The following list gives the most common tasks.

1. programming (This involves an evaluation of current and future needs.)
2. space standards (This component establishes different kinds of workstations and offices based on function and status, and standardizes sizes of rooms and furniture.)
3. personnel/space projections (The estimation of future needs based on best estimates or curve fitting.)
4. stacking plans (The allocation of departments and spaces throughout several floors of a multifloor building.)
5. affinity analysis (Proximity requirements are taken from programming information and translated into departmental adjacency needs.)
6. block plans (This planning component lays out the required spaces in a given building according to the parameters established by the affinity analysis.)

7. space planning (After stacking and block plans, this graphic component allows the facility manager to lay out the office space in detail showing offices, furniture locations, electrical and other construction items.)

8. furniture and equipment inventories (These account for all the items in a facility and the attributes of each.)

9. space and personnel inventories (This component maintains a listing of current personnel, the departments to which they are assigned and the spaces they occupy.)

10. space utilization (Utilization involves keeping track of vacancies, conformance of use to approved space standards, usable to rentable ratios and assignable space to total space (efficiency).)

11. cost analysis (This component may range from simple cost budgeting to complex life cycle cost analyses or lease versus buy evaluations.)

12. project scheduling (This can help a company plan and organize the construction of new space or remodeling of existing space. It is also used for long-term planning of multifacility companies.)

13. maintenance scheduling (Necessary repair, replacement and regular maintenance are coordinated with this component.)

14. computer-aided drafting (This is used to produce space planning presentations as well as working drawings for construction.)

15. lease management (This tracks the start and stop dates of various leases, the square footage involved, lease rates and any options available.)

16. business graphics (Simple bar charts, graphs and similar two-dimensional graphics are produced from data in any of the other components.)

Requirements of Hardware

Hardware requirements vary considerably for this application depending on the sophistication of the software. Some systems only require a microcomputer with a dot-matrix printer while the CADD-based systems need the full complement of hard disk storage, color terminals, plotters and digitizers.

One of your first decisions is to determine whether you need just the data base functions without graphics or whether you need both. However, you will find that the bulk of work can be performed with non-graphic software. A few low-cost CAD systems, such as AutoCAD, do allow you to assign attributes (data base record fields) to graphic entities and print out reports.

Cost Variables

As with hardware, the costs involved with setting up an integrated facility management system can range from a few thousand dollars to well over $160,000 for one system. Again, determining your needs is critical to setting the price range you will be considering.

No matter how sophisticated a system you choose, data entry will require much of your time and efforts. For large projects, initial keyboarding of data is extensive and maintaining the data base over several years consumes a great deal of time. When estimating your time and writing fee proposals make sure you allow enough for ongoing maintenance. If you are new to offering this service, try to negotiate an hourly rate.

Implementation Procedures

1. Before you automate, make sure you have a workable manual system and you know specifically what kinds of tasks you need to perform. If you have been offering facility management services before this will probably not be a problem. If you are thinking of expanding services, proceed cautiously with computerized facility management.

2. Define your needs, both initially and for the future. These will depend on how much of your office's business you want to devote to facility management and how much money you want to spend. An integrated package makes it much easier to do a lot of work, but you can also set up separate applications as described elsewhere in this book using data base management programs and spreadsheets.

3. Based on your defined needs and the basic application requirements described above, review the various software available. Use the list at the end of this section as a starting point for your shopping. Also, consult one of the many software directories available for design professionals. See Appendix C.

4. Establish procedures for gathering information and maintaining the data base. This includes designing forms for data collection that are compatible with data entry into the system.

5. Train your staff in the procedures and method of data entry as well as the intricacies of the software you purchase. For this application, training may require a commitment of significant time and money. You should be prepared for this and allow enough time for everyone to become familiar with the system before expecting high efficiency.

Sources for More Information

International Facility Management Association
11 Greenway Plaza, Suite 1410
Houston, TX 77046

Automated Facilities Management: A Buyer's Guide

The Current State of Facilities Management Automation
Both Available from:

Graphic Systems, Inc.
180 Franklin Street
Cambridge, MA 02139

Hales, H. Lee. *Computer-Aided Facilities Planning.* New York: Marcel Dekker, Inc., 1984.

Software:

FAMES
Decision Graphics, Inc.
P.O. Box 306
Southboro, MA 01772

SPACE/1000
DFI Systems
P.O. Box 22787
Lake Buena Vista, FL 32830

FACILITIES MANAGEMENT SYSTEM
Formative Technologies, Inc.
5001 Baum Boulevard
Pittsburgh, PA 15213

BOS 1
Facility Design Group, Inc.
One South Main Street
Wilkes-Barre, PA 18701

FACILITIES MANAGEMENT SOFTWARE
Information Displays, Inc.
28 Kaysal Court
Armonk, NY 10504

RDI/PC
Resource Dynamics, Inc.
150 East 58th Street
New York, NY 10155

CADG+FM[tm]
The Computer-Aided Design Group
2407 Main
Santa Monica, CA 90405

GFS-PS
Basicomp, Inc.
4040 East McDowell Suite 305
Phoenix, AZ 85008–4447

CAP 2.0
Computer-Aided Planning, Inc.
169 C Monroe Avenue
Grand Rapids, MI 49503

DESIGNPAK
Design Network, International
P.O. Box 10129
Chicago, IL 60610

SpaceTRACKER
Facilities Management Systems, Inc.
774 Post Road
Scarsdale, NY 10583

SPACE PLANNING AND FACILITIES MANAGEMENT SYSTEM
Micro-Vector, Inc.
1 Byram Brook Place
Armonk, NY 10504

8.4

UPGRADING YOUR SERVICES
WITH PROJECT MAINTENANCE MANUALS

One of the most valuable facility management services an architect or interior designer can offer to a client is assistance with using the new facility properly. The information provided may range from broad issues that explain why the space planning was done a particular way to specific instructions such as the kind of replacement bulbs that should be used in the light fixtures.

Providing a maintenance manual with this kind of information not only helps the client get the most from the investment, but also provides you with a valuable marketing tool. Using computers for this kind of task can make the job easy while still allowing you to do a thorough job.

Basic Application Requirements

A maintenance manual can be defined as a document that describes the design and operation of a building or interior with particular emphasis on care and replacement of materials, proper operation of systems and components and correct maintenance procedures. Maintenance manuals must be tailored to the requirements of a particular job, but they are usually comprised of standard sections of text with an occasional chart or graph. For example, instructions on how to maintain a particular flooring material may not be needed for every job you do, but when that flooring is specified, the maintenance instructions will be the same.

A word processing program is a natural for this application if it can read standard "boilerplate" text files into your working file. This may be done either with a program's ability to transfer other files into the file you are currently working on or with a "merge" program that allows one file to "call" other files while it is printing so that the final copy is a combination of several individual pieces of text.

Additional Application Requirements

If your maintenance manuals contain a large number of tabular charts and other graphic material, you may find it useful to have a word processing program integrated with a spreadsheet and graphics program, or at least a word processing program that can read files from other types of programs.

If your manuals are lengthy you may also find it useful to be able to automatically index or create a table of contents. Some of the more expensive word processing programs have this built in; in other cases you need to purchase a separate program.

Requirements of Software

Software for this application must have all the basic features of a good word processing program for document entry, editing, file handling, document formatting and printing. In addition, the software must have the capability to read several "boilerplate" files into the file you are working on or at least have the ability to "chain" several of these files together at print time in the order you define. However, simple chaining of files at the time of printing is not very desirable since you will almost always want to include additional information.

Requirements of Hardware

RAM. Most word processing programs will operate with a minimum amount of internal memory—48K or 64K is usually sufficient. More RAM is only necessary if you are using an integrated package or want this application to run a little faster.

Disks. Since the total amount of text in any one maintenance manual is minimal from the standpoint of the computer, disk capacity is usually not a problem. Even if your practice involves very large jobs and you build up a large file of "boilerplate" text to include in your manuals this can be saved on one disk and used to compile a manual on the same disk. If you run short of disk space once you are finished with a job's manual, the file for that project can be copied to another archival disk and deleted from your working disk to give you room for the next job.

244

Printer. You can use a dot-matrix printer, but a daisywheel or ink-jet printer capable of producing a finished typewritten report is easier to read and makes a better impression on your client.

Cost Variables

Hardware. A basic word processing setup is inexpensive due to the minimal requirements of RAM and mass storage. A complete configuration with a letter-quality printer can be purchased for $3,000 or less.

Software. Some fairly good word processing programs can be purchased for under $200, but you should consider spending $300 to $700 for the kind of features you will need for all of your office's work—not just this application.

Setup. If you have never produced a maintenance manual before, the initial research and text entry will be substantial. You can spread out the work and assign much of the cost to several jobs if you do a little each time you produce a manual. The first one, of course, will take the most time since everything will need to be done from scratch.

Spend some time organizing your "boilerplate" setup so the project manager or job captain can simply note the standard text sections he or she needs on an index form. The secretary can then take this checklist and print out a rough draft of the manual for editing.

Data entry. You should plan on extra time for initial entry of text but once that is done, producing a maintenance manual should take no more time than what would normally be required for typing.

Implementation Procedures

1. Decide on a general outline and format to use on all the maintenance manuals you produce. Having this standard format will make it easier to produce individual "boilerplate" text and to assemble individual manuals. Use the outline shown in Figure 8.4-1 as a guide and modify it according to your needs.

2. Research and write the individual paragraphs and sections of text you will use repeatedly. If you don't want to do this at one time, complete those sections required for the particular job you are working on. As you do more manuals for additional jobs you will slowly build up a valuable collection of standard text.

3. Make sure the procedures you write are correct. Submit them to factory representatives, colleagues, trade associations and others to verify the accuracy of the information.

4. Make an index of the standard sections you have. The project manager can use this list to identify which sections to include for a particular project.

5. To assemble a maintenance manual, first read in the appropriate "boilerplate" sections into your working file or set up a "merge" file if your program

```
I.    Introduction

II.   Design statement

III.  Replacement materials

      List of names, manufacturers and suppliers of replacement

      materials such as paint colors, flooring, and similar

      items.

IV.   Maintenance procedures

      Information on how the facility should be maintained.

      For example, how the specified carpet should be

      cleaned, proper methods of maintaining the exterior

      finish, proper replacement bulbs for light fixtures,

      and so forth.  Also include who to call for repairs.

V.    Operating requirements and procedures of the mechanical

      system.
```

Figure 8.4-1
Maintenance Manual Contents Outline

has that capability. Next, edit the standard text as required by the job and add additional information unique to the project.

Additional Tips

- Don't try to bunch too much information into each individual file. This will decrease the flexibility of assembling many standard sections into your working file.
- If your word processing program has "file merging" capabilities, name each "boilerplate" file with a number that corresponds to your master outline. When the time comes to assemble your working file, simply list the numbers of the sections you want in your merging file. When you run the merge program most of your work will be complete.
- Print out all the standard text with file names to put in a reference notebook. These can be reviewed by the project manager if necessary when making the list of sections to include.

246

- Don't fall into the trap of thinking that just because you have written standard text that it will always be accurate. You must make a commitment to keep your files up to date.

Sources for More Information

Operation and Maintenance Manual: Preparation and Format, #MP-2-5. Washington, DC: The Construction Specifications Institute, 1981.

CHAPTER 9

How to Outdistance the Competition with Information Management

A design office is a processor of vast quantities of information. In spite of this fact, most offices do a very poor job of handling the lifeblood of their business. Two of the reasons for this are the sheer quantity and variety of data every office is inundated with daily. Since designers are not trained in information management this job is usually relegated to a position of importance below design and the production of construction documents. It is absolutely vital that professional design firms improve their organization, storage, and retrieval of information, not only for reasons of productivity but also for legal purposes.

This chapter provides guidance for architects, design firm librarians and secretaries in the process of using computers for information management. It shows how to automate the tedious tasks of keeping track of the tens of thousands of pieces of data every office must be able to access in order to run a successful design practice.

9.1

ORGANIZING CATALOGS AND SAMPLES

Product catalogs, loose pamphlets of product information and samples are some of the most important resources in an architect's office, but are often disorganized and out of date. This makes it difficult to find the information they contain and feel confident that it is current. Although the 16-division Masterformat system of the Construction Specifications Institute is an ideal way to classify and file catalogs and product literature, several problems remain that a computerized system can solve.

The first of these problems is being able to quickly identify manufacturers and their catalogs that contain information on one particular product type that the architect is researching. For example, product literature on special wood wall treatments may be physically located in separate binders (no problem locating these), binders that contain other types of wall finishes filed under another Masterformat number and in vertical files with the loose product pamphlets. The architect who is short on time may easily find the wood wall treatment binders in the Division 6 (Wood and Plastics) section, but not have the time to search through other binders that might contain just what is needed.

The second problem is keeping the information current. Ideally, the local product representatives should automatically update catalogs when new information is published. As every professional knows, this does not happen as often as it should. An additional problem is that for many catalogs there is no local representative; the catalog must be obtained from an out-of-state representative or directly from the factory. It is often the architect's responsibility to call for updating, but once a catalog is on the shelf its currency is unknown until someone refers to it.

Samples pose a third, unique problem because of the wide variety of their sizes, shapes and weights. Samples may be kept as reference for future jobs or for legal reasons—as a record of the approved form of a product for a particular job (a terrazzo mix, for example). Every office should have a way to track what samples they have, what date the samples were submitted to the office, whether they pertain to a job, when they can be disposed of and where they are located.

Basic Application Requirements

A data base management system is best suited for this application because information needs to be easily added, deleted, changed and viewed in various ways. This is an application where the information structure becomes complicated enough to require a relational data base management system (RDBMS) for best performance. Refer to Appendix A, Fundamentals of Data Base Management Systems, for a more complete explanation of this type of software. The example in the appendix relates to this application as well as the next one on product representatives so you may want to review it before proceeding.

Although a RDBMS is best, if your collection of catalogs is small and you want to keep things as simple as possible you can use a file management system (FMS). This section will show how to use *both* a FMS as well as a simple, two-file RDBMS for organizing catalogs and samples. Section 9.2 illustrates how you can set up a more complex, and powerful, relational data base management system linking product representatives, catalogs and other product information.

For the basic file management system (FMS) application you will want to:

1. Find all catalogs and pamphlets listing a particular product type even if they are in different Masterformat divisions or physically filed in different places.

Catalog Name	Product Type	Master-Format #	Location	Date
AmMaCo	Marble flooring	09615	Files	86/01/05
Everyfloor	Wood flooring	09550	Shelves	85/11/18
	Tile flooring	09300	Shelves	85/11/18
Super Paint	Interior paint	09920	Shelves	85/02/06
	Wood stain	09930	Shelves	85/02/06
Wonderwood	Wood flooring	09550	Files	85/09/18

Figure 9.1-1
Tabular Representation of FMS Type Data Base

2. Find the product information published by a particular manufacturer whether it is in a single catalog binder or filed as loose product information sheets.

3. List the catalogs that have not been updated within a specified period of time.

4. List the samples your office keeps, organized by Masterformat number and showing location.

5. List the catalogs in your office's library arranged alphabetically by manufacturer.

The most basic FMS application in controlling catalogs and samples deals only with the catalog or sample itself, the product information it contains, and its location. This is shown in tabular form in Figure 9.1-1 where the rows are records in the data base and columns are data fields. Information concerning the representative's address, phone number, the manufacturer's address, phone and contact are located elsewhere, presumably in the catalog itself. Additional data, such as trade names of products, jobs a particular product was used on and so forth are likewise not a part of the most basic computerized setup.

This table shows the same problem discussed in Appendix A, that one catalog may have more than one product type in it. If you want to separate one catalog into several product types, there is a redundancy of data in each data base record.

Additional Application Requirements

Using a simple, two-file relational data base management system (RDBMS) you can add the following application features:

Organizing Catalogs and Samples

1. Maintain two separate but related files: one containing information on the catalog and one containing a list of product types and the catalogs in which they can be found. This solves the problem of data redundancy and updating caused by using a file management system. Refer to Appendix A for a complete explanation of this. A tabular representation of these two files is shown in Figure 9.1-2.
2. Add trade names to the file of product types. This is useful if you hear of a product by name, but don't know where to find more information about it.
3. Add information concerning the product, such as what jobs you used it on, how it performed and similar data.

Catalog Name	Catalog Number	Master-format #	Location	Date
AmMaCo	09600.13	09615	Files	86/01/05
Everyfloor	09000.33	09000	Shelves	85/11/18
Super Paint	09900.05	09900	Shelves	85/02/06
Wonderwood	09950.01	09950	Files	85/09/18

Catalog file

Product type	Trade name	Catalog Number
Interior paint	Paintall	09900.05
Marble flooring	Lox Marble	09600.13
Tile flooring	Flortron	09000.33
Wood flooring	AceFloor	09000.33
Wood flooring	Gymlock	09950.01
Wood stain	B-Stain	09900.05

Product type file

Figure 9.1-2
Tabular Representation of a Two-File RDBMS Design

4. Add information concerning the representative of each catalog. This may be simply the name of the representative's company and a phone number. More complete information can still be written out in each catalog. The problem here, again, is that one company may supply several manufacturers' catalogs, so you may have to repeat representative's information on several catalog records in your data base. Section 9.2 will discuss in more detail how to solve this problem.

Requirements of Software

In addition to the basic selection criteria mentioned in Appendix A on data base management systems, your program for the FMS and RDBMS should have the following minimum capabilities. These apply to organizing samples as well as catalogs. For a file management system (FMS):

1. You should be able to index on a minimum of three fields: the catalog name, Masterformat number and date. Ideally, you should be able to index on any of the fields in the record you set up.

2. Your program should allow you to sort on more than one key. For example, you may want to list all your product catalogs by Masterformat number, then alphabetically by manufacturer's name within each number.

3. You need the basic relational query capabilities so you can find out-of-date catalogs. For instance, you will want to find all the catalogs in your data base that are dated after a particular time.

4. It is helpful if your program has the ability to make mass changes. Rather than searching and changing every record if a catalog's representative changes from "Smith" to "Jones," you could do this just once, instructing your data base to find all occurrences of "Smith" in the representative field and change it to "Jones."

For a relational data base management system (RDBMS):

1. As stated, this application requires that at least two files be open at one time.

2. Your software must allow a flexible way to display on the screen or print out reports, extracting whatever data you want from both files and organizing it the way you want.

Requirements of Hardware

RAM. Many file management systems will work with as little as 64K of RAM. The more sophisticated relational data base management systems usually require 128K or more.

253

Disks. Two disks are usually sufficient for this application. Even for large offices, the usual number of catalogs found in most libraries and the relatively short records recommended in this section don't require a great deal of disk space.

Printer. A dot-matrix printer is acceptable for this application.

Cost Variables

Hardware. A complete setup with two disk drives and a dot-matrix printer can be purchased for $2,000 or less.

Software. Simple file management programs range from under $100 to $400 with a few costing more than $400. Relational data base management programs range from about $400 to over $1,000, but with many very good programs under $800.

Setup. Setup costs depend on the complexity of your application. The FMS approach described in this section can be set up with most programs in less than 15 minutes. A RDBMS with two files may take from four to eight hours.

Data entry. Data entry is the big variable in this application because of the number of individual records you need to enter. If you choose to use a FMS and simply consider each catalog binder as a record in the data base you will make as many entries as you have catalogs. If you add to this all the loose pamphlets you may have in separate files, the number increases dramatically. Estimating the number of entries you will have and multiplying by the expected time required to make each entry will give you an idea of how much time will have to be devoted to this activity.

Using the RDBMS will require even more time because there will be several records for each physical catalog. For example, a catalog from a brick manufacturer may contain data on face brick, brick pavers, glazed brick and preassembled panels, each of which would require a separate data entry in your product type file. Remember though, that the increased number would be offset by the short length of each record, possibly containing only three or four fields.

Implementation Procedures

1. Decide on whether to use a simple file management system or a relational system. Refer to Section 9.2 to decide if you want to implement an even more comprehensive system than described here. Your choice will depend on the number of catalogs and samples you have, who will maintain the data base and how much time they can devote to it and how important this application is to you. For some architects, simply keeping track of when catalogs were last updated is all that is required. For other firms, the time saved and the improved access to product information will justify an extensive data base management system.

2. Decide on the data fields that you want in each record. Some of the possible

fields for both the FMS and the RDBMS are shown in Figures 9.1-3, 9.1-4 and 9.1-5.

3. If you decide to use a RDBMS, determine how detailed you want to be with product type categories. You can use the Masterformat "Broadscope" classifications or the "Narrowscope" divisions. Another possibility is to use the headings found in the Sweet's catalog index that include *properties* of many products as well as types of products. Remember that as the categories become more detailed, more care is necessary in classifying each catalog.

Establishing product type categories is where you can really customize this application to make it work for *your offices'* needs. For example, you may want to be more detailed in one area because your firm specializes in a particular building type.

4. Purge your existing shelves and files of unused and dated material. Order catalogs you really need, but don't have.

5. Set up the system according to your needs and the instructions with the

```
1. CATALOG NAME      Super Paint
2. MANUFACTURER      Super Paint Company, Inc.
3. MASTERFORMAT #    09900
4. PRODUCT TYPE      Painting
5. DATE (YY/MM/DD)   85/10/15
6. LOCAL REP         Smith Associates, Inc.
7. LOCATION          Shelves
```

Figure 9.1-3
File Management System Data Record

```
1. CATALOG NAME      Super Paint
2. CATALOG #         09900.37
3. MANUFACTURER      Super Paint Company, Inc.
4. DATE (YY/MM/DD)   85/10/15
5. LOCATION          Shelves
6. LOCAL REP         Smith Associates, Inc.
7. REP'S PHONE       555-1234
```

Figure 9.1-4
RDBMS Catalog File Record

```
1. PRODUCT TYPE      Interior paint
2. MASTERFORMAT #    09920
3. TRADE NAME        Paintall
4. CATALOG #         09900.37
5. COMMENTS          Excellent paint, meets gov. specs
```

Figure 9.1-5
RDBMS Product Type File Record

255

software you select. Enter all existing catalogs, pamphlets and samples into the system.

6. Establish a standard policy for who maintains the system, how often it is done and what reports are regularly produced. Assign someone the responsibility to order updated material on a regular basis.

Examples

Figure 9.1-3 shows how a simple FMS record might appear as part of a data base to organize catalogs. One similar to this could also be used to maintain a separate data base for samples. With this short, simple setup you can satisfy all five functions listed in the Basic Application Requirements portion of this Section, realizing, of course, that in some cases you may have to compromise on the detail with which you classify product types. For example, a catalog of wood windows may also contain data on wood sliding glass doors. The product type data field has to include one or the other, but not both.

Figures 9.1-4 and 9.1-5 illustrate data entry formats for the two files of a relational data base management approach using the same catalog information shown in 9.1-3 with some additional data. Figure 9.1-4 shows the *catalog file* data entry format with information unique to the catalog, and Figure 9.1-5 shows the *product type* file data entry format. The two are related by the catalog number so that when you query the data base for all catalogs containing information on interior paint, it first searches the *product type* file for matches on interior paint (or the corresponding Masterformat number if you use that) and uses the catalog number to search the *catalog file* for the desired information concerning the catalog.

Kaplan/McLaughlin/Diaz, San Francisco, uses a simple file management system in the technical library to maintain its collection of catalogs and representatives. Figure 9.1-6 shows a data entry format they use and Figure 9.1-7 shows a partial listing of one report format for printing out a portion of the data in each record.

Additional Tips

- Print up form letters to manufacturers and representatives to make it easier to request that they update their catalogs. If your data base management system is part of an integrated program or can otherwise transfer data to a word processing program, writing request letters will be easy.

- Be sure to spend some time thinking through this kind of application before you start entering data. Make sure you have enough data fields for expansion and that whatever classification of product types you select will be helpful for day-to-day use of the system.

256

```
File: INTERIORS              REVIEW/ADD/CHANGE    Escape: Restore former entry

Selection: All records

Record 99 of 343
================================================================================
COMPANY: DU PONT (CORIAN)
CITY: WILMINGTON DE
PHONE: 302/774-8472
LOCAL: BUTLER JOHNSON
REP: JACK MACKALL
PHONE: 408/259-1800
PRODUCT1: CORIAN
PRODUCT2: -
PRODUCT3: -
CATALOG: 06200/DU PONT (TECHNICAL LIB.)
UPDATE: Jun 85
SAMPLES: SAMPLE CORRIDOR
UPDATE: Apr 84

--------------------------------------------------------------------------------
Type entry or use @ commands                                        11K Avail.
```

Figure 9.1-6
Library Data Entry Form

File: CATALOGS   REVIEW/ADD/CHANGE   Escape: Main Menu

Selection: All records

CATALOG	NUMBER	REP PHONE	REP NAME	UPDATE
TIMCO DOORS	08200	800/527-7626	STEVE ROYALS	Aug 84
TIME & SOUND	16700	213/698-0601	DOUG KAPLAN	Mar 85
TITUS REGISTERS	15880	415/788-8384	-	Jan 85
TNEMEC COATINGS	09800	707/226-1801	GLEN AMOS	May 85
TNEMEC FIRE-RESISTANCE	07200	707/226-1801	GLEN AMOS	Feb 85
TOCH CARBOLINE	07100	408/684-0972	ROCK MARCHIONE	Apr 84
TRASK & SQUIER LOCKERS	10500	415/392-1338	MAC BARKER	Mar 84
TREMCO ROOFING	07500	415/348-0926	ANDREW SMITH	May 85
TREMCO SEALANTS	07900	415/838-8844	MARV RAUPP	Aug 83
TRUS JOIST	06170	415/239-6432	ROGER ERICKSON	Mar 85
TRUSSBILT	08100	612/646-7181	-	Jul 83
TUBELITE	08400	415/282-8220	JOHN SCHMIDT	-
TUBULAR SPECIALITIES	10800	415/652-2945	R.E. EDWARDS	Apr 85
U. S. CERAMIC TILE	-	415/788-6880	INTERTILE	-
U.S. ALUMINUM	08400	415/487-1166	STEVE KITT	Jun 85

Type entry or use @ commands   @-? for Help

Figure 9.1-7
Catalog Report

258

9.2
MAINTAINING A PRODUCT REPRESENTATIVE DATA BASE

In Section 9.1 the applications illustrated for organizing catalogs and samples assumed that most of the information concerning representatives and manufacturers would be maintained within the catalog in written form or in some other place. The reason for this was that since one person may represent several product lines the information on that representative would have to be repeated each time a catalog was entered into the computer. If the representative changed address or phone number, for example, you would have the tedious task of changing several records.

Of course, you can maintain a simple "mailing list" type of file on representatives with a simple note on your catalogs or catalog data base referring you to the name and address file. However, you can develop a very powerful integrated system that links representatives, product catalogs, manufacturers, and an index based on trade names and product types to give you a flexible way to access some of your office's most valuable information.

Basic Application Requirements

A relational data base management system is the only type of "generic" software that can be used for this application. If you are unfamiliar with this type of software, refer to Appendix A, Fundamentals of Data Base Management Systems. The example used in this section will be an expansion of the example described in Appendix A.

Integrating information about product representatives with other files requires software that can have several files open at one time. In the RDBMS discussed in Section 9.1, only two files were needed. In this application the program capability must include having at least four files open at once.

For this application you will want to:

1. Identify and locate all catalogs and pamphlets listing a particular product type.

2. Find the local representative for a given product or manufacturing company along with that representative's address and phone number.

3. Find the product information published by a particular manufacturer, whether it is in a single catalog binder or filed as loose product information sheets.

4. List the catalogs that have not been updated within a specified period of time.

259

5. List all the manufacturers in the data base along with their local representatives' names.

6. Find the manufacturer and representative using a trade name.

7. List the catalogs in your office's library arranged alphabetically by manufacturer.

There are other variations of these requirements, but these represent the primary ones. One advantage of a well-designed relational data base management system is that it gives you a great deal of flexibility in manipulating the information you have in the data base.

Additional Application Requirements

In order to make this application even more powerful, you may want to consider adding the following features.

Custom menus. Since the mechanics of this application can get rather complex, setting up custom screen menus can guide both the experienced and nonexperienced user through the process. You can list the tasks that your office needs the most and with the touch of one keystroke have what you need.

Custom screen display. Rather than just listing the various data fields, you may want to "design" how a data entry or reporting screen looks. This often makes entering information easier and aids in the readability of the screen output.

Program integration. A data base management program is much more valuable if you can use the information it contains in other ways in other programs—word processing and spreadsheets, for instance. For example, you may want to use your list of representative's names and addresses to generate request letters for updating catalogs. Of course, existing integrated programs have this capability, but many of them sacrifice data base power for flexibility. Keep this in mind when shopping.

Requirements of Software

If you are going to set up a rather complex relational system for this application and have not purchased the software, there are some additional software attributes to look for when selecting a RDBMS program in addition to the ones listed in Appendix A:

1. the ability to have at least six files open at once

2. the ability to add data fields after the system is set up and operating

3. custom menu generation and batch file processing so you only need to set up complex procedures once; after that, a one-keystroke selection from the custom menu will complete the task.

4. custom screen definition

5. the ability to transfer data to other programs such as a word processing program

Requirements of Hardware

RAM.   Some RDBM systems will operate with as little as 64K of memory. The more sophisticated packages require 128K or more.

Disks.   At least two disk drives are necessary, but a complex relational data base management system will work faster with a hard disk. However, you need to determine if you want some of the capacity of the hard disk to be taken up by this application. For large-capacity hard disks this is usually not a problem but for small-capacity disks you may find yourself short on disk space if you have several other applications. If you decide to keep the data on a floppy disk and read it onto the hard disk, the time required to do this is a factor to consider.

Printer.   Any kind of printer is usable for this application.

Cost Variables

Hardware.   A complete system with two disk drives and a dot-matrix printer can be purchased for $2,000 or less.

Software.   Relational data base management programs range from about $400 to over $1,000, but with many very good programs under $800.

Setup.   Since this is a complex application, designing the system and setting up custom menus and data entry screens will take a considerable amount of time—from eight to twenty hours depending on how easy your program is to work with and how familiar you are with it. If some custom programming is required, the time will be extended.

Data entry.   As with any data base management application data entry consumes a great deal of time. Once the system is established, a secretary or even part-time help can go through your collection of catalogs and enter the data. Additional research will probably be needed to find things such as manufacturer's addresses or representatives for some catalogs.

Implementation Procedures

1. Decide which separate files you need. For the basic application you will need at least a "Catalog File," a "Representative File" and a "Product File." In addition, you may want a "Manufacturer's File" that contains information on the main manufacturing factory, its address, who to contact and so forth. It is also possible to set up files containing information on samples you have in the office,

local suppliers of a product and showrooms or locations where the product is on display, but this level of detail is usually not needed by most architects.

2. Develop a schema for your data base. This will allow you to see the big picture before getting involved in the details of setting up the system. An example of one schema is shown in Figure 9.2-1 using a tabular format. This is an expansion of the example shown in Appendix A, Fundamentals of Data Base Management. The rows in the tables represent individual records in each file and the columns represent data fields in each record. Each file is linked to another with a common field. For example, the product file contains a catalog number field.

3. As you develop your schema, decide what information you feel is vital to your office's work that you want to maintain in each file. For example, in the "Product File" you may not want to maintain a list of trade names; the product type may be sufficient. Further, in your field for product type, you must determine what level of detail is best for you. Is it sufficient to list product types by Masterformat's Narrowscope list of products or do you need more detail? For instance, you can list "Wood Doors" (08210) or you can develop headings that describe functions, properties, and types of wood doors, much as Sweet's catalog does in their index. In this case you could have "Flush Wood Doors," "Stile and Rail Wood Doors," "Louvered Wood Doors," "Fire-rated Wood Doors" and so on.

4. Estimate how much disk storage space you will need. To do this, establish how long each data field in each file will be in bytes (characters). Add these to get the total size of each record. Next, determine how many records in each file you are likely to have. For the catalog file, this number will be the number of catalogs you have now plus whatever number you will add in the future. For the product file, estimating is more difficult and depends on the level of detail decided upon in step 4. One way is to establish an average number of products that you think each catalog contains and multiply this by the number of catalogs. The representative file will contain fewer records than the catalog file since one company will represent several manufacturer's catalogs.

Determining how much disk space you are likely to need is important in this application because the size of the data base can be substantial. If you don't already have a program or hardware, this calculation will help you purchase the right software and capacity of disk storage you need.

5. Following the instructions of your RDBMS, set up the data entry formats, screen, custom menus (if any) and any other components required by the software. Before starting the actual implementation and spending a lot of time entering data, you should test your data base design by entering some data and retrieving selected information. Have several people in the office review the system and make suggestions. You may want to make modifications.

6. Before entering data, go through your catalog collection and purge out-of-date material and information that you don't use. If information on who represents a particular catalog is not in the binder or stamped on the data sheet, assign someone the responsibility of researching this.

Catalog File

Cat. No.	Catalogue Name	Date of update	Representative number	Mfg. No.

Representative File

Rep. No.	Name	Company	Address	City	State	Zip	Phone	Contact

Product File

Trade name	Product type	Masterformat number	Catalog number

Manufacturer File

Mfg. No.	Manufacturer	Address	City	State	Zip	Phone	Contact

Figure 9.2-1
Relational Data Base Schema

7. Entering data for the first time is the most difficult part. If a secretary or part-time help will be entering the information, you will probably need to print some data entry forms so that someone on the professional or library staff can review the representatives and catalogs to determine such things as whether or not to keep the catalog, what subject headings to assign to the products in the catalog and make similar "professional judgement" determinations. Once this is done and unknown items researched, data entry can then proceed quickly and efficiently.

If you decide to use paper forms to organize your efforts proceed in the following manner. First, start with each catalog. Fill in the information that will be part of, and unique to the catalog file such as name, date of last update, catalog number and so on.

Since each catalog will have a representative (even if it is just the factory), the next step is to make a form for the first representative that handles the first catalog you are reviewing. If you don't know the representative, find out about him (or her). As you proceed from catalog to catalog, make up a form for each new representative. Maintain them in alphabetical order. When you come to a catalog that has the same representative as a previous one, simply note on the catalog form the representative's name (or number if you are going to relate the files by number rather than name). You don't need to note on the representatives form what products he or she handles because the data base management program will be able to do this for you. All you need is an identical field in the catalog file and representative file. See Figure 9.2-1 for an example of this relation.

Next, as you review each catalog, fill out a product type form for as many products as there are in the catalog and in as much detail as you want. You may find the task of listing all the products in your catalog collection a formidable task. In this case just list a general type—a Masterformat Broadscope or Narrow-scope heading, for example. The advantage with a relational data base management system is that you can add information at a later time so initially you may have only one record in the Product File that relates to a catalog on wood windows. Your subject heading may be "wood windows." Later, if you need a more detailed listing of product types you can list the several types of wood windows found in that catalog: wood casement windows, wood sliding windows, wood sliding doors and so on. Data entry is easy because you only have to enter the subject heading, trade name (if part of your system), Masterformat number and the catalog name or number. You don't even need to worry about who the representative is because that is linked to the product type through the relation between the catalog file and the representative file.

8. Using the paper forms generated in step 7 enter the data into the system.

9. Establish a clear policy concerning how the system will be maintained: who will be responsible for entering new catalogs and updating the files, when updating will take place, and when reports will be printed. Be realistic with the

kind of system you set up—an extensive data base requires a great deal of maintenance. If you are not prepared for this, use a more modest system.

Examples

Refer to Appendix A, Fundamentals of Data Base Management Systems for an example of this type of system.

Additional Tips

- Try to keep the number of data fields in each file record to a minimum. Because a data base management system can handle a lot of information easily you will find it tempting to overload your system with data that may not be used enough to justify the extra time for data entry. You can avoid this by defining precisely what you want the system to do for you before setting it up.

- Consider carefully the need for a manufacturer's file. Not all offices will require it. Either the product representative or written information in each catalog can provide the place to record this data.

- Use an identifying number for each representative, catalog and manufacturer. With some software, using a shorter number field will make the system work faster than using a longer, alphanumeric data field for the relation field. Using a unique identifying number also lessens the possibility for error. When a program looks for relations, fields are compared *exactly*, so "Super Paint Co." is not the same as "Super Paint Company."

- When assigning unique numbers to catalogs, use the primary Masterformat number under which the catalog is filed, add a period and then number the catalogs sequentially in that Broadscope or Narrowscope division. The suffix numbers can be loosely based on an alphabetical order of manufacturer's names or any arbitrary system. Remember, since the computer record will have the catalog's name, manufacturer's name and other information, you can generate any kind of list based on any field sorted in any way you want. For this reason maintaining strict alphabetic sequence on the shelves is not necessary if they are arranged by your numbering system.

- Regardless of the level of detail you decide to use when categorizing product types, use the same terms utilized by the Construction Specifications Institute's Masterformat system as much as possible. There may be instances where your firm's practice is so unique or specialized that you have to develop new terms but keep this to a minimum.

DEVELOPING A CUSTOM CLASSIFICATION SYSTEM

Organization and management of catalogs, samples and representatives as discussed in Sections 9.1 and 9.2 is based on simple classification categories: trade name, product type, representative's name, Masterformat number and so on. As you fully develop the use of computers for other types of information management you will need a comprehensive, uniform method for classifying, indexing and storing your data. This section will describe how you can develop a system tailored to your office's individual needs. The following sections in this chapter will describe how you can apply the classification system you develop to specific applications.

Every architect has experienced the frustration of trying to keep track of all the diverse types of information the office accumulates. Of course, the Masterformat system developed by the Construction Specifications Institute is excellent for organizing *product* information, but does not work well for subject matter that is not strictly single-product oriented. For example, where is material on the growing subject of "indoor air pollution" filed? Is it filed in that dreaded black hole of "miscellaneous" where things are never seen again? If a separate file is set up how does someone else find the pertinent material six months later when he or she is looking for data on "material toxicity," or "outgassing," or "office hazards"?

The solution to these and other problems of information management in architectural offices can be solved by developing a classification system and thesaurus customized for the unique needs of your firm. The American National Standards Institute in their standard Z39.19 defines a thesaurus as "a compilation of words and phrases showing synonymous, hierarchical, and other relationships and dependencies, the function of which is to provide a standardized vocabulary for information storage and retrieval." With a classification system and thesaurus you can fully utilize your computer for advanced information management.

Basic Application Requirements

Any classification system you develop should be oriented for the type of work you do. Since offices vary widely in their information management needs your first step is to decide what you want your system to do for you. The following checklist will give you a starting point for making these decisions.

1. It must provide a basis for subject-oriented *storage* as well as *indexing.* Information needs in the building industry are usually subject-oriented rather than title or author specific. Browsing is also often useful and the serendipity that can occur should not be underestimated.

2. Classification and indexing should be based on subjects within broad categories that relate to the *time* of need during the design process: program-

ming, schematic design, design development and so on. These time phases are established in the architectural and interior design professions, and information requests are nearly always within the context of this variable.

3. It should be flexible enough to allow for expansion when new terms are required, or when more detailed classification is needed on a particular heading.

4. The descriptors should be based on current usage of familiar terms in the design professions.

5. The system should respond to the unique type of work your firm does and to the amount of information you have to manage.

6. It should be flexible enough to allow for varying degrees of detail under different subject headings.

7. It must be easy for anyone in the office to use. Search assistance should be built into the system with such aids as "see" and "see also" references as well as an alphabetical index.

8. The system should allow for various forms of material to be classified (books, photographs, drawings, tear sheets, etc.) and allow for consistent shelving of this material. The following sections in this chapter will describe how individual types of material can be organized.

9. Finally, the system you develop must have an acceptable cost associated with its design, preparation, use and maintenance.

Additional Application Requirements

For small offices or for applications in which you are only managing a limited amount of information, the requirements listed above may be sufficient. As you begin to organize a broad collection of data in large quantities you will need more sophisticated features built into your system. You may want to consider the following advanced requirements:

1. It should allow you to access your information from different points of view such as subject, building type, design concept, Masterformat number, author, title or geographical area. In the case of special collections such as codes and standards, you will also need the information indexed by the numbering or coding system of the collection you are managing.

2. The system should allow for broad or narrow searches as required by the information request.

3. Is should be systematic enough so that a single concept or piece of information can be retrieved as well as one concept in relation to other subjects. For example, one time you may want to retrieve information on "atriums" while another time you may want data on "smoke exhaust" from "atriums." In information management terms this is coordinate indexing.

Coordinate indexing is the process of assigning several terms to a document, each of which describes some aspect of that document. A search can then be made on just one term or several depending on how specific the searcher wants to be.

For example, a report on the effects of acid rain on exterior facing material of schools might be assigned the terms "acid rain," "exterior finishes," "educational facilities" and "corrosion." If you were interested in all information in the collection concerning educational facilities you would only use that term. If you were specifically interested in the problems caused by acid rain on schools you could "coordinate" two terms and ask for documents that only contained the keywords "educational facilities" *and* "acid rain." How this is accomplished will be described in more detail in the following sections.

4. The wide variety of information needed by the design professions should be accommodated by the classification scheme and the descriptors. The system should provide you with a way to manage information in addition to the product orientation of Masterformat. This information includes subjects related to allied disciplines, management, legal concerns and the like. However, you may decide to focus on just one aspect of your practice rather than the entire field of architectural information.

5. It should provide both an acceptable "recall ratio" and "precision ratio." The recall ratio is the number of relevant items retrieved in a search divided by the total number of relevant items in the index and the precision ratio is the number of relevant items retrieved divided by the total number of items retrieved. Ideally, you want to retrieve *all* the documents in your collection that relate to your need for information and to have *all* of them be of use to you. This never happens, however, and the recall and precision ratios are ways of measuring how successful your system is. Generally, as the recall ratio increases the precision ratio decreases. You should establish a system that comes as close to this ideal as you need within your limits of time and money.

Requirements of Software

A simple file management type of data base management system is sufficient to assist you in developing your thesaurus and classification system. If you are unfamiliar with these types of programs refer to Appendix A. The program you use must be capable of sorting alphabetically and numerically on the various data fields you establish.

Requirements of Hardware

RAM. Practically all file management systems (FMS) will operate with a minimal amount of RAM; 48K is sufficient in most instances. However, if you will be purchasing a relational data base management system for other applications, all hardware will have to be purchased with that in mind.

Cost Variables

Hardware.   Any hardware you purchase for other applications will support this application.

Software.   Simple file management programs range from under $100 to $400 with a few costing more than $400.

Setup.   Setup for this application is simple and you will probably be able to do it in less than a half an hour. The largest cost variable in this application is the thought process of establishing the classification system and refining your choice of descriptor terms.

Implementation Procedures

In order to satisfy the application requirements you should consider a hierarchically classified system. This simply means that you establish broad categories of subjects and further subdivide them to suit your needs.

However, instead of just arbitrarily selecting subject headings (as many offices do now), the development of your classification scheme should be done in conjunction with the thesaurus. Do this by actually using the data you have and the *process* of indexing the daily influx of information to help you focus on the unique requirements of your office. This will result in a more "customized" system for your use and it makes the job easier to start and continue because you have something concrete to work with (the reports, books, etc. in your hands). You aren't faced with the formidable task of sitting down and starting from scratch—a job most architects would find impossible anyway given their daily work load.

1. Begin by reviewing the kinds of information your office needs to organize. This process will suggest broad subject categories. Setting up a "first level" list of categories will make subsequent grouping of terms easier. Expand and refine these subject categories until you are satisfied that they cover all areas of your firm's practice that you want to organize. Try to limit the number of categories to between five and ten. This not only makes the next step more manageable but also allows a quick, first glance division for either cataloging or searching, and it is easy to remember.

Consider basing the first level of classification on the normal time sequence of the design process. For example, if you wanted to develop a thesaurus for all aspects of your practice you could base the first division on the time sequence of the design process, bracketed on one end by "Professional Practice," that group of subjects necessary for the functioning of a design office but apart from project-

```
10   PROFESSIONAL PRACTICE
     11   Education
     12   Cost estimating
     13   Law
     14   Design profession
     15   Office management
     16   Marketing
     17   Project management
     18   Financial management

20   PROGRAMMING
     21   Codes and standards
     22   Programming data
     23   Interiors types
     24   Building types
     25   Programming
     26   Completed programs

30   SCHEMATIC DESIGN
     31   Environmental psychology
     32   Design methods
     33   Site planning
     34   Energy
     35   Architectural form
     36   Reuse

40   DESIGN DEVELOPMENT AND DOCUMENTATION
     41   Building products
     42   Building systems
     43   Product selection
     44   Specifications
     45   Drawing production
     46   Standard details

50   CONSTRUCTION
     51   Construction industry
     52   Construction techniques
     53   Construction management
     54   Furniture industry

60   EVALUATION
     61   Competitions and awards
     62   Exhibits
     63   Evaluation methods
     64   Completed evaluations

70   ALLIED DISCIPLINES
     71   Planning and urban design
     72   Facility management
     73   Graphic design
     74   Product design
     75   Architectural history
```

Figure 9.3-1
First and Second Level Classification Headings

related information, and by "Allied Disciplines" on the other end. See Figure 9.3-1. You may want to just limit your system to technical subjects.

2. If the first-level classification covers all your present and expected future classification needs, you can now start the process of developing your list of terms for the controlled vocabulary and a second level of division under each of the first-level categories. As suggested earlier, use the material you have in house and the items that cross your desk as a starting point. Periodicals are very useful for this because they contain the latest developments in a field and use the terminology that describes your area of interest.

Review the title of the document first for possible terms. Next, review the abstract (if there is one), and finally read the text itself for terms used. Note the ones that seem to describe the document best. Assign a new term if you think you need to add depth to the description. This is especially true if your office may later find a document useful from a point of view different from what its author intended.

3. Review the list you are developing with other "authority lists" such as construction dictionaries, other thesauri, indexes such as the *Architectural Index* and *Art Index* and reference books. These will give the terminology others in your field are using to describe various subjects and will give more uniformity to your system compared with industry standards. Reviewing these sources may also give you some ideas about concepts or terms you left out of your list.

4. Assign each term to one of the broad first level categories you established in Step 1. Do this by recording candidate terms using the data base management program. Every time you review a term keep track of its frequency by increasing by one the number in the "frequency" data field. The frequency of a term's occurrence will be valuable later in making the final list of keywords. Also note any related terms or concepts that come to mind when you list the word. Figure 9.3-2 shows what a typical FMS data entry screen might look like. The terms grouped into five to ten divisions will make it easier to proceed to the second level.

5. After you have compiled a representative sample of terms begin to organize them into groups. Start this process by sorting the terms alphabetically. This will point out similar spellings and versions of the same concept and suggest more subdivisions or candidate terms. In Figure 9.3-3 for example, several terms listed alphabetically are closely related, but with some occurring more frequently than others. Since "Teleconferencing" occurs most often this is a likely candidate for the preferred term with the others referring to it. Depending on your office's needs more detailed terms may be listed.

6. Review other parts of your list for words that may be grouped with your first alphabetical list. In Figure 9.3-3 the term "facsimile" may be appropriately grouped with "telecommunications" for your offices' particular needs. You also have to determine which form of similar terms is the preferred version. In the

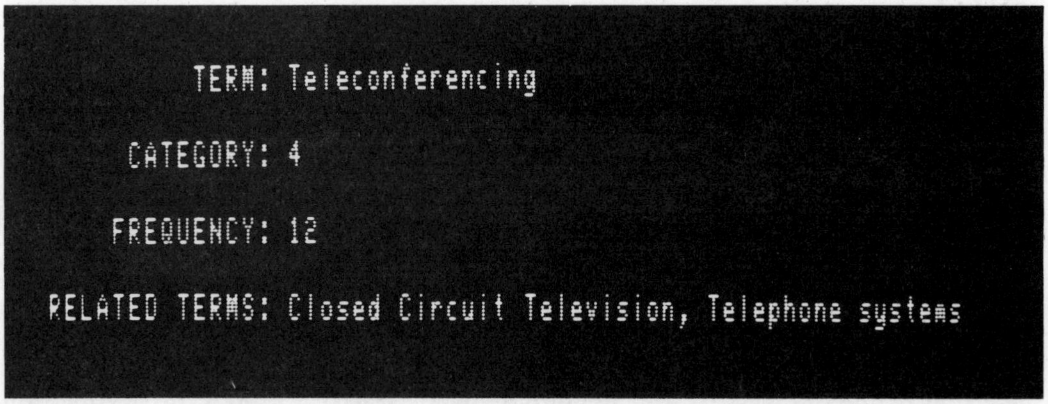

Figure 9.3-2
Thesaurus Data Entry Screen

example do you want "CCTV" or "Closed Circuit Television" as the preferred term?

7. You will find many candidate terms that have a very low frequency of use; that is, you put them on your list as you reviewed your collection or examined incoming literature, but they only came up a few times. These terms can be grouped

Term	Frequency	Related terms
Telecommunications	5	Local area networks "Smart" buildings Facsimile
Teleconferencing	12	Closed Circuit Television CCTV
Teleconferencing space layout	2	
Telegraphic images	1	
Telephone equipment rooms	3	Mechanical equipment space needs
Telephone systems	6	
Telephones	4	Telecommunications

Figure 9.3-3
Alphabetical List of Candidate Terms

with other low-frequency terms that mean about the same thing or represent the same concept that you are interested in. You will then need to assign only one term to do the work of all the others. However, in your final list, you can list the infrequently used terms and refer the user to the "approved" term with a "USE" reference. Documents later indexed are assigned only the "approved" term, giving you the "controlled vocabulary" that makes retrieval more accurate.

At this point you need to develop consistency in the forms of the terms such as whether a word is in the plural or singular form. There are well-established conventions for this such as ANSI Standard Z39.19.

8. The ultimate goal of developing a thesaurus is to give you terms that can provide effective access to your collection of information. Having terms that are too general will result in retrieving irrelevant information, and having overly specific terms will cause you to miss many relevant items. Keep in mind, however, that a term that is too general for one office might be just fine for another office. "Energy Conservation" would not be specific enough for an architectural firm doing solar energy work, but would be sufficient for an interior design firm that only occasionally indexed material on the subject.

The advantage to using a coordinate indexing system is that you can combine two or more terms from your thesaurus to add precision to your search and reduce the number of references you need to review. You can ask your computer to find all the references to items assigned the keywords "masonry" *and* "earthquake resistant construction" and get fewer items than if you searched on either word alone.

9. At this point you must make a decision about how you are going to physically store the material you classify and index using your thesaurus. This depends on the physical form of the material (books, reports, drawings, samples, catalogs, etc.) as well as how much browsing ability you want to build into the system. If you file (or shelve) all material in the same way you classify it on paper, you will probably need to create a third level (possibly a fourth) to subdivide those subjects on which you collect a lot of information. The development of your thesaurus will continue in a similar manner to the way you developed the second level.

You can still assign two or more keywords to each document to give you multiple access to the same item, but you will always have to decide on the primary keyword to give it a place on the shelf. For example, a technical report on atrium construction might discuss design considerations, fire protection, egress from atriums and lighting of atriums. You would have to choose which subject to physically file it under while assigning at least four different keywords.

You can also decide to file material chronologically, by arbitrary accession number or by some other method unrelated to subject matter. You may even store material in different locations—on the book shelves, in files, in dead storage and so on. The advantage of using a computer for information management is that classification and indexing *can* be separate from the actual storage of the

150000 OFFICE MANAGEMENT

150100   Business Management
         RT Personnel management, 150300
         RT Money management, 190200
         RT Financial planning, 190300

    150101   Business plan
    150102   Quality control
    150103   Ownership transition
             RT Ownership liability, 130407
             RT Design firm valuation, 180600
    150104   International practice
             RT International marketing, 160201
    150105   Time management
    150106   Mergers and acquisitions
             RT Design firm valuation, 180600

150200   Insurance
         RT Insurance law, 131300

    150201   Liability insurance
             RT Liability, 130400
    150202   Errors and omissions insurance
             RT Errors and omissions, 130902
    150203   Valuable papers insurance
    150204   Automobile insurance
    150205   Disability insurance

150300   Personnel management
         RT Business management, 150100

    150301   Personnel practices
    150302   Personnel practice surveys
    150303   Compensation
    150304   Personnel manual
    150305   Statutory personnel requirements
    150306   Personnel evaluation

150400   Information management
         RT Office automation 350702

    150401   Records management (procedures)
             RT Records retention, 131601
             RT Project management documentation, 170205
    150402   Filing systems   (equipment)
    150403   Design firm library
    150404   Archival storage
    150405   Data base management (systems)
    150406   Networking
             RT Computer networks, 150707
             RT Local area networks, 350703
    150407   Information sources (includes directories)

Figure 9.3-4
Thesaurus Sample Page

274

material if it is more convenient. Once the reference to the material is found, the index citation directs the user to the correct file, shelf or drawer.

10. Establish a separate term for general reference works that deal with a variety of subjects into one category. Books like *Architectural Graphic Standards* and *Time-Saver Standards* would be in this category. Since every architect knows what is in these types of references, no further indexing or classification is necessary.

Examples

Figure 9.3-4 shows one page from a detailed thesaurus developed from the first- and second-level classification system shown in Figure 9.3-1. The terms are arranged in hierarchical order. There is an alphabetical listing of all terms that accompanies this. In the example, "RT" stands for "related term," directing the user to other entries that could be useful.

Sources for More Information

American National Standards Institute. *Guidelines for Thesaurus Structure, Construction, and Use,* ANSI Z39.19. New York: American National Standards Institute, 1980.

Johoda, Gerald. *Information Storage and Retrieval Systems for Individual Researchers.* New York: Wiley-Interscience, 1970.

Kalt, Kathleen L. *Organizing and Managing Information in Architectural, Engineering and Consulting Firms.* Newington, CT: Professional Services Management Journal, 1979. Available from PSMJ, P. O. Box 11316, Newington, CT 06111.

Lane, N. D. *An Evaluation of Architectural Information Systems.* Champaign, IL: Army Construction Engineering Research Laboratory, October, 1974. Available from the National Technical Information Service, Document #AD/A-001 616.

Manual for Building a Technical Thesaurus. Available from the National Technical Information Service, Document #AD 633279.

van Erp, William. *The Architectural/Interior Design/Engineering Library.* Newington, CT: Professional Services Management Journal, 1981. Available from PSMJ, P.O. Box 11316, Newington, CT 06111.

Wynar, Bohdan S. *Introduction to Cataloging and Classification, 6th ed.* Littleton, CO: Libraries Unlimited, Inc., 1980.

9.4

IMPROVING ACCESS TO IN-HOUSE TECHNICAL DATA

One of the most difficult aspects of information management in a design office is keeping track of all the miscellaneous bits and pieces of data that do not fit neatly into an existing organizational scheme as product catalogs do. These data include such things as reprints of magazine articles, reports, correspondence containing technical information, notes taken at seminars and the like. Many architects simply keep separate files on the subjects that interest them and drop in the information as it accumulates. If the number of files is small and confined to one person's filing system this casual approach works perfectly well. However, as the number of files and people that the files must serve increases, a better method is needed.

This section outlines a method for using a microcomputer to organize this kind of technical data. Although other kinds of information commonly found in an architect's office can be included with this application you may want to separate the applications because there are some unique features of each. The next section will discuss organization and indexing of books and references and the following section describes the indexing of codes and standards. In all cases, you will find it extremely helpful to utilize a classification system and thesaurus developed for your office that was discussed in Section 9.3.

Basic Application Requirements

Organizing in-house technical data requires that you have a method for recording bibliographic information about a report, reprint and so on, and are able to access your files based on whatever search criteria you require. For example, you will probably want to find information based on subject matter as well as title. Either a file management system (FMS) or a relational data base management system (RDBMS) will meet your needs. However, you will need a RDBMS if you want to integrate this application with files containing data on books, references and codes and standards. If you are unfamiliar with this type of software refer to Appendix A, Fundamentals of Data Base Management Systems.

As a minimum, you will want your system to perform the following functions:

1. It should assist you in finding information based on subject headings. These subject headings should be part of a controlled vocabulary outlined in Section 9.3.

2. It should provide access to your information in various ways in addition to subject-oriented indexes. These should satisfy your particular needs. For example, some people may be able to remember that they took notes at a particular conference, but cannot remember exactly what topic heading it was filed under or what the title of the conference session was. Having a system that could extract only conference notes within a given time period would make the search much more manageable. Other offices may require access to their data based on geographical location.

3. The system should be able to print out lists of your current holdings sorted by subject, title or other order determined by you.

4. It should allow you to identify out-of-date information so you can purge your files periodically or, for legal purposes, to archive information on which you based design decisions.

Additional Application Requirements

One refinement to this application is to make it a part of a larger data management system that includes books, periodical indexing, codes and standards and other data. This requires relational data base management software that is capable of having several files open at once. Different types of information need to have their own files since the data fields are different. They are linked, however, by subject fields so that an information request instructs the system to find records on the same topic in all files and report these, either on screen or in printed form.

For most relational data base systems this requires some additional programming in the particular software's procedural language. If you are shopping for a RDBMS package, make sure that this kind of custom programming is possible.

Requirements of Software

If you use either a file management system or a relational data base management system, the majority of available programs will have the features you need for the basic application requirements. Refer to Appendix A, Fundamentals of Data Base Management Systems for a complete discussion of features to match to your requirements.

Requirements of Hardware

RAM. Most file management systems and some relational programs will work with as little as 64K and practically all with 128K. Many of the integrated programs need 128K or more to work.

Disks. For short, simple file management systems two floppy disks will serve your needs. As the length and number of your records increase you may find the increased storage and faster access time of a hard disk worth the investment.

Printer. A dot-matrix printer is the minimum requirement.

Cost Variables

Hardware. A complete setup with two disk drives and a dot-matrix printer can be purchased for $2,000 or less.

Software.   Simple file management programs range from under $100 to $400 with a few costing more than $400. Relational data base management programs range from about $400 to over $1,000, but with many very good programs under $800.

Setup.   As with any data base management system, setup time depends on the complexity of the application. A simple file management system can be set up in less than an hour. A more complex relational system linking several files as described above in the Additional Application Requirements may take more than a day, especially if customized programming is required.

Data entry.   Data entry can be done by whoever is in charge of the office's information management whether that person is a librarian, specification writer, secretary or project manager.

Implementation Procedures

1. Establish what kinds of technical data your office needs better access to. Some offices may have a preponderance of technical reports while others collect periodical reprints and seminar notes. What types of material you index will determine the data fields required in your data base management system.

2. Decide on whether you want to keep this application separate or integrate it with other files such as codes and standards. If so, you will need a relational data base management system. Review Section 9.5 to see if you may want to include books and trade association literature with this application.

3. Decide on the data fields you will need in each record. These depend on the kinds of information you are indexing as well as the points of access you want. Consider the following list as a starting point.

document number (if you assign a unique identifying number to each piece of information)

title of document (if a periodical reprint, the title of the article)

author

document type (reprint, notes, research report, etc.)

subject(s) (based on your office's controlled vocabulary)

location in your office

publisher

publisher's address

report number (useful for reordering or reference)

periodical name in which the document was located

number of pages

date

price

abstract or brief description of the document

masterformat number (if product related)

name of conference or seminar from which the data came

geograhical area the document relates to

building type involved

You will not need or want all these data fields. Select the ones that will give you the easiest and most complete access to your collection. When you select the fields to be used as "keys" for indexing and sorting, keep in mind the way you and others in the office actually remember things. Subjects, document types and sometimes well-known authors are likely candidates for key fields.

4. Since the size of this kind of file can be substantial, estimate how much storage you will need. Determine the number of bytes (characters) in each of the data fields established in Step 3. Add these to get the total bytes in each record and multiply by the estimated number of records you are likely to have. This information will help you decide on how to allocate floppy disks or hard disks for this application and whether to incorporate this application with other information management functions. If you are shopping for a computer system, this will also help you define your needs more precisely.

5. Set up the data entry formats, indexes, report formats and other components of the system following the instructions of your data base management software.

6. Decide on how to treat existing documents. You can enter all data on existing documents as a separate file and start fresh with new data that come into your office or you can purge seldom-used and obsolete documents and just enter the most useful ones. Remember, before you throw something away make sure you do not need it to back up previous design decisions in case legal problems develop.

7. As with all data base management, establish an office policy on who maintains the system, who enters data and when and what reports are regularly produced.

Additional Tips

- There should be only one person designated as the central control point for classifying and entering information into the system. This will give you consistency in indexing and storage and improve the chances for accurate retrieval.

- Instead of logging each piece of information as it comes into the office, set up a separate "in-basket" for the material and establish a regular schedule of data entry. You will spend your time more efficiently and classification of the material will be more uniform if you do it in groups.

- If the storage capacity of your existing system is limited, consider logical divisions of files. For example, you can assign a year's worth of information to one disk. Since much of the data in the profession is timely it makes sense not to clutter the most current data base with what could be outdated information. However, you still have it if you need it.

9.5
A SYSTEMATIC WAY TO INDEX BOOKS AND REFERENCES

Organizing books and trade association literature is similar to the application discussed in section 9.4, but somewhat simpler. Unlike the variety of formats of technical data discussed in the previous section, books and association literature can be catalogued according to a consistent bibliographic format. The quantity of books and trade association literature most architectural offices maintain is minimal and this makes it easier to access the valuable information they contain.

Basic Application Requirements

This application should fulfill the standard requirements of any library by providing access to your reference collection based on title, author and subject. You can think of it as setting up an electronic card catalog, but instead of having separate cards for title, author and subjects, you just enter the desired information on each reference once and index on any fields you like.

A simple file management type of data base management system is adequate for this application. Refer to Appendix A, Fundamentals of Data Base Management Systems, if you are unfamiliar with this type of software. At a minimum, each record in your data base should contain the following fields:

author

title

publisher

date of publication

call number

subject

In addition, consider including additional data fields:

author 2 (You may want to search on more than one name or simply have this extra field for complete bibliographic information) reference type (For example, you may search on book, pamphlet, video tape, etc.)

location (Your reference material may be spread out on shelves, in file cabinets, in someone's office)

subject 2, subject 3, etc. (One of the real advantages to a computerized index is being able to search on multiple subject headings. Include as many as your material requires.)

pages (This is useful to give the searcher an idea of the scope of the reference.)

Additional Application Requirements

For the simplest file management systems, you will have to separate multiple subject headings into distinct fields in your data base record so that you can search on more than one topic. This will usually not be a problem because most software will allow you to search for a keyword that is either in the "Subject 1" field *or* the "Subject 2" field *or* the "Subject 3" field. Thus, if two references had the same subject headings assigned to them, but in different order in the data fields, this kind of search would find them both. In a similar way, you could look for references that only have keywords in the "Subject 1" field *and* the "Subject 2" field.

Some data base software has the capability to search for a string (any combination of letters and numbers) anywhere in the data field. This is an advantage for subject searching because you don't have to be as careful with the setup of subject fields. You could, for example, search the "Title" field for a subject word as well as a long subject field containing several subject headings. It takes a program longer to make this kind of search than a search on an indexed file, but the advantages outweigh the extra wait. If you are shopping for a data base management system, look for this feature.

If you want to set up a comprehensive system for your office's information retrieval, this application can be part of a relational data base management system that includes in-house technical data, codes and standards and periodical indexing as well as books. Each of these separate files can be linked by subject fields so that an information request would result in the data base returning all records in all files on the topic requested.

Requirements of Software

Your data base management software should be able to index and sort on any of the data fields. You may want to create a "shelf list," for example, of all your holdings for inventory purposes. This would include a listing by document number.

The program should also allow you to search on more than one field at a time using relational operators such as "less than" and "equal to" and the Boolean operators of "or" and "and" so you can use multiple subject fields or, for example, search for all references on a particular topic published after a particular date.

Refer to Appendix A on data base management systems for a more complete discussion of specific program features.

Requirements of Hardward

RAM.   Many file management systems will work with as little as 64K and practically all with 128K. The more sophisticated relational data base management systems usually require 128K or more.

Disks.   For small files, two floppy disks are adequate, one for the program and one for data. Floppy disks may be preferable to a hard disk because you can assign a distinct file to a particular disk without taking up hard disk space.

Printer.   Any type of printer will work, but for this application, a faster dot-matrix or laser printer may be desirable for in-house searching and complete listings of your data base.

Cost Variables

Hardware.   A complete setup with two disk drives and a dot-matrix printer can be purchased for $2,000 or less.

Software.   Simple file management programs range from under $100 to $400 with a few costing more than $400. Relational data base management programs range from about $400 to over $1,000, but with many very good programs under $800.

Setup.   A simple file management system can be set up in an hour or two depending on the software.

Data entry.   Data entry for this application is time consuming. If you already have standard library cards for your references, data entry is simply a matter of keyboarding this information into your system. If you are starting with your collection of references "on the shelf" it will take longer.

Implementation Procedures

1. If you don't already have cataloging cards, make one for each reference you will be indexing. This adds extra time to the process, but serves several valuable functions:

   a. It forces you to decide if you need the reference at all, or whether you need to order a more current copy.

b. It provides the opportunity for someone knowledgeable in the subject field to assign usable keywords. These may be based on an existing classification system or one you devise (See Section 9.3). The actual keyboarding can then be done by a secretary or temporary clerical help.

c. It forces you to classify each reference so it can be shelved or filed in an assigned position.

2. Decide on the data fields you need in each record. For many applications you may only need to keep track of the author, title, date, call number and one or more subject fields.

3. Set up the data entry formats, indexes and report formats following the instructions of your software.

4. Enter the data from the cards you created in Step 1. Establish an office policy of who enters new information, at what intervals it is done and who maintains the system.

Example

The San Francisco office of Gensler and Associates uses an IBM Displaywriter to produce and maintain their library list of about 500 volumes. For subject headings they use the Library of Congress system. Each record contains the following data fields:

author 1

author 2

title

publisher

date of publication

medium (book, video tape, etc.)

location

call number

subject 1

subject 2

subject 3

With this as the basis for their system, the librarian can produce a subject catalog, title list and shelf list for inventory. A sample page of their title list is shown in Figure 9.5-1.

Additional Tips

- If you do not have your own classification system and don't want to establish one (See Section 9.3), consider using the Library of Congress system. Most

Author 1	Engineering News-Record	Engineering News-Record
Author 2		
Title	ENR directory of contractors, 1981-1982.	ENR directory of design firms, 1984-85.
Publisher	McGraw-Hill Book Co. 1980	McGraw-Hill Inc. 1984
Med/Loc	BOOK LIB	BOOK LIB
Call No.	TA12 E	TA12 E
Series Sta.	Fourth Edition	Sixth Edition
Subject 1	Contractors-Directories	Architects-Directories
Subject 2		
Subject 3		
Subject 4		
Subject 5		

Author 1	Kelly, J. Frederick	Whitehead, Russell, ed.
Author 2		Brown, Frank Choutaeu, ed.
Title	Early domestic architecture of Connecticut.	Early homes of Massachusetts.
Publisher	Dover Publications Inc. 1952	Arno Press Inc. 1977
Med/Loc	BOOK LIB	BOOK LIB
Call No.	NA7235 K	NA7235 W
Series Sta.		Architectural Treasures of Early America
Subject 1	Architecture, domestic-Connecticut	Massachusetts-Historic houses, etc.
Subject 2	Connecticut-Historic houses, etc.	Architecture, domestic-Massachusetts
Subject 3	Housing-Design and construction	Housing-Design and construction
Subject 4		
Subject 5		

Author 1	Fields, Randy	Hozumi, Nobuo
Author 2		
Title	Economic analysis and personal investment strategy.	Eero Saarinen: TWA Terminal (New York), Dulles Int'l Airport (Washington, D.C.)
Publisher	1978	A.D.A. EDITA Tokyo 1973
Med/Loc	AUD LIB	BOOK LIB
Call No.	AUD	NA6 G
Series Sta.		Global Architecture 26
Subject 1	Business-Technique	Saarinen, Eero-Architecture
Subject 2		Airports-Architecture
Subject 3		
Subject 4		
Subject 5		

Author 1	Rossman, Wendell, E.	Drucker, Peter F.
Author 2		
Title	Effective architect.	Effective executive.
Publisher	Prentice-Hall Inc. 1972	Harper and Row 1966
Med/Loc	BOOK LIB	BOOK LIB
Call No.	NA1996 R	HD38 D
Series Sta.		
Subject 1	Architectural services marketing-Technique	Management-Technique
Subject 2	Office practice-Technique	Organizational behavior-Technique
Subject 3		
Subject 4		
Subject 5		

Figure 9.5-1
Title List Report

books already have the call number and subject headings assigned in the book (called "cataloging in print"). This speeds assigning keywords and for other references, the Library of Congress' *Guide to Subject Headings* is available.

- The subject heading data fields are the most important for successful use of your system. Most architects need information based on subjects and not titles or authors. Carefully evaluate how you want to be able to search and find the software that lets you do it according to *your* needs.

9.6

ACCESSING CODES AND STANDARDS

Codes and standards present a unique information management problem for architects and interior designers. On any given job, the number of standards mentioned in the specifications and those made part of a building code by reference may number in the hundreds. The architect and interior designer must be aware of the requirements of all of these and either have copies in the office or be able to quickly find them if necessary. An additional problem is the rate with which codes and standards are revised. The advantages to having a comprehensive data base of codes and standards targeted to the unique needs of your practice outweigh the time involved in setting up and maintaining the data base.

There are several reasons why indexing codes and standards should be a separate computer application instead of being combined with other indexing. More active updating is required, the types of access points required are different from other information (alphanumeric designations, unique subject headings and so forth), and there is the possibility that the physical location of the standard may be outside the office (in a university or public library, for example).

Basic Application Requirements

Indexing codes and standards is best accomplished with a data base management system because you need a way to easily update your listings and sort and search them in various ways. In setting up your operation you will need to decide if your data base will simply keep track of the codes and standards you have in your office or whether you want to be able to locate copies in your geographical region. For example, it may not be cost effective to own all the ASTM standards. Knowing what local library has them may be sufficient for those times when you need a particular reference.

In either case, for standards, you should list each individual standard that is applicable to your practice, not just the compilation such as *ASTM Standards in Building Codes.* This allows you to pull out applicable standards when writing specifications, update them when you learn a revision has taken place and easily refer to a particular standard when it is referenced in a building code. Initially, the time and effort required to set up the data base will be significant, but once that is done, updating and adding new codes and standards is easy.

However, codes and standards should be kept in separate computer files because they will contain slightly different data fields and you will want to access them in different ways.

You may find it desirable to maintain a "retrospective" codes and standards file to keep a historical record of the regulations your office used on past jobs. This kind of archival information could be vital to your defense if a legal problem developed on a project you completed. However, if you decide to index past codes and specifications, these should be kept in a separate file to avoid inadvertently using one on a current job.

If you have a limited number of codes, or your office does work in a limited geographical area you may not need to set up a data base for codes, but rather focus your efforts on standards.

Additional Application Requirements

A simple listing of both codes that apply to your practice and geographical areas in which you work, and the standards that you use most often, is probably sufficient for most people. A more advanced (and difficult) application is to take the building code you use the most and index it section by section. You could then search by keyword, building type, occupancy group or any other method most useful to you. Your data base would not have to contain the actual text, but simply keywords or summaries of each section.

You could make queries of the data base on screen or produce printed reports that would be "checklists" for a particular building type and occupancy group.

Requirements of Software

A simple file management type of data base management software is sufficient for this application and the majority of programs of this type will have the features you need for the basic application requirements. Refer to Appendix A, Fundamentals of Data Base Management Systems, for a complete discussion of features you should consider. At a minimum, you will want software that can index and sort on any of the data fields, and that can select records based on criteria on one or more fields.

Requirements of Hardware

RAM. Many file management systems will work with as little as 64K and practically all with 128K.

Disks.   Two floppy disks will meet the requirements of this application since the size of the data base will be relatively small.

Printer.   Any type of printer will work for this application, but you may want a dot-matrix or laser printer for faster output.

Cost Variables

Hardware.   A complete setup with two disk drives and a dot-matrix printer can be purchased for $2,000 or less.

Software.   Simple file management programs range from under $100 to $400 with a few costing more than $400.

Setup.   Initial definition of the data base parameters can be set up in very little time depending on the software. Usually, less than one hour is required.

Data entry.   Initial data entry is the most time-consuming part of this application. Rather than attack the problem all at once, you can begin by entering data applicable to one job you are working on. As you complete additional projects, more codes and standards can be entered into the data base. You will find that certain standards are repeated over and over, so as you build your data base, the data entry time will decrease.

However, you may need to devote additional time and money to researching codes and standards that are applicable to your practice but that you have not used in the past.

Implementation Procedures

1. Decide if you need to set up *both* a codes data base and a standards data base. If your practice is small or you do work in a limited geographical region, you may use so few codes that it isn't necessary to do both.

2. Using your data base management software, set up the data entry formats, indexes and report formats required. For your standards data base use the following data fields:

> standard number (This is the alphanumeric designation given by the issuing organization such as ASTM E-119. Do not include the date, however, which is usually a suffix to the standard number. If all standards you index have an acronym as a prefix, you do not need to set up a separate data field for the issuing organization.)
>
> title
>
> standard date (You may want to put this in a format as required by your data base management software so you can search by date; for example, YY/MM/DD)
>
> date of your in-house copy

cross-reference to other organization's number (For example, many Underwriter Laboratories, ASTM and ANSI standards have different designations for the same test or standard)

location (This can be either the location in your office or where you can find a hard copy of the standard in your region)

masterformat number (This data field refers to the specification section or sections for which the standard is most appropriate. It can be used to assist in writing specifications by pulling out all those standards in the data base that the specifier may want to include in the project manual.)

subject(s) (This field is used for keyword searches such as finding all the standards relating to "fire resistance" or "wood doors." Use a controlled vocabulary discussed in Section 9.3 for assigning keywords.)

For a codes data base use the following data fields:

issuing agency (For example, the city publishing the code, the state, or one of the model code agencies.)

code type (Building code, zoning ordinance, land use, etc.)

title

date of the latest edition of the code

date of your in-house copy

geographical area served (This is useful if you want to search out all the applicable codes that apply to a particular area in which you are beginning a project)

location in your library

3. Begin entering data with the standards you have in your office. As you do, verify that the ones you have are current. One of the easiest ways to do this is obtain a current index from the various standards-producing agencies such as ASTM and ANSI.

4. If you have the time and personnel, collect the standards you have used in past jobs, verify their currency and enter them in the data base. If you cannot do this at once, select one project you are starting and as you research the standards and specifications required, enter these into your system. Continue to add more as you complete additional jobs.

Additional Tip

Before you update your data base, make a copy of the codes and standards disk to serve as an archival copy. You then have a permanent record of the regulations you used during any particular time period.

Sources for More Information

ASTM Standards in Building Codes. American Society for Testing and Materials, 1916 Race Street, Philadelphia, PA 19103.

Index and Directory of U.S. Industry Standards. Englewood, CO: Information Handling Services, 1983.

KWIC Index of U.S. Voluntary Engineering Standards. Washington: National Bureau of Standards, 1982. Available on computer printout and microfiche.

Goldberg, Alfred. *Design Guide to the 1985 Uniform Building Code.* Mill Valley, CA: GRDA Publications, 1985.

Associations

Information Handling Services
15 Inverness Way East
Englewood, CO 80150
IHS produces the Industry and International Standards data base available through BRS (See Appendix B) and the Tech-Net data base available through Information Handling Services.

National Center for Standards and Certification Information
Office of Product Standards Policy, National Bureau of Standards
U.S. Department of Commerce
Technology Building
Washington, DC, 20234

National Standards Association, Inc.
5161 River Road
Bethesda, MD 20816
NSA produces the Standard and Specifications Data Base available through DIALOG (See Appendix B). The information is also produced on microfiche.

CHAPTER 10

How to Gain Additional Value from Your Computer: Commercial Data Bases, Computer Conferencing, Networking and Electronic Mail

One of the most exciting aspects of a computer is its ability to connect us with the outside world in ways never before possible. For the first time, the microcomputer can bring such concepts as the "global village" and the "electronic cottage" to fruition. For architectural and interior design firms the implications are vast. Not only can you communicate faster and more completely but you can also benefit from the incredible amount of information contained in hundreds of data bases.

The sections in this chapter show how you can use the computer as a communication tool. They give you step-by-step guidance for tapping into large data bases, describe how to connect your hardware for even more power, and illustrate how to take advantage of electronic connections with your clients and other professionals away from your office. Appendix A provides the essentials of data base management systems. Appendix B details the dozens and dozens of on-line data bases where you will find a wealth of information you can use in your practice every day.

10.1

TAPPING THE WEALTH OF INFORMATION IN COMMERCIAL DATA BASES

With the continued development of on-line data bases the architect has an enormous amount of information available at his or her fingertips. This information can be accessed easily through a personal computer equipped with a modem and communications software.

Commercial data bases are files of information on a particular subject stored in computer memory and retrievable through simple commands. The most common type of data base record is "bibliographic" in which each record in the data base contains enough information to enable the user to decide if the complete document should be consulted. The record may contain the title of the reference, author, publisher, date, "descriptors" and an abstract, and other information. In this sense, computer data bases are similar in concept to printed indexes such as *Architectural Index* and *Business Periodicals Index.*

Other types of data bases are full-text, in which the complete document is reproduced, and statistical, in which the data is numerical as in a cost-estimating data base.

There are many benefits for the architect:

1. The information is current. In most cases data is input into a computer data base long before the equivalent printed version is available.

2. A data base search is cost effective. Most well-planned searches can be conducted for twenty to forty dollars in about fifteen minutes. The time required to search the same number of records manually might take several hours or days.

3. The search is comprehensive. You can search millions of records in minutes for the information you need.

4. You can make the search as broad or as narrow as necessary. By combining search descriptors (words that describe the topic you are interested in) with "and," "or" and "not," and searching on ranges, you can be very precise (or general) with your request. This is something you cannot do with simple printed indexes that list subject under only one heading at a time.

Data bases are produced by various kinds of organizations in a specific field from trade associations to government agencies. For example, World Aluminum Abstracts is produced by the Aluminum Association while the Federal Energy Data Index is produced by the U.S. Department of Energy. Access to most data bases is provided by "search services." These are companies who buy individual data bases from many sources and provide the computers, communication links, programming and administrative services to make it all work.

The three most widely used search services are DIALOG, ORBIT and BRS. For more information and a current catalog of the data bases these companies provided access to, write to them at the following addresses.

DIALOG Information Services, Inc.
Marketing Department
3460 Hillview Avenue
Palo Alto, CA 94304

ORBIT Search Service
SDC Information Services
2500 Colorado Avenue
Santa Monica, CA 90406

BRS
1200 Route 7
Latham, NY 12110

In addition to these, there is *The Source,* a popular consumer-oriented information service that includes access to many data bases as well as offering electronic mail, electronic "bulletin boards" and computer conferences. The American Institute of Architects uses *The Source* for its networking system (See Section 10.2 for more details). Some of the data bases available include the *Commerce Business Daily,* UPI reports on national and local news, stock market quotations and Management Contents. For more information write to them at *The Source,* 1616 Anderson Road, McLean, VA 22102.

Unfortunately, there is not one computer data base that provides complete coverage of the wide range of information useful for architecture and interior design. You have to select the one that will provide you with the best information for your particular need. Refer to Figure 10.1-1 for a summary of the available data bases and the information needs for which they are most appropriate. Appendix B gives a complete listing of these along with a description of the kinds of data they contain.

Basic Application Requirements

For this application you only need to send commands to the search service and have a printer to record your "conversation" and retrieved data from the supplier. Contact the search services you are interested in using to get their specific software and hardware requirements. The following software and hardware requirements outline what you will need.

Requirements of Software

There are two basic approaches you can take with accessing commercial data bases. One is to use a terminal supplied by or recommended by the search service. These are simply keyboards with an integral printer (no screen) that serve no function other than to connect you with the central computer. The other approach is to use your microcomputer with software that turns your computer into a "communications terminal" rather than a computer. If you plan on conducting data base searches during most of the work day, you may want to consider a dedicated terminal so you don't tie up your micro.

If you use a personal computer for accessing commercial data bases you will need communications software. This performs the basic function of sending signals

Figure 10.1-1
Data Bases Useful for Architectural and Design Practice

	General information	Management	Marketing	Programming	Regulations	Schematic design	Energy/Environment	Post occupancy evaluation	Building system technology	Product information	Specifications	Building costs	Construction industry	Transportation design	Government affairs	DIALOG	BRS	SDC	OWN COMPANY
ABI/INFORM		•	•												•	•	•	•	
API	•	•	•	•	•	•	•	•	•	•	•	•	•		•				•
ASI			•									•	•			•		•	
AVERY	•	•	•	•	•	•	•	•	•	•		•	•	•					•
B/P SOFTWARE		•														•			
BEIS							•												•
BEK SYSTEM										•									•
CBD			•													•			
CDD	•	•	•			•	•	•					•		•	•	•		
CIS/INDEX						•	•						•		•	•		•	
COLD						•	•	•										•	
COMPENDEX	•						•		•	•	•	•	•	•	•	•	•	•	
COMPUSOURCE										•									•
COMSPEC											•								•
CRECORD	•					•		•					•		•	•		•	
DISCLOSURE II		•	•													•			•
DMI			•																•
DODGE CIS												•							•
DS			•																•
EA	•															•			
EIS IP			•													•			
ENERGYLINE						•	•	•	•				•		•	•		•	
ENERGYNET	•						•								•	•			
ENVIROLINE	•						•									•		•	
FEDREG					•											•		•	
FEDRIP	•							•	•							•		•	
JSAH	•																•		
M & S COST												•							•
M & S REM												•							•
MC	•	•	•										•		•	•	•	•	
MDD			•													•			
MLSS						•						•					•		
NCJRS				•		•										•			•
NDEX	•																	•	
NNI	•															•			
NTIS							•	•	•				•	•	•	•	•	•	•
PTS AR			•													•	•		
PTS F & S			•													•	•		
SHOWROOM										•									•
STD AND SPECS				•							•					•			
STDS				•							•						•		
TECHNET				•						•	•								•
TI	•	•											•		•	•			
TRIS-ON-LINE														•		•			
TTD										•									•
WAA										•						•			
WT										•						•			

294

from your keyboard to the data base and receiving signals from the data base and making them understandable to your computer. Additionally, the software controls the various communications parameters that must be set to allow you to "talk" to the data base.

There are other things communication software can do. One is to allow you to download or upload information from a disk file rather than from the keyboard. This saves time and often money because most of the work can be done off line and then sent to the data base at a rate much faster than you could type it. You should consider getting this feature in any software you are thinking of purchasing. Another software feature is the ability to program keys so you can dial the data base, enter the log-on procedure and your password with one or two keystrokes.

There is additional software that may be of use to you. It is called on-line access software and it makes using certain data bases faster, easier and more complete. Some types of software simplify the commands you need to enter for certain data bases; others, such as that created for the Dow Jones News/Retrieval Service, help you extract only the information of interest to you in the quickest way possible.

Requirements of Hardware

Modem. A modem (modulator/demodulator) converts the digital signals of your computer into analog signals that can be transmitted over telephone lines, and converts the analog signals from the data base back into digital signals your computer can understand. It is the primary piece of additional hardware you will need to implement this application (assuming you already have some kind of micro). Some computers are being sold with modems built in. If you are shopping and plan to communicate with the outside world, this may be one feature you should consider when making comparisons.

Most modems operate at either 300 baud or 1200 baud. A "baud" is a unit of operating speed; ten baud equals one character sent or received per second so a 300 baud modem operates at 30 characters per second while a 1200 baud modem operates at 120.

Some modems use an acoustic coupler to connect with the telephone while others connect directly. There are some problems with acoustic couplers so only consider the direct connect variety for most reliable operation.

Modems connect to the computer with a serial port (much like some printers). Some computers may require you to get a separate communications card that fits inside the computer and provides the point of connection. Check with your dealer to see what you must do to hook up your computer.

Disks. Typically, only one disk is required to load the communication software and hold downloaded files.

Printer. Any kind of printer is acceptable for this application, but you may want to consider the fastest printer you can find since you pay for every second you are on line.

Cost Variables

Hardware. A basic 300 baud direct connect modem costs in the range of $200 to $300. A 1200 baud modem (which will also work at 300 baud) costs in the range of $500 to $800 depending on the "extras" you get with it.

Software. Communications software ranges from about $50 to $200 depending on how many features it has.

Setup. You can expect to spend from about one hour to several hours initially setting up your hardware, communications software and modem controls.

Start-up fees. Some data bases or search services charge a nominal, one-time start-up fee while others do not.

On-line charges. This charge accounts for the majority of the ongoing cost of accessing commercial data bases. Each data base charges a different rate per hour of connect time (the time you are actually accessing the data base). These rates range from a low of about $25 per hour to over $100 per hour at the time of this writing. Keep in mind, however, that you typically are connected to a data base for only a fraction of an hour and that your connect time is recorded down to the thousandth of an hour so a "long" 15 minute search on a $100 per hour data base would only cost $25. One of the advantages of using a high-speed modem (1200 baud or higher) is to minimize the connect time.

Communication charges. Depending on the service you use, these charges range from about $6.00 per hour to $20.00 per hour at the time of this writing.

Output. Most of the online query of the data base is part of the direct connection charges. When you want to have a complete citation displayed or printed, there is an extra charge per citation. Data base citations are least expensive if they are printed "off line" by the search service and mailed to you. The trade-off for saving money is having to wait several days to receive them. Citations printed off line range from about $0.10 to $0.50 per record.

Some data bases charge for the display of a full record while online. Most of these cost from $0.05 to $0.35 with some charging more. If you want to print a full record online you are charged for display itself, the connect time and communication time while that record is being printed. The cost, therefore, depends on the connect time charge for the data base, the length of record being printed, and the speed of communication (baud rate and printer speed).

As an example, assume you are connected to a data base charging $90 per hour. This works out to $.025 per second. If the record being printed takes 20 seconds to type then your cost is approximately $.50 plus whatever communication charges you are paying. If the data base charges $.25 for offline printing you are paying double for the convenience of having the information immediately. The cost is nominal if you only have a few records, but the cost of printing dozens can add up fast.

Implementation Procedures

1. Review your office's needs for data base information to determine which kinds of services would benefit you the most. Use the listing of data bases in Appendix B as a starting point.

2. From the information given in the appendix, determine which search services supply access to the data bases you want. You may find that you need two or more, one of the large services listed earlier and another, specialized data base that provides its own access to subscribers.

3. Write to your selected search services for catalogues and subscription information. You should specifically ask for technical requirements of software, modems and communication services so you can buy the right kind of hardware.

4. If you already have a microcomputer, purchase the communication software and modem required for your setup. If you want to have a dedicated terminal for this application consider purchasing or leasing one. Leases may range from about $75–$150 per month depending on the brand and features included.

5. Subscribe to the search service you select. They will send you a password for access to the system and specific instructions about log-on procedures and the specific methods of querying the data bases. Read the information they send you thoroughly! Your instructions to the computer must be exact and making many mistakes while on line will cost you money. Some search services give you a few free hours of use when you first subscribe so you can learn the system, but after that you are charged for every fraction of a second.

6. When you are ready to do a search, plan your strategy *before* getting on line. Consider the following items:

- Determine what individual data bases you are going to search. Some will be more appropriate for particular information needs than others.

- Think of all the possible descriptors (keywords) that describe the subject you are researching. Some data bases (such as Compendex) use preferred words listed in a printed thesaurus (in the case of Compendex, they use the *Engineering Index Thesaurus*). If such thesauri are available, use them. They will usually lead you to what you need faster and more accurately. Many data bases have on-line thesauri as well.

- Think of how you want to combine your descriptors. You can coordinate terms in certain ways to narrow your search. For example, you can ask the data base to find citations described with word "A" *and* word "B" but *not* word "C."

- If you are searching a bibliographic data base, think of any prominent authors that might have written on your subject. You can search based on authors' names and this is often a good way to find pertinent citations.

Additional Tips

- Check to see if the search services you are using have special rates for evenings or weekend use—you can often save money working off hours. An additional benefit is that the response time is faster because there are fewer people using the system.

- Consider taking a training course if one is offered by the search service or data base company you are going to use. Each has their own form of commands and investing a little time up front may save a considerable amount of money later by avoiding wasted search time.

- If you are not sure which data bases may be best for you consider contracting with an independent researcher, public library or university library in your area to do a few searches. You can "get the feel" of researching this way without buying any of the necessary equipment. You are only charged the costs of the search (access, citation printing, communication time, etc.) as well as whatever fee is involved. An added advantage is that the researcher can help you structure your search to be most efficient.

- To save money in having citations displayed or printed on line, have just a few displayed while you are searching. These are usually enough to let you know if your chosen descriptors are finding the kinds of information you need.

Sources for More Information

Directories

Computer-Readable Data Bases: A Directory and Data Sourcebook
Latest edition
American Library Association, Publishing Services
50 East Huron
Chicago, IL 60611

Database Directory
Latest edition
Knowledge Industry Publications, Inc.
701 Westchester Avenue
White Plains, NY 10604

Datapro Directory of On-line Services
Datapro Research Corporation
1805 Underwood Boulevard
Delran, NJ 08075

Directory of Online Data Bases
Latest edition
Cuandra Associates
2001 Wilshire Boulevard Suite 305
Santa Monica, CA 90403

Encyclopedia of Information Systems and Services
Latest edition
Gale Research Company
Book Tower
Detroit, MI 48226

Guide to Dial-Up Databases
Latest edition
Datapro Research Corporation
1805 Underwood Boulevard
Delran, NJ 08075

Online Bibliographic Databases
Latest edition
Gale Research Company
Book Tower
Detroit, MI 48226

Public Data Bases for Design Firms
American Consulting Engineers Council
1015 Fifteenth St. N.W.
Washington, DC 20005

Basics of Online Searching. Meadow, Charles T., Cochrane, Pauline (Atherton). New York: John Wiley & Sons, 1981.

The Executives Guide to Online Information Services. Hoover, Ryan E. White Plains, NY: Industry Publications, Inc., 1984.

10.2

VALUABLE IDEAS FOR COMPUTER CONFERENCING

There are several ways architects and interior designers can use a computer's power for communicating. This section describes how to apply microcomputers

299

for discussing or exploring a particular issue by using computer conferencing. This application differs somewhat from local area networks, multiuser systems and electronic mail in that there is usually a particular group of participants involved with computer conferencing and they tend to "communicate" about one subject at a time just as in a standard conference. Other applications will be discussed in Sections 10.3 and 10.4.

With computer conferencing, or electronic text messaging as it is sometimes called, the participants in a conference can be in different parts of the country (or world) and can access the system anytime it is convenient for them. Thus, an architect in the San Francisco office of a firm can place a message on the system late in the afternoon so his colleague in a New York office can read it the next morning. Later, the field representative on the job site in Kansas City can review the "discussion."

In another instance, there may be an "open" conference dealing with problems of single-ply roofing. Architects, roofing contractors, suppliers and others may contribute their questions, experiences and solutions on an ongoing basis over a long period of time. Anyone may join in at any time to contribute. The collected knowledge base built up becomes a valuable electronic library of information on this one subject.

Computer conferencing does not replace a telephone call for instant communication or regular mail (or electronic mail) for transmitting paper-based information. Rather, it's best use is for ongoing discussions and development of management directions for a company who has many employees in many locations, or for people in many firms who want to "talk" about a particular subject. The conference can either be "closed" to a select number of people or "open" to anyone who wants to participate.

Basic Application Requirements

Computer conferencing requires a central computer that provides the software to run the system and serves as the storage center for incoming messages. Each participant in the system needs a terminal to send and receive messages as well as a modem to send signals over telephone lines. Large companies can set up their own systems based on in-house mainframes and their own software, but most people take part in computer conferencing by tapping into one of the many publicly available services. The service provides the computer and software. For the cost of on-line time and communication charges you can start a conference.

For architects, one type of conferencing system is available through ArchNet, a computer network offered by the American Institute of Architects through *The Source*. With the program PARTI, subscribers can participate in either open forums or in private conferences with other members.

300

Additional Application Requirements

In addition to basic text messaging, you may want to consider graphic capabilities. Of course, this is more expensive, but could be useful to large firms who need to exchange marketing and report-type graphics between many offices. With some of the more sophisticated systems it is also possible to access commercial data bases online while a conference is taking place.

Requirements of Software

Special software is required for this application. This ranges from the simple communications programs that allow your computer to answer an incoming call, to mainframe-based applications. Since most architects and designers who decide to implement this application will be using one of the available services, actually selecting software is not a problem; that is already provided. Rather, you may want to evaluate what features are offered by several services you are considering. Use the following list in your evaluation. Not all these features may be necessary for your needs; you will have to make the final determination.

- Do you have the option of a "closed," "open," or "read-only" type of conference? A closed conference is limited to a select group of people who have a password to take part in the conference while an open one allows anyone to access it. With a read-only conference, anyone can read messages but only those with passwords can add comments.
- Does the system allow several people to be on line at the same time?
- Does the system automatically notify you of any messages received since you last signed on? This way you don't have to reread messages you may have already seen—a real time saver when hundreds of comments are put onto the system.
- Can you search for open conferences by keywords included in their descriptions?
- Is there on-line help?
- Does the system include a word processor or some kind of text editor so you can write and edit longer messages to include in the conference?
- Is there an electronic mail option?
- Does the system have a voting option so you can poll the participants on issues being discussed?

Requirements of Hardware

Unless you plan to set up a dedicated, in-house system on a mini- or mainframe computer, hardware requirements are fairly simple. All you need is a microcomputer, modem and appropriate communications software. With these, you can log on to one of the publicly available systems such as The Source and begin a conference.

Cost Variables

If you use one of the available systems, the primary cost variables are on-line time charges and communications charges. Of course, if you are starting from scratch you will need to purchase a microcomputer, modem and communications software. As with most on-line charges, rates vary depending on the time of day you use the system, normal business hours being the most expensive, and evenings and weekends being much less expensive. The baud rate you use also determines the charge; 1200 baud generally being more than 300 baud. Contact each company for their current rates and method of billing.

Implementation Procedures

1. Select the system you want to use. If you are thinking of developing your own in-house system the time and expense will be significant—only the largest firms may be able to justify this approach. If you are going to tap into one of the existing services, use the list provided above under "Requirements of Software" to help guide your decisions. Since both ArchNet and PARTI are on The Source you may want to investigate them first.

2. If you are going to use computer conferencing primarily for in-house use among several remote offices, clients and others, assign someone the responsibility of being the central coordinator. This person can organize the conferences, help answer questions about the system and encourage everyone to make the best use of the concept.

3. Once you decide to hold a conference, decide if it is to be "open," "closed," or "read-only." Give the conference a name and write a brief description of its purpose, the topics to be discussed, who should participate and similar information. This is equivalent to developing a detailed agenda for any meeting. If you set up an open conference, this description is important to help others decide if they are interested. If it is a closed conference it keeps everyone focused on the issue at hand. Also, if the conference is closed, assign everyone a password.

4. Following the procedures of the particular system you are using simply log-on and start. The advantage of electronic conferencing is that you can partici-

pate when you want to or when you have the time—day or night—not according to some prearranged schedule. You will find that the ongoing dialog may actually be more stimulating and thought provoking than a face-to-face meeting with all of its distractions of personalities, body language, formalities and protocol.

Additional Tips

- Implementation of a successful computer conferencing system requires new ways of communicating. Be prepared to do a lot of "coaching" and motivating of the participants until everyone gets used to the system.
- Support from top management is essential. Everyone must feel that implementation of computer conferencing is important enough to warrant involvement from senior people in the firm.
- Find the most "user-friendly" software possible to make it easy for everyone to use. Complicated commands and procedures will discourage people.
- Keep personal communications off the system. Computer conferencing is designed to focus on one subject and extraneous messages just get in the way.
- Hundreds of people can participate in a conference, but for practical purposes you should limit the number to 30 or less.

Sources for More Information

Books

Glossbrenner, Alfred. *The Complete Handbook of Personal Computer Communications.* New York: St. Martin's Press, 1983.

Hiltz, Starr R. *Online Communities.* Norwood, NJ: Ablex Publishing Corp., 1984.

Kerr, Elaine B., and Hiltz, Starr Roxanne. *Computer-Mediated Communication Systems.* New York: Academic press, 1982.

Selected List of Services That Provide Computer Conferencing

PARTI (PARTICIPATE)
The Source
Source Telecomputing Corporation
1616 Anderson Road
McLean, VA 22102

ARCHNET
Also available through *The Source*
Contact the AIA ArchNet Manager, AIA Service Corporation, 1735 New York Avenue, N.W., Washington, DC 20005.

EIES (Electronic Information Exchange System)
Telenet
Accessible by Telenet and Uninet. Membership is subject to approval since the primary objective is the development of computer conferencing itself as the topic.

AUGMENT
Tymshare, Inc.
20705 Valley Green Drive
Cupertino, CA 95014

GTE Telenet Communications
8229 Boone Boulevard
Vienna, VA 22180

CONEXUS
New Era Technologies
1252 Columbia Rd. N.W.
Washington, DC 20009

CompuServe, Inc.
5000 Arlington Centre Blvd.
Columbus, OH 43220

10.3

CONNECTING YOUR COMPUTERS FOR ADDED POWER

As architectural offices add applications to their arsenal of computer power they also tend to add computers. A typical firm may find that the first unit they bought for general office word processing and specifications is now on the secretary's desk, one for accounting is with the office manager, and another used for scheduling, project management and other project-oriented applications is with the production department. Seldom are these connected. In some cases a connection is not necessary, but for most design firms there are definite advantages in planning an overall *system* for computer use.

One of the most obvious advantages is sharing of expensive peripherals—printers, hard disks, modems and the like. The real advantage is sharing of *information*—project files, in-house developed data bases, standard detail drawing files and other data that is useful to more than one person at a time.

There are two ways that several computers and peripheral devices can be connected. One is with a local area network (LAN) and the other is with a multiuser system. There are advantages and disadvantages to both and situations where one is warranted and another is not. This section will briefly describe both methods and how you can begin to evaluate which is best for your situation.

A local area network (LAN) is a group of computer devices (terminals, CPU's, printers, plotters, modems) within a limited geographical area (usually within a few thousand feet) connected to each other with a private communications connection, usually a coaxial cable or pair of wires. The system also includes the software required to enable the signals to proceed from one device to another in an orderly manner. Since there are physical limits on how far apart the various devices may be, LANs are limited to one office, building or nearby group of buildings.

A multiuser system is very similar in concept to a LAN but requires the majority of the equipment to be supplied by one source specifically configured to work as a system. The effect is the same, however; several people are able to share the computer's resources. Multiterminal computer-aided design and drafting installations are an example of a multiuser system.

A local area network is usually placed in a situation where there is a variety of previously installed computer devices that need to be tied together for high-speed data transfer. Hardware and software is added to allow these devices to "talk" to one another and make the system work when several people are trying to access the same information or hardware at the same time.

One of the primary disadvantages of a LAN is its cost. A small, six- or eight-user LAN may cost more than double what a multiuser system would to serve the same number of people assuming both were purchases as complete systems without using existing equipment.

Basic Application Requirements

Basic application requirements will vary depending on each user's particular needs. If you are considering a LAN or a multiuser system keep the following features in mind.

1. The system must provide all users with access to all devices: hard disks, printers and plotters.

2. The system must allow concurrent access to files (within the bounds of security limitations) with lock-out facilities so simultaneous updating does not damage a file.

3. The system must provide for access to external communication through a modem to allow for contact with another computer that is not part of the system. Additionally, access to a commercial data base, electronic mail or computer conferencing should be possible.

4. For LANs, the system must allow for a simple connection to the types and brands of equipment you currently have.

5. The system must be compatible with modems and other telecommunications devices.

305

6. Security features to protect unauthorized file access must be built into the system.

7. There must be reliability and a configuration such that a failure of one part of the system does not create total system failure.

8. The system should allow multitasking.

Additional Application Requirements

1. A LAN should be able to support simultaneous voice, video and data transmission.

2. The system should support color graphics and multiple windowing.

3. You may want the ability to interface with a mainframe computer.

4. The system should allow you to send messages (electronic mail) to other users on the system. This would probably only be desired if your office is large and spread out over several floors or buildings.

5. The system should have the ability for a microcomputer in a remote location to tap into the LAN through a modem connection.

Cost Variables

It is impossible to give accurate cost ranges for local area networks or multiuser systems because there are so many variables involved including the number of users, the sophistication of the software selected, whether printer and file servers are required, as well as other items. For example, in addition to some initial installation prices, a LAN workstation connection may cost from several hundred dollars to several thousand dollars.

If you decide to set up a local area network you should consider the following items that will add to the overall cost:

interface cards

network software

wiring

print servers

file servers

communications servers

installation

hard disk systems

protocol converters

maintenance

Of course, not all these will be required for every installation, but they do indicate the additional equipment needed to make a LAN work.

As mentioned above, multiuser systems are generally less expensive—sometimes about one half the cost of a LAN for the same number of users.

Implementation Procedures

Setting up a local area network or multiuser system can be a complex procedure involving a multitude of technical questions. You should enlist the help of a local dealer, consultant or someone else who regularly deals in these systems. There are, however, some steps you can take to get started.

1. Determine what your needs are and how much you are willing to spend on setting up a system. Do you have a great deal of information that must be shared by several people at the same time? How much do you have invested in existing equipment? Is is becoming obsolete? Do you need to just share data or is there a need for voice and video communication? Will you need to add users to the system in the future? Answering these types of questions will guide your decision.

2. Make your best prediction for future requirements. This should include how many people and devices will be on the system ultimately, whether you will be moving or how often you change office layouts. All these may affect which network you select.

3. Decide on an implementation plan. This includes what kind of ultimate configuration you will need (as best as you can determine) and a timetable for reaching your goal. Most systems can be set up in modules. You may only need a minimum configuration to begin.

4. If you decide to go with a local area network, contact suppliers. You may find these in several different ways. In larger cities there are "value-added dealers" that specialize in architectural applications. In addition to selling hardware and software, they can tailor a total system to your needs, including a local area network to connect the equipment you may already have as well as any new items you may purchase.

Office information suppliers who originally developed LANs can also help with your selection, but they will probably suggest their own. You will also find help from independent communications suppliers or consultants.

Additional Tips

- Make sure the network you decide on is capable of running all the software you have and intend to have. In some cases there is enough incompatibility to cause problems with some programs.

307

- When deciding on a system based on your estimates of the number of people using it and their frequency of communication, keep in mind that use will probably increase *above* your estimates. Once people become familiar with the advantages of a LAN their electronic interactions will increase.

- Select the vendor of your system carefully. There are dozens of vendors for this increasingly popular method of data communications and new ones are starting business all the time. Select one that has a good track record and supports a variety of devices. Make sure that they offer a good program of support and maintenance.

Sources for More Information

Brooks, Tom, ed. *The Local Area Network Reference Guide.* Englewood Cliffs, NJ: Prentice-Hall, Inc., 1985.

Byers, T.J. *Guide to Local Area Networks.* Englewood Cliffs, NJ: Prentice-Hall, Inc., 1985.

Chorafas, Dimitris N. *Designing and Implementing Local Area Networks.* New York: McGraw-Hill, 1984.

Derfler, Frank J. Jr. *A Manager's Guide to Local Networks.* Englewood Cliffs, NJ: Prentice-Hall, Inc., 1983.

McNamara, John E. *Local Area Networks: An Introduction to the Technology.* Bedford, MA: Digital Press, 1985.

All About 66 Local Area Networks and 35 PABX Systems

and

Local Area Networks and the Data Communications Capabilities of PABXs

There two reports available from:

Datapro Research Corporation
1805 Underwood Boulevard
Delran, NJ 08075

For a comprehensive list of local area networks check the following directory. It is available in most large libraries.

Data Sources
Ziff-Davis Publishing Co.
One Park Avenue
New York, NY 10016

Published quarterly, this directory is a comprehensive guide to available data processing and data communications equipment, software and companies.

10.4

SAVING TIME AND MONEY WITH ELECTRONIC MAIL

Establishing instant or overnight communication is becoming increasingly important to architects. Whether it is sending information to a remote job site or assembling a proposal for a big job, every designer frequently needs a fast, reliable method for transmitting the written word. The telephone, overnight delivery services and facsimile are some of the traditional ways, but electronic mail can provide the best features of all three.

Microcomputer-based electronic mail is simply sending a message in digital form over some kind of common carrier transmission system to another user's "electronic mailbox" where it can be viewed immediately or stored for later recall. Electronic mail differs from computer conferencing in that the messages are usually on a one-to-one basis, cover a wide range of subjects and are sent and received by anyone using the system. Computer conferencing, on the other hand, typically involves a limited group of people "discussing" a particular topic, just as with a standard conference.

The differences are subtle (in fact, some electronic mail services offer computer conferencing as an optional service), but important in helping you decide which application to implement. You may have a greater need to communicate on a variety of topics with a large number of people than with a few people on one subject at a time. In this case, the hardware and method of implementation will be different. Refer to Section 10.2 for a discussion of computer conferencing.

Electronic mail offers several advantages to the architect and interior designer. The foremost is its ability to overcome the problem of "telephone tag." Most telephone calls do not reach the person for whom they are intended the first time. In some cases, two people can spend days trying to catch each other in the office at the same time. With electronic mail, one person can send a message anytime day or night, have it stored in someone else's mailbox, and it can be retrieved anytime.

Instant communication is another advantage. Messages can be sent faster than overnight delivery and can be more complex than those sent by telephone. Instant communication and the ability to transcend time zones are features especially appealing to firms who do business overseas.

Electronic mail can also provide a hard copy for permanent records—something an "instant" telephone call cannot do. This lessens the chances of miscommunication and makes it easier to send long, complicated messages. Electronic mail can be edited, searched by keyword and integrated with word processing systems.

One disadvantage is that all the people who want to participate must subscribe to the same service. For a firm whose primary interest is "talking" to branch offices and specific job sites this is not a problem. However, it can cause difficulties if you try to send a message to a new client who subscribes to another service.

There are ways around this, however. With some systems, mixed-mode, high-speed facsimile transmission is possible, allowing one "electronic" office to send a message to a "nonelectronic" office if they have a facsimile machine. Another way is to subscribe to a service who provides hardcopy delivery. In this case, an office sends an electronic message to the electronic mail station nearest the intended receiver. It is printed out and either delivered by courier within hours if both are in the same city or sent by standard mail. MCI Mail is one example of this type of service.

Basic Application Requirements

An electronic mail service can offer you many features. The following should be considered basic requirements to look for in selecting one.

1. The system must have private "mailboxes" accessible only with the use of passwords.
2. All users should be advised by the system of the number of messages pending in their mailbox when they sign on.
3. Editing of text should include the usual range of word processing functions.
4. Sending options should include marking for urgent priority delivery, delivery notification and receipt confirmation.
5. There should be on-line help to make the system easy to use. A menu driven system is also preferable.
6. The system should allow you to send the same message to several mailboxes without having to retype your message.
7. All messages should be automatically dated and time-stamped.
8. You should be able to display messages in the order in which they were sent.

Additional Application Requirements

There are many more options possible. You may want to consider the following list as useful additional features:

1. the ability to search and retrieve messages by date, sender, receiver, subject and keywords
2. the ability to add, change and delete mailboxes, passwords and names in an interactive, on-line mode

3. the availability of several security levels as well as answerback validation
4. the inclusion of tickler files, system bulletin boards and computer conferencing
5. the ability to reread "old mail"
6. the capability of communicating with nonsystem users through facsimile or some other method

Requirements of Hardware

Electronic mail messages can be sent using a variety of devices including personal computers, dedicated terminals, telex terminals and some electronic typewriters. If you already have some of these in place, make sure the system you choose can use them. Buying new terminals adds to the overall installation expense and, in most cases, is not necessary. The supplier of the service will provide detailed information on other equipment required.

Cost Variables

As with computer conferencing or a local area network, giving general costs for establishing an electronic mail capability is difficult due to the many variables. Once you are up and running the primary cost will be that of transmission of messages, just as with regular mail or overnight delivery services. In most cases transmitting electronic mail will be less expensive than other forms of delivery and can pay for initial costs in a few years. As an example, the cost of sending an electronic mail message may be about one dollar while the same document sent by an overnight delivery service or express mail may cost from nine to thirteen dollars.

Pricing for most systems is based either on the system time used or by the transaction. At the time of this writing, for example, MCI Mail charged $1.00 per 7,500 characters sent electronically while Western Union charged $.30 per minute for messages transmitted at 300 baud and $.45 for messages transmitted at 1,200 baud. A one-page letter with 2,500 characters would then cost about $.57 for 300 baud and $.31 for 1,200 baud. There are additional costs for hardcopy delivery. Some services also charge a registration fee and mailbox rental fee while others include these charges in their message pricing structure.

The overall "soft" costs can also be reduced if the people sending the "mail" compose their own messages directly on the computer screen rather than dictating to a secretary or writing the message out longhand. For many people, old habits may be hard to change, but to make the most efficient use of the technology this should be a serious consideration.

311

Implementation Procedures

Electronic mail can be accessed in one of two ways. You can either use a public data network such as *The Source* or set up your system through a computer hardware supplier. For most architectural firms selecting one of the popular public data networks is probably the best choice. You only have to have the terminals, a modem and communications software; the electronic mail service takes care of the rest.

A partial list of some of the more popular electronic mail companies is given at the end of this section. Write to them for more information on features and costs. If computer conferencing is also an application you want to implement, check to see what companies might offer that service as well.

Additional Tips

- Different hardware maintained by various users on the system may be incompatible. Verify that the service you select and the equipment of the people you want to communicate with can all work together.

- Just as with a telephone system, you should institute management controls including policies for when and when not to use the system, careful recording of messages sent so costs can be recovered as reimbursable expenses and as a way of controlling system use for personal messages. Some companies provide detailed billing information to their customers including such things as number of messages sent, average length of messages and similar accounting data.

- Sometimes messages are not urgent. Consider saving these on disk until the evening when transmission rates are often lower.

- Make sure that the service you select offers both clear documentation and operator's manuals as well as telephone support for those times when you have problems.

Sources for More Information

Electronic Mail Association
1919 Pennsylvania Avenue N.W. Suite 300
Washington, DC 20006

Newsletter

Electronic Mail and Message Systems
International Resource Development, Inc.
30 High Street
Norwalk, CT 06851

Books

Dordick, H.S.; Bradley, H.G.; Nanus, B. *The Emerging Network Marketplace.* Norwood, NJ: Ablex Publishing Corporation, 1980.

Trudell, Libby; Bruman, Janet; and Oliver, Dennis. *Options for Electronic Mail.* New York: John Wiley & Sons, 1984.

All About 57 Electronic Mail Systems

Datapro Research Corporation
1805 Underwood Boulevard
Delran, NJ 08075

Selected List of Electronic Mail Vendors

SOURCEMAIL
The Source
Source Telecomputing Corporation
1616 Anderson Road
McLean, VA 22102

EMAIL
CompuServe, Inc.
5000 Arlington Centre Blvd.
Columbus, OH 43220

MCI MAIL
MCI Digital Information Services Corp.
2000 M Street N.W. Suite 300
Washington, DC 20036

DIALCOM
ITT Dialcom, Inc.
1109 Spring Street
Silver Springs, MD 20910

EASYLINK
Western Union Telegraph Co.
1 Lake Street
Upper Saddle River, NJ 07458

TELEMAIL
GTE Telenet
8229 Boone Boulevard
Vienna, VA 22180

ONTYME II
Tymshare, Inc.
20665 Valley Green Drive
Cupertino, CA 95014

COMET
Computer Corporation of America
675 Massachusetts Avenue
Cambridge, MA 02139

QUICK-COMM
General Electric Information Services Co.
401 N. Washington St.
Rockville, MD 20850

APPENDIX A

Essentials of Data Base Management Systems

A good data base management program is one of the most useful software purchases an architect or interior designer can make. With it, you can automate many of your firm's business functions using only one program instead of buying several distinct application programs. This section briefly describes data base management systems (DBMS) for those unfamiliar with them, and outlines some of the most important criteria to consider when purchasing software. Implementation of particular applications using a DBMS are described in each chapter section when a DBMS is appropriate. For a complete discussion of data base management systems refer to the sources listed at the end of this section.

For the purposes of this book, a data base is an organized collection of related information that can be stored, manipulated and retrieved with a computer. A common analogy of a noncomputer data base is that of a card file used to maintain a mailing list. Each card contains information on one person on the mailing list, including such things as last name, first name, address, city, state, zip code and telephone number. Each card contains related information in a similar format and the cards are organized alphabetically by last name. See Figure A-1. The same type of data base can easily be maintained on a computer except that the information is stored electronically instead of on paper.

Certain terms have been agreed on to describe the elements of a computer data base. The largest element that describes a definable unit is the *file.* This corresponds to the total collection of cards in the mailing list file. The file contains a number of *records* that each contain information on one uniquely identifiable element. In the case of the mailing list file, a record is one card containing the information for one person. Each record contains a number of data *fields* that contain information unique to the record. For example, in the mailing list analogy, the name is one data field, the city another, the zip code another and so on.

A number of separate files can be combined to form a larger "data base." If there is a way to relate them (assuming there is also a need) the data base becomes much more flexible and useful. For example, one file in the data base

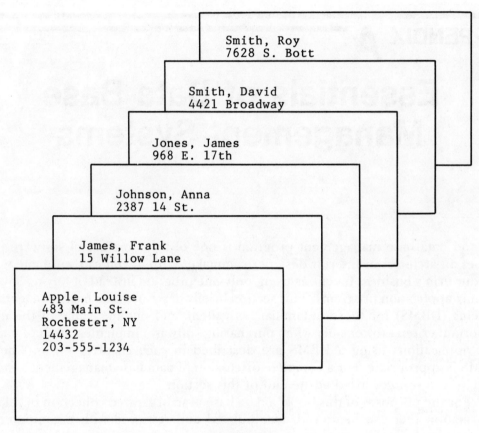

Figure A-1
Card File Data Base

can contain the mailing list information and another can contain records of when you made sales calls on each person. Assuming your DBMS has the capability, the two can be related by last name and first name so at any time you can view your client's address as well as a listing of when you made sales calls. You can also retrieve a list of clients who you have not contacted in the last six months, along with their phone numbers. There are several advantages of maintaining two or more files instead of one large one. These will be discussed later in this section.

Another way to look at the organization of information in a data base is to combine the fields and records in a file into a table format with rows and columns as shown in Figure A-2. Each row represents a record and each column represents a data field that is present in each record. This is a more accurate diagrammatic way of looking at a file of information and is a helpful way to understand how data base management files should be set up.

Last	First	Address	City	St	Zip	Last contact
Apple	Louise	483 Main St.	Rochester	NY	14432	Oct. 25, 1985
James	Frank	15 Willow Lane	Medford	OR	97843	
Johnson	Anna	2387 14th St.	Oakland	CA	94124	June 4, 1985
Jones	James	968 E. 17th	Sacramento	CA	95630	Aug. 16, 1985
Smith	David	4421 Broadway	Chicago	IL	60606	
Smith	Roy	7628 S. Bott	Boise	ID	83501	

Figure A-2
Table Representation of a Data Base

As shown in the example, some fields need not contain any data at all while at least one field must always contain information that uniquely identifies a record. This field (or combination of fields) is called the *key* field and is the primary way the records are organized. In the example, the key is the combination of last name and first name because it is possible for there to be two "Smiths" as a last name. (Of course, in a large mailing list file there can even be duplicates of first and last names so another unique identifier is needed.)

The advantages to a computerized DBMS over manual methods are that the same information can be quickly accessed many different ways with various indexes, the information can be sorted in any manner desired, and records can be selectively retrieved based on given criteria. For instance, you can retrieve just the names of people who live in California and Oregon, or you can sort your mailing list according to zip codes for presorted mailing.

Types of Data Base Management Systems

There are four major types of data base management systems based on how information is structured and manipulated: file management systems, relational, network and hierarchical. The theories behind the last three can become quite complex, but a detailed understanding of how they operate is not necessary for using most of the programs available for microcomputers. In fact, you will probably only be concerned with two, file management systems and relational data base management systems.

A file management system (FMS) is the simpler of the two and almost always costs less. It is very similar to the mailing list analogy discussed previously where

317

there is only one file (the set of address cards), and each record (an individual address card) contains a limited number of fields (data elements such as name, city, etc.). The records can be organized according to last name and first name (the primary key) and can also be sorted and accessed by other arrangements (by zip code, in the example).

Although some features of one type of system will often be found on another, the primary difference is the ability of a FMS to only access *one* file at a time. Therefore, all the information you need must be included in the records of one file. For simple applications this works perfectly well, but there are instances where problems arise that a relational DBMS can solve.

A relational data base management system (RDBMS) consists of several different files that are related in some way so the information in each can be manipulated according to the user's needs. One way to view a relational system is to set up the information in a table as shown in Figure A-2. In data base management theory, such a table is called a relation, which is the origin of the term. As mentioned before, the rows are the individual records and the columns are the fields.

Relational Data Base Management System Example

To illustrate how a RDBMS might work and how it is better than a FMS for many applications, consider the problem of keeping track of local manufacturer's representatives, the products they represent and the catalogues they supply to an architectural office. At any time you might want to answer the following questions:

1. Knowing a trade name, ask who the local representative is, their address and phone number, and also what is the address and who is the person to contact at the factory?

2. Who are all the manufacturers and local representatives who deal in wood flooring so I can evaluate them for a particular project?

3. What catalogues have not been updated in the last six months so I can notify the representatives to bring me a current catalog?

There are other information management aspects of this situation you may want to consider, but for the purposes of this example, we will deal with just these. For a more complete discussion of this data base application refer to Sections 9.1 and 9.2.

Since the primary interest is keeping track of local trade representatives you can start by basing each record on an individual representative as shown in Figure A-3. (This example has been simplified for purposes of explanation. In addition to the data fields shown you would have additional information such as the manufacturer's address, phone and so forth.) However, one representative may handle several manufacturers and products *or* just one so you will never know how many

318

Local rep	Address	Trade name	Manufacturer	Product type
A	15 N 18th	B-Stain	Super Paint Co.	Wood stain
		Paintall	Super Paint Co.	Paint
B	249 Lance	Gymlock	Wonderwood Co.	Wood flooring
C	123 Main	AceFloor	Everyfloor	Wood flooring
		Flortron	Everyfloor	Tile flooring
		Lox Marble	AmMaCo, Inc.	Marble flooring
none		none	Slateco	Slate flooring
none		Wonderwall	Amalgamated, Inc.	Wall fabric

Figure A-3
Invalid Relational Representation
of Manufacturer's Representatives Data Base

data fields to set up. Too many will result in wasted space on your disk and too few will not allow you to list all the products of some representatives. In addition, there may be some products that do not have local representatives or even trade names so this format would not accommodate them.

To solve these problems for use with a simple file management system that uses only one file, you can reorganize the table as shown in Figure A-4. This repeats the representative listing for as many times as the number of products he or she represents. If the representative adds a product line, you would simply add another record. The primary key, or unique identifier of each record, would then have to be a combination of representative's name and trade name.

Another way is to organize the information according to trade name which is better since each trade name is unique and can also serve as the primary key to the data base. See Figure A-5. For products that do not have a separate trade name you can use the manufacturer's name. To isolate individual representatives and the products they handle, you can create an index based on the local representative data field and sort the index according to the representative's name.

Both of these methods, however, create additional problems. The first is the redundancy of data. For each local representative, the name and address of the representative has to be repeated several times. The same is true of the manufactur-

Local rep	Address	Trade name	Manufacturer	Product type
A	15 N 18th	B-Stain	Super Paint Co.	Wood stain
A	15 N 18th	Paintall	Super Paint Co.	Paint
B	249 Lance	Gymlock	Wonderwood Co.	Wood flooring
C	123 Main	AceFloor	Everyfloor	Wood flooring
C	123 Main	Flortron	Everyfloor	Tile flooring
C	123 Main	Lox Marble	AmMaCo, Inc.	Marble flooring
none		none	Slateco	Slate flooring
none		Wonderwall	Amalgamated, Inc.	Wall fabric

Figure A-4
Reorganized Table of Manufacturer's Representatives

Trade name	Product type	Manufacturer	Local rep	Address	Catalog date
AceFloor	Wood flooring	Everyfloor	D	123 Main	85/11/18
B-Stain	Wood stain	Super Paint Co.	A	15 N 18th	85/02/06
Flortron	Tile flooring	Everyfloor	D	123 Main	
Gymlock	Wood flooring	Wonderwood Co.	C	249 Lance	85/09/18
Lox Marble	Marble flooring	AmMaCo, Inc.	D	123 Main	86/01/05
Paintall	Paint	Super Paint Co.	A	15 N 18th	85/02/06
"Slateco"	Slate flooring	Slateco			
Wonderwall	Wall fabric	Amalgamated, Inc.			84/10/19

Figure A-5
Manufacturer's Representatives by Trade Name
Represented

er's name and address, although for brevity the manufacturer's address is not shown in the example. This not only wastes computer memory but also increases the chances for errors each time the name and address are entered.

The second problem concerns changes. For example, if a representative changes his or her phone number, the phone number data field for every record concerning that representative has to be changed, a very time-consuming and error-prone process unless you have software that can perform a global replace.

The third problem is that such a redundant data base often makes it impossible to easily pull out just selected information—subfiles as they are called. Suppose you wanted to print out a current list of representatives and their addresses to send out invitations to an office open house. Most data base management systems will allow you to selectively print just the data fields concerning the representative's name, company name and address, but there would be no way to tell the system to ignore repeat printing of a representatives' listing after the first time.

A relational data base management system provides the means to solve these kinds of problems and provides you with a powerful tool for many different applications. Once again, the full theory behind data base design can become very complicated, but the following discussion will illustrate enough points to allow you to begin your own application designs based on a RDBMS.

The first step is to identify the different unique entities in your total collection of information. In our example, one entity is the local representative, another is the manufacturer and yet another is the trade name. For each of these entities there is certain information concerning that entity only, and not the others. The local representative has its address, telephone number and name of the person in the company to contact for information. The manufacturer has *its* address, telephone and other data unique to it, *including the name of the representative in your geographical area that handles the manufacturer's product.* This is the link, or relation, between what will become two separate files in your data base design.

Finally, the trade name represents a product that is of a certain type, has a catalog in your office with a date, possibly has a listed price, availability, and a myriad of other information uniquely associated with it. Each trade name (or an assigned name if no trade name exists such as "Slateco" in the example) also has an associated representative and manufacturer that provide the relations between this file and the representative file and manufacturer file. The revised tables representing a design for a relational data base design for this example are shown in Figure A-6. These have been expanded somewhat to illustrate more of the data fields that might be associated with each entity type.

Although the three separate files (tables) appear to be much larger than the one in Figure A-5 because of the added information, they have actually eliminated the data redundancy and therefore the chances for error in either entering or changing data. They also make it possible to extract information in many ways

Representative file

Local rep	Address	City	St	Zip	Phone	Contact
A	15 N 18th	Denver	CO	80202	303.888.7654	Joe Smith
B	249 Lance	Lakewood	CO	80226	303.555.1212	Bill Jones
C	123 Main	Aurora	CO	80012	303.258.2145	Janet Kind

Manufacturers file

Mfg.	Address	City	St	Zip	Local rep
Amalgamated, Inc.	968 E. 17th	Sacramento	CA	95639	
AmMaCo, Inc.	483 Main St.	Rochester	NY	14432	C
Everyfloor	7628 S. Baum	Boise	ID	83501	C
Slateco	15 Willow Lane	Medford	OR	97843	
Super Paint Co.	2387 14th St.	Oakland	CA	94124	A
Wonderwood Co.	4421 Broadway	Chicago	IL	60606	B

Trade name file

Trade name	Product type	Manufacturer	Local rep	Master-format #	Catalog date
AceFloor	Wood flooring	Everyfloor	D	09550	85/11/18
B-Stain	Wood stain	Super Paint Co.	A	09930	85/02/06
Flortron	Tile flooring	Everyfloor	D	09650	
Gymlock	Wood flooring	Wonderwood Co.	C	09550	85/09/18
Lox Marble	Marble flooring	AmMaCo, Inc.	D	09615	86/01/05
Paintall	Paint	Super Paint Co.	A	09220	85/02/06
"Slateco"	Slate flooring	Slateco		09625	
Wonderwall	Wall fabric	Amalgamated, Inc.		09975	84/10/19

Figure A-6
Relational Data Base Design

322

different from the three ways it was entered—this is the real power of relational data base management systems.

For example, with the data base designed the way it is, you can now answer the original three questions stated in this example. Knowing a trade name of a product, for instance, a RDBMS can find the trade name in the trade name file, find that its associated representative was "C" (or whatever it happened to be), look in the representative file for "C" and then extract the address, phone number and other desired information about that representative. It can also find the manufacturer's name as the link to information in the manufacturer's file. If representative "C" changes its address, only one record in one file has to be updated to maintain the currency of the entire data base.

Relational data base management systems vary in their ability to handle multiple files and in how the operator passes instructions to the program. Some allow fairly simple natural language interface while others require more complex programming in the software's procedural language.

Criteria for Software Selection

For architectural and interior design office use, one of the first decisions you need to make in selecting data base management software is whether you need a relational system or can get by with a simple file management system. If you want to set up several applications you may find that having both will be worth the small extra cost since many times a FMS is easier to learn and use. Review the applications in each section of this book to see whether a FMS or RDBMS is recommended.

After this fundamental decision, there are many criteria to consider in making your purchase. I will outline some of the more important ones here. If some criteria are critical for a particular application those will be highlighted in the application's section under "Requirements of Software."

The capabilities of any FMS or RDBMS can be categorized in five broad areas: General system specifications, Data entry, Maintenance, Query and Reports. Your review of a software package should include all of these.

General

Records/file. What is the maximum number of records that is possible with the software? For many systems this is limited only by available disk space; for less expensive systems it may be a few thousand.

Fields/record. What is the maximum number of fields that is possible in each record? This may range from as few as 20 to as many as limited by disk space. Evaluate your intended needs to decide what your minimum number is. This is especially important if you are going to use a FMS where all the data needs to be packed into one record. Also, consider what the total maximum size in bytes (characters) the record can be.

Field size.   What is the maximum number of characters allowed in each field? The range spans from 30 bytes to tens of thousands. Usually, you will seldom need or want anything that exceeds the width of the screen or the width of the paper your reports will be on. If the field size can exceed the size of the screen or paper, can the software "wrap" the excess to the next line?

Open files.   If the data base is relational, how many files can be open at one time?

Number of indexes.   How many different data fields can have indexes associated with them? Indexes provide a very fast way to retrieve data without sequentially searching each record. Simple, low-cost file management systems often provide only one index, the one associated with the primary key. Your software should have the capability for *at least* five indexes, more if possible.

Keys/record.   As mentioned in the discussion above, every record in a file must have one unique identifying field so the program can tell one record from another. This may be a unique name like a trade name, an arbitrary employee number or some combination of fields that is unique. This key is called the primary key and is the way the main data file is organized. The record or its associated index is sorted in alphabetical or numeric order and gives the primary access to your data. It is also critical to be able to access records in other ways or you may just as well keep a card file. In the example given, you will want to access your product file by "type of product" as well as by trade name. This key is called a secondary key. The more keys allowed per record, the better.

Number of sort keys.   Some low-cost programs only allow you to sort your data based on one key. There are times, however, when you will want to organize your information based on two or more keys. For example, you might want to sort product information first by product type and then alphabetically by manufacturer's name.

Field types.   All programs allow you to have either numeric or alphanumeric field types for entering text or numbers. Some allow variable-length fields that can save disk space when you have a field that may contain an unknown amount of information. If you make just a short entry, the rest of the field is not "padded" as fixed-length fields are, but you still have the ability to enter a long field. Beyond these three types, some programs allow you to set the format of the field. For instance, a dollar's field would have a leading dollar sign and a decimal point two places to the left of the last digit.

Security.   Programs differ in their ability to let you assign passwords to files or to provide some other method of security for your files.

Procedural language.   More sophisticated programs come with their own high-level language that allows you to custom design very complex applications. For

324

simple needs such as list management this is not necessary, but it can be quite useful for more advanced applications.

Compatibility with other programs. The question here is whether the DBMS can import or export data to other programs such as a spreadsheet or word processing program and, if so, how difficult is it to do.

Menu vs. command driven. Menu driven software packages are easier for the first-time and occasional user to manipulate, but command driven systems offer more power and flexibility. The better software packages will allow you to use commands or set up your own custom menus for your applications.

Data Entry

Screen definition. Screen set-up for data entry can either be automatic or allow the user to define how the screen should look. Custom formatting of the screen can make data entry easier by more closely emulating a paper form.

Screens per record. Since the number of fields that can appear on a screen at one time is limited, the program should allow more than one screen per record. When you complete one screen, hitting the return key shows the next "page" of data. Many of the less expensive file management systems allow only one screen.

Required field entry. Some programs will allow you to mark certain fields that must have data entered before going on to the next field. This is useful for primary and secondary key fields and keeps the person entering data from overlooking a field.

Range test for values. This feature will check the entered data against a previously defined range of acceptable values and not let you go on until the mistake is corrected.

Default values. To make data entry easier, the better data base management programs can provide automatic entry of a set value for a field unless you enter something else. An example is the current date. Pressing one key for each record is much easier, faster and less error-prone than typing the same data repeatedly.

Entry editing. Any program should make it easy to correct typing mistakes. You should look for a program that lets you edit a field entry before going on to the next one and that lets you review and edit the entire screen before proceeding to the next record.

Maintenance

Add, delete, change records. Being able to perform these basic functions is mandatory for any program. All programs allow for modifications to records but some are easier and more flexible to use than others. With some DBM systems you have to reindex and sort your file before you can use it which takes more time and often is overlooked by the user.

Mass changes.   This feature allows you to enter a desired change for one field and have the change made on all records. It is especially useful for such things as increasing the value of a certain field by a given percentage or changing a date.

Adding fields.   Many data base management programs, once they are defined, do not allow the total length of each record to be changed, therefore precluding the addition of one or more fields. The programs that let you add or delete a field after you start using the file give you much more flexibility.

Adding indexes.   You should be able to add indexes at any time. When you first set up the data base, the first index will be on the primary key which may be all you need. Later, you may want to establish other ways to index the data base.

Sorting.   As you add records and indexes, and delete records, you will need to sort the data. Programs differ widely in their speed of sorting, especially with large data files. When you evaluate programs make sure you know the capabilities of its sort feature.

Query

Method of query.   Querying a data base involves asking questions about the data that meet certain conditions. The output may be either on the screen or in a report. For instance, you may want to look at a list of people on your mailing list that have offices only in one particular city. The method and ease with which you can do this is critical in any evaluation of a DBMS.

Relational query.   Can you define your query conditions based on the "greater than," "less than," "equal to," "not equal to," "greater than or equal to" and "less than or equal to" conditions?

Boolean searches.   Can you use the Boolean operators of "and," "or" and "not" to specify conditions of your search?

Partial string search.   There are times when you don't know the complete name of someone or can remember only the first few letters of an item. With the ability to search on partial strings (a string is any group of letters or numbers) you can query your data base to look for the names "Ander*" where the asterisk represented any additional characters. You would get back the names Anders, Andersen, Andersohn and Anderson if they were in your data base. Some programs can find strings only if you enter at least the first letter of the field while others can find a string embedded anywhere in a larger field of characters.

Batch files.   If you make the same request of your data base repeatedly, it is easier if you can define your query once and save it as a file for future use with a simpler and quicker series of keystrokes. This is useful if your program's query language requires a lengthy and complicated set of instructions.

Reports

Method of defining reports. Are printed reports defined through a programming language or a report generator? Report generators built into the program make it easier to define how you want your data base output to look on paper and are usually the best to have.

Layout flexibility. Does the report generator provide you with various options for the appearance of the final report? These include such things as column format, headers, footers, titles, page totals of numerical values, report totals and partial printing of text fields.

Multifile access. This is only valid if the program can have more than one file open at a time. If this is possible, can the report generator extract data from more than one file?

Calculation. As a minimum, the program and report generator should be able to perform basic four-function arithmetic on your data. In addition, the better programs will have such features as averages, minimum, maximum, counting and percentages. More complex mathematical functions are usually not included so if your requirements are for a lot of involved "number crunching" a generic data base management program may not be for you.

Sorting and selection. Of course, the report generator should have all the sorting features and relational and Boolean selection features mentioned previously. The ability to sort on multiple fields is especially important.

Sources for More Information

Byers, Robert A. *Everyman's Database Primer, featuring dBaseII.* Reston, VA: Reston Publishing Company, Inc., 1982.

Date, C. J. *Database: A Primer.* Reading, MA: Addison-Wesley Publishing Co., 1983.

Deakin, Rose. *Database Primer.* New York: New American Library, 1984.

Kruglinski, David. *Data Base Management Systems, A Guide to Microcomputer Software.* Berkeley, CA: Osborne/McGraw-Hill, 1983.

Lewis, Bryan. *Data Management for Professionals.* Culver City, CA: Ashton-Tate, 1983.

APPENDIX B

On-Line Data Bases Useful for Architecture and Interior Design

Interactive, on-line computer data bases provide the architect and interior designer with powerful, cost-effective tools to obtain information quickly, accurately and comprehensively. There are dozens of individual data bases that can provide the wide variety of information designers need. Refer to Section 10.1 for how to make the best use of on-line data bases. Also, review Figure 10.1-1 for suggestions on the areas of design practice each data base is most appropriate for.

The following listing gives the acronym used in Figure 10.1-1, the name of the data base, its supplier, a brief description of the information contained and its availability. The availability describes how you can access the data base. Most of the following are offered through one or more of the major search services such as DIALOG, BRS and SDC. Addresses of these search services are given in Section 10.1. Some are available only through less well-known services or require that you arrange for access through the supplying company.

Since the on-line commercial data base industry changes frequently, refer to the latest edition of one of the directories listed in Section 10.1 for new data bases or changes to those listed below. Where addresses are given they are current at the time of this writing, but you should check with current directories for any changes. This list includes the data bases most firms will find useful. There are, of course, hundreds of others. For example, Books in Print can be used to find pertinent references to a specific topic more thoroughly than looking through a library's card catalogue. If your firm works in a specialized area you should consult one of the directories listed in Section 10.1 to examine the full range of possibilities.

ABI/INFORM
ABI/Inform
Data Courier, Inc.
620 South Fifth Street
Louisville, KY 40208

This is a bibliographic data base including abstracts of the principal articles in over 610 journals in the fields of business management, marketing, information management, economics and other business topics.

Available through DIALOG, SDC and BRS among other services.

API
Architectural Periodicals Index
British Architectural Library
66 Portland Place
London, UK W1N 4AD

The API is the data base version of the printed *Architectural Periodicals Index,* which indexes about 300 journals published in about 45 countries covering architecture and related fields.

Available on magnetic tape.

ASI
American Statistics Index
Congressional Information Service, Inc.
4520 East-West Highway Suite 800
Bethesda, MD 20814

ASI is an index to statistical publications of the United States Government from periodicals, one-time reports, report series and annual reports.

Available through DIALOG and SDC.

AVERY
Avery Index to Architectural Periodicals
Avery Library, Columbia University
Broadway & 116th Street
New York, NY 10027

The Avery Index is a bibliographic index to selected articles from periodicals received in the Avery Architectural and Fine Arts Library. Over 500 Western language periodicals are scanned in the fields of architecture, interior design, landscape architecture, decorative arts, city planning and housing. It is the data base version of the printed index.

Available through the Research Libraries Information Network (RLIN), Jordan Quad, Stanford, CA 94305.

B/P SOFTWARE
Business/Professional Software Database (tm)
Data Courier Inc. & Information Sources
620 South Fifth Street
Louisville, KY 40202

B/P SOFTWARE contains descriptive citations of major software packages used in business and professional applications that run on personal and mini-computers.

Available through DIALOG.

BEIS
Building Energy Information System
AIA Foundation
1735 New York Avenue, N.W.
Washington, DC 20006

BEK SYSTEM
Computer Cost Estimating Services
American Appraisal Associates, Inc.
525 East Michigan Street
Milwaukee, WI 53202
    The BEK System contains labor and material rates from over 800 research locations in the U.S. and Canada processed through a series of formulas to generate detailed models of all types of construction with costs and allocations.
    Available through General Electric Information Systems Co. and on purchased disks.

CBD
Commerce Business Daily
433 West Van Buren Street Room 1304
Chicago, IL 60607
    CBD is the full-text equivalent of the printed Commerce Business Daily announcing services and products wanted by the U.S. Government.
    Available through DIALOG and *The Source.*

CDD
Comprehensive Dissertation Database
University Microfilms International
300 N. Zeeb Road
Ann Arbor, MI 48106
    This data base provides access to citations on every doctoral dissertation accepted at North American Universities since 1861 and over 15,000 Masters theses.
    Available through DIALOG and BRS.

CIS/INDEX
CIS Index to Publications of the U.S. Congress
Congressional Information Service, Inc.
4520 East-West Highway Suite 800
Bethesda, MD 20814
    This is the data base version of the printed index. It provides access to all working papers, hearing transcripts, special publications, reports and other proceedings of Congress.
    Available through DIALOG and SDC.

COLD
Cold Regions Data Base
CRREL, U.S. Army Corps of Engineers
72 Lyme Road
Hanover, NH 03755

Cold Regions covers areas that are temporarily or permanently affected by freezing temperatures including the Artic, Antarctica, the Antarctic Ocean and the sub-Antarctic islands. Topics of interest to designers include civil engineering and the behavior of materials in cold regions.

Available through SDC.

COMPENDEX
Computerized Engineering Index
Engineering Information, Inc.
345 East 47th Street
New York, NY 10017

Compendex is the data base version of the *Engineering Index* providing international abstracted information coverage of approximately 3500 journals, conference proceedings, government reports and engineering society publications.

Available through DIALOG, SDC and BRS.

COMPUSOURCE
CompuSource
CompuSource, Inc.
2825 Sacramento Street
San Francisco, CA 94115

CompuSource provides product information to architects and interior designers covering such areas as furniture, wall covering, carpeting and fabrics.

Available through CompuSource.

COMSPEC
Computer-based System for Preparing Specifications
Bowne Information Systems, Inc.
777 Northern Boulevard
Great Neck, NY 11021

Comspec includes full-text specifications of SPECTEXT (Construction Specifications Institute), NAVFAC (U.S. Navy Facilities Master), FAA (Federal Aviation Agency), VA (Veterans Administration Master Specifications), U.S. Army Corps of Engineers Master and the Coast Guard Master Specifications.

Available on-line through Bowne Information Systems or on disks.

CRECORD
Congressional Record Abstracts
Capitol Services, Inc.
415 Second Street, N.E.
Washington, DC 20002

CRECORD draws from the Congressional Record indexing about 250 subject areas divided into 30 broad topics. Indexed material includes new bills, debates, statements, hearing notices and a daily digest of proceedings.

Available through DIALOG and SDC.

DISCLOSURE II
Disclosure II
Disclosure Partners
5161 River Road
Bethesda, MD 20816

Disclosure II provides information extracted from reports filed with the U.S. Securities and Exchange Commission by approximately 8,000 publicly owned companies with at least one million dollars in assets.

Available through DIALOG, New York Times Information Service, the Dow Jones News/Retrieval Service, and Control Data Corporation's Business Information Services.

DMI
Dun's Market Identifiers
Dun & Bradstreet Corporation
3 Century Drive
Parsippany, NJ 07054

DMI provides detailed information on over 1,400,000 U.S. businesses with more than ten employees, and with fewer than ten employees if they have annual sales over one million dollars. Information includes current address, product, financial and marketing information.

DODGE CIS
Dodge Cost Information Systems
Cost Information Systems Division
McGraw-Hill Information Systems
1221 Avenue of the Americas
New York, NY 10020

CIS provides access to the building cost data bases maintained by McGraw-Hill including the Dodge Conceptual Budget Analysis, the Dodge Detailed Construction Cost Estimate and the Energy Requirement Analysis.

Available through McGraw-Hill Information Systems.

DS
Design Search
Design Search
2215 Broadway Street
Vancouver, WA 98663

Design Search is a data base of architectural, engineering and other design firms. It is used by companies to find design firms, and by design firms to locate appropriate joint venture partners or consulting firms.

Available to subscribers through phone inquiry.

EA
Encyclopedia of Associations
Gale Research Company
1109 Book Tower
Detroit, MI 48226

This data base corresponds to the printed version listing thousands of professional societies, trade associations, labor unions and other groups. These groups are often invaluable as a source of detailed information on almost any topic.

Available through DIALOG.

EIS IP
EIS Industrial Plants
Economic Information Systems, Inc.
310 Madison Avenue
New York, NY 10017

This data base provides access to information on over 150,000 industrial plants and over 250,000 nonmanufacturing establishments that employ 20 or more people. Combined, these listings represent over 80 percent of the U.S. industrial and nonmanufacturing activity.

Available through DIALOG and Control Data Corporation.

ENERGYLINE
Energyline
EIC/Intelligence, Inc.
48 West 38th Street
New York, NY 10018

Energyline is the on-line counterpart to *Energy Information Abstracts* covering over 40,000 energy records dating from 1971. Coverage includes journals, books, research reports, congressional hearings, conference proceedings, government reports and statistics.

Available through DIALOG and SDC.

ENERGYNET
Energynet
EIC/Intelligence, Inc.
48 West 38th Street
New York, NY 10018

The Energynet data base contains directory-type information on over 2,500 organizations and 8,000 people in energy-related fields including the congressional establishment, the federal executive establishment, state energy officials, energy associations, energy companies and information/publishing companies.

Available through DIALOG.

ENVIROLINE
Enviroline
EIC/Intelligence, Inc.
48 West 38th Street
New York, NY 10018
    Enviroline is the data base version of *Environment Abstracts* providing coverage of all aspects of the environment including management, technology, planning, law, political science, economics, geology, biology and chemistry as they relate to environmental issues.
    Available through DIALOG and SDC.

FEDREG
Federal Register Abstracts
Capitol Services, Inc.
415 Second Street, N.E.
Washington, DC 20002
    FEDREG contains complete coverage of the *Federal Register*. It is useful to insure compliance with federal building and product standards.
    Available through DIALOG and SDC.

FEDRIP
Federal Research in Progress
National Technical Information Service
5285 Port Royal Road
Springfield, VA 22161
    FEDRIP summarizes ongoing, federally-funded research projects giving the project title, principal researcher, sponsoring agency and a project summary. Participating agencies of interest to architects include the National Bureau of Standards, the Department of Energy and the National Institute for Occupational Safety and Health.
    Available through DIALOG.

JSAH
Journal of the Society of Architectural Historians
Society of Architectural Historians
1700 Walnut Street Suite 716
Philadelphia, PA 19103
    This data base provides coverage of all articles published in the *Journal of the Society of Architectural Historians* since 1941.
    Available through BRS.

M & S COST
Building Cost Programs
Marshall and Swift
1617 Beverly Boulevard
Los Angeles, CA 90026

This Marshall and Swift Building Cost Program produces replacement and depreciated cost reports for vitually all types of commercial, agricultural and residential buildings. Report options include component (segregated cost), square foot (calculator) and residential options. The cost information is updated monthly.

Available on-line through Marshall and Swift and on disk for microcomputer use.

M & S REM
Repair and Remodel Programs
Marshall and Swift
1617 Beverly Boulevard
Los Angeles, CA 90026

This program produces reports estimating the cost of making repairs, renovations, or remodeling work to a building. The reports itemize the costs associated with removing, replacing, resetting, cleaning, painting and refinishing construction and appliance items within a building.

Available on-line from Marshall and Swift and on disk for microcomputer use.

MC
Management Contents
Management Contents
2256 Carlson Drive
Northbrook, IL 60062

MC provides access to over 700 U.S. and international journals as well as newsletters, research reports and other proceedings on business and management topics.

Available through DIALOG, SDC, BRS and *The Source*.

MDD
Million Dollar Directory
Dun & Bradstreet Corporation
3 Century Drive
Parsippany, NJ 07054

This data base gives business information on over 115,000 U.S. companies with a net worth of $500,000 or more.

Available through DIALOG.

MLSS
Military and Federal Specifications and Standards
Information Handling Services
15 Inverness Way East
Englewood, CO 80150

MLSS is the most complete source available for information on the active and historical standards and specifications of the Department of Defense and Federal Government. Hard copy and microform versions of the full text are available.

Available through BRS.

NCJRS
National Criminal Justice Reference Service
National Institute of Justice
Box 6000
Rockville, MD 20850

This data base covers the literature related to law enforcement and criminal justice. One of the subject categories available is "architecture and design."

Available through DIALOG and the National Institute of Justice.

NDEX
Newspaper Index
Bell and Howell Co.
Old Mansfield Road
Wooster, OH 44691

Nine major U.S. newspapers and ten black newspapers are covered in this data base.

Available through SDC.

NNI
National Newspaper Index [tm]
Information Access Company
11 Davis Drive
Belmont, CA 94002

NNI indexes the Los Angeles Times, The Christian Science Monitor, The New York Times, The Wall Street Journal and The Washington Post.

Available through DIALOG.

NTIS
National Technical Information Service
5285 Port Royal Road
Springfield, VA 22161

NTIS serves as the central source for the sale of all government-sponsored and government-conducted, nonclassified research. The data base includes the fields of building industry technology, energy and materials technology among many others.

Available through DIALOG, SDC and BRS.

PTS AR
PTS Annual Reports Abstracts
Predicasts, Inc.
11001 Cedar Avenue
Cleveland, OH 44106

This data base gives coverage of annual reports issued by over 3,000 publicly held U.S. corporations and some international companies.

Available through DIALOG and BRS.

PTS F & S
PTS Funk and Scott Indexes
Predicasts, Inc.
11001 Cedar Avenue
Cleveland, OH 44106

The Funk and Scott Indexes provide a wide range of business and financial information on domestic and international companies. They include abstracts from over 2500 journals and newsletters, data on corporate acquisitions and mergers, new products and forecasts of company sales, among other information.

Available through DIALOG and BRS.

SHOWROOM
Showroom Online
1211 Avenue of the Americas
New York, NY 10036

This service offers data on over 400,000 products for interior design use. The system uses a self-contained computer for searching on several categories and a videodisk for displaying product information.

Available as a self-contained unit through Showroom Online.

STD AND SPECS
Standards and Specifications
National Standards Association, Inc.
5161 River Road
Bethesda, MD 20816

Standards and Specifications provides access to government and industry standards, specifications and related documents that specify terminology, performance, testing, safety, materials, products or other requirements and characteristics of interest to a particular industry or technology. It contains information to identify standards and specifications such as issuing organization, the Federal Supply Classification code, whether the document has been cancelled or superseded, if it was adopted by a U.S. Government agency, designated an American National Standard and, for international standards, whether approved for use by an agency of the U.S. government.

Available through DIALOG.

STDS
Industry and International Standards
Information Handling Services
15 Inverness Way East
Englewood, CO 80150

STDS contains voluntary engineering standards from private sector societies and organizations in the United States in addition to selected foreign national standards and international standards. Hard copy and microform versions of the full text are available.

Available through BRS.

TECHNET
Tech-Net
Information Handling Services
15 Inverness Way East
Englewood, CO 80150

Tech-Net offers on-line searching of engineering and architectural products, manufacturers, and related standards. It covers over eight million pages of catalogs, codes and standards and other technical documents. Full-text copies are also available.

Available through Information Handling Services.

TI
Trade and Industry Index [tm]
Information Access Company
11 Davis Drive
Belmont, CA 94002

This data base indexes over 300 trade-specific journals, general business journals, news releases from PR newswire as well as selective coverage from over 1000 general-interest periodicals. Architecture-related journals covered include *Builder, Building Design & Construction, Building Supply News, Construction Review, Interior Design, Progressive Architecture* and *Solar Age*.

Available through DIALOG.

TRIS-ON-LINE
Transportation Research Information Service
Transportation Research Board
2101 Constitution Avenue, N.W.
Washington, DC 20418

TRIS provides research information on all types of transportation modes on subjects including environmental and safety concerns, materials, design, construction technology and operations, among others.

Available through DIALOG.

TTD
Textile Technology Digest
Institute of Textile Technology
P.O. Box 391
Charlottesville, VA 22902

TTD provides access to *Textile Technology Digest,* a monthly journal abstracting literature related to textile technology.

Available by subscription from the Institute of Textile Technology.

WAA
World Aluminum Abstracts
American Society for Metals
Metals Park, OH 44073

WAA provides coverage of the world's technical literature on aluminum from ore processing through end use.

Available through DIALOG.

WT
World Textiles Data Base
Shirley Institute
Didsbury, Manchester, England M20 8RX

This is the data base version of *World Textile Abstracts* indexing the world literature on the science and technology of textiles and related materials.

Available through DIALOG.

APPENDIX C

Sources for More Information

As with all other aspects of the A/E computer marketplace, new literature is being published at a rapid rate. The following listing of books, reports, periodicals, directories and other material was current at the time of this writing. Contact each supplier or publisher for a current list of available publications and their prices. Also, check with your library for new books, directories and periodicals.

Books and Reports

The Architect and the Computer. Nigel Evans, (RIBA Publications, London) ISBS/ Timber Press, P.O. Box 1632, Beaverton, OR 97075.

Automation in Architectural Practice. Robert Babbin, 1340 Astor Street, Chicago, IL 60610, 1983.

CAD/CAM Handbook. Eric Teicholz, McGraw-Hill, 1984.

CAD/CAM Systems Planning and Implementation. Charles Know, Marcel Dekker, New York, 1983.

Computer Aided Architectural Design. William J. Mitchell, Van Nostrand Reinhold, Co., New York, 1977.

Computer-Aided Architectural Graphics. Daniel Ryan, Marcel Dekker, New York, 1983.

Computer-Aided Design and Drafting for Design Professionals. American Consulting Engineers Council, 1015 Fifteenth Street N.W., Washington, DC 20005, 1983.

Computer-Aided Facilities Planning. H. Lee Hales, Marcel Dekker, New York, 1984.

Computers in the Architectural Office. Natalie Langue Leighton, Van Nostrand Reinhold, 1984.

Construction Project Management Using Small Computers. Glen Peters, Nichols Publishing Company, New York, 1984.

The Guide for the Evaluation and Implementation of CAD/CAM Systems. S. H. Chasen and J. W. Dow, CAD/CAM Decisions, Box 76042, Atlanta, GA 30328, 1983.

Implementing and Managing CADD in the Design Office. GSB Associates, Inc., 3400 Edge Land, Thorndale, PA 19372.

94 Computers in the Design Professions. American Consulting Engineers Council, 1015 Fifteenth Street N.W., Washington, DC 20005, 1985.

Pioneers of CAD in Architecture. Alfred M. Kemper, ed., Pacifica, CA: Hurland/ Swenson Publishers, 1985.

Public Data Bases for Design Firms. American Consulting Engineers Council, 1015 Fifteenth Street N.W., Washington, DC 20005, 1984.

The Small Computer & Architectural Practice. John Perry, Nichols Publishing Co., 1983.

The following reports and workbooks are supplied by A/E Systems Report, P.O. Box 11316, Newington, CT 06111:

Automation from A to Z

Computer Graphics in Architecture & Engineering

Justifying the Cost of CADD: Alternative Methods

Low Cost CADD for Architects and Engineers

Using Computers in A/E Firms

Word Processing for A/E Marketers

The following are published by Graphic Systems, Inc., 180 Franklin Street, Cambridge, MA 02139:

Automated Facilities Management: A Buyer's Guide

The Current State of Design Automation

The Current State of Facilities Management Automation

PC CADD: A Buyer's Guide

The following are published by Guidelines, P.O. Box 456, Orinda, CA 94563:

Guidelines A/E Computerization Manual

How to Set up a Microcomputer CADD System

How to Set up an Office Computer Filing System

101 A/E Uses for the Microcomputer

The following are published by Practice Management Associates, LTD., 126 Harvard Street, Brookline, MA 02146:

Computer-Aided Design and Drafting Directory

Financial Management Directory

How to Select a Data Processing System

Project Cost Accounting, Scheduling and Budgeting/Estimating Directory
Service Bureau Directory
Specification/Construction Management and Consultants Directory
Using Microcomputers in the Professional Design Firm

Directories

Computer Graphics, CAD and CAD/CAM Product Guide
Frost and Sullivan
106 Fulton Street
New York, NY 10038

Computer Literature Index
Applied Computer Research
P.O. Box 9280
Phoenix, AZ 85068

Construction Computer Applications Directory
Construction Industry Press
1105-F Spring St.
Silver Spring, MD 20910

DAEDALUS—The Accounting and Management Information Software Directory
Publication 95–1.
American Consulting Engineers Council
1015 Fifteenth St. N.W.
Washington, DC 20005

The following are available from Datapro Research Corporation, 1805 Underwood Boulevard, Delran, NJ 08075:

All About 50 Personal Computers

All About Personal Computer Communications

All About 232 Personal Computer Software Packages

In-Depth Analyses of the dBase and PFS Families, and 121 Other Database Management Packages

Data Sources
Ziff-Davis Publishing Co.
One Park Avenue
New York, NY 10016
Published quarterly, this directory is a comprehensive guide to available data processing and data communications equipment, software and companies. It is available at most large libraries.

Design Compudata
Volume 1: Computer Aided Design and Drafting Directory
Volume 2: Application Software Directory
Volume 3: Time-sharing, Service Bureaus and Consultants Directory
Graphic Systems, Inc.
180 Franklin Street
Cambridge, MA 02139

Low-Cost CAD Systems
Leading Edge Publishing Inc.
P.O. Box 8100
Dallas, TX 75205

Microcomputer Market Place
Dekotek
2248 Broadway
New York, NY 10024

The S. Klein Directory of Computer Graphics Suppliers: Hardware, Software, Systems and Services
Computer Graphics Suppliers
P.O. Box 89
Sudbury, MA 01776

Turnkey CAD/CAM Computer Graphics: A Survey and Buyer's Guide
Daratech Associates
P.O. Box 410
Cambridge, MA 02238

Periodicals

Computers for Design & Construction
310 E. 44th Street
New York, NY 10017

Computer Graphics World
Computer Graphics World Publishing Co.
1714 Stockton
San Francisco, CA 94133

Design Graphics World
St. Regis Publications, Inc.
390 Fifth Avenue
New York, NY 10018

Plan and Print
AIDD, Inc.
10116 Franklin Avenue
Franklin Park, IL 60131

Newsletters

A/E Computerization Bulletin
Guidelines Publications
P.O. Box 456
Orinda, CA 94563

A/E Systems Report
P.O. Box 11316
Newington, CT 06111

AEC Automation Newsletter
7209 Wisteria Way
Carlsbad, CA 92008

ASN Quarterly
Architect's Software Network
1610 Washington Plaza
Reston, VA 22090

Construction Computer Applications Newsletter
Construction Industry Press
1105-F Spring St.
Silver Spring, MD 20910

ECAN: Engineering Computer Applications Newsletter
5 Denver Tech Center
P.O. Box 3109
Englewood, CO 80155

The S. Klein Newsletter on Computer Graphics
P.O. Box 89
Sudbury, MA 01776

Today's SCIP (Small Computers in Practice)
EMA Management Associates, Inc.
1145 Gaskins Road
Richmond, VA 23233

Conferences and Conventions

Contact each sponsoring organization for current schedules and costs.

A/E Systems, The International Conference on Automation and Reprographics in Design Firms
and
A/E Systems Fall
A/E Systems Report
P.O. Box 11318
Newington, CT 06111

AIDD: National Convention and Annual Design/Drafting CAD/CAM Exposition
American Institute for Design and Drafting
102 N. Elm Place, Suite F
Broken Arrow, OK 74012

CEPA: Society for Computer Applications in Engineering, Planning and Architecture, Inc.
CEPA
358 Hungerford Dr.
Rockville, MD 20850

Computer-Aided Space Design and Management Conference
Gralla Conferences
1515 Broadway
New York, NY 10036

National Computer Graphics Association Conference and Exposition
National Computer Graphics Association
8401 Arlington Boulevard, Suite 601
Fairfax, VA 22031

Computer Graphics in the Building Process Conference and Exhibition
World Computer Graphics Association
2033 M Street N.W. Suite 399
Washington, DC 20036

Seminar Programs

The following are some of the organizations offering seminars and other continuing education courses. Contact each for a current list of topics and schedules.

American Institute of Architects Professional Development Programs
1735 New York Avenue N.W.
Washington, DC 20006

CAD/CAM Institute
21 Chambers Road
Danbury, CT 06810

EMA Management Associates, Inc.
1145 Gaskins Road
Richmond, VA 23233

Guidelines
P.O. Box 456
Orinda, CA 94563

University of Wisconsin-Extension
929 North Sixth Street
Milwaukee, WI 53203

Software

Architect's Software Network, Ltd.
1610 Washington Plaza
Reston, VA 22090

Designer Software Exchange
Laboratory of Architecture and Planning
Massachusetts Institute of Technology
77 Massachusetts Avenue
Cambridge, MA 02139

Index

Index